Praise for
Einstein Never Used Flash Cards

WINNER
BEST PSYCHOLOGY BOOK
Books for a Better Life Award, 2003

HIGHLY RECOMMENDED

"Reviewing decades of developmental research, [the authors] dispute the effects of accelerated learning on children reported by the media and recommend that children be left to develop curiosity on their own (much like Einstein and other intellectuals) rather than through "canned" academic programs. Parents will better comprehend each of the significant areas of development—math, reading, verbal communication, science, self-awareness, and social skills—and get a grasp of what is scientifically proven to help children learn and grow. Highly recommended . . ."
—Library Journal

VALUABLE

". . . Parents will find a valuable message if they stick with the program, ultimately relieving themselves and their offspring of stress and creating a more balanced life."
—Publishers Weekly

A SIGH OF RELIEF

"Any mom who's ever fretted over the 'magical' 0–3 window for learning (who hasn't?) can breathe a big sigh of relief, thanks to Einstein Never Used Flash Cards. *This get-real guide, from two mothers who are also developmental psychologists, explodes overhyped education myths and tells you why relaxing and reclaiming your child's childhood is the best way to nurture his growing mind."*
—Parenting magazine

EINSTEIN NEVER USED FLASH CARDS

HOW OUR CHILDREN REALLY Learn— AND WHY THEY NEED TO PLAY MORE AND MEMORIZE LESS

KATHY HIRSH-PASEK, PH.D., AND
ROBERTA MICHNICK GOLINKOFF, PH.D.,
WITH DIANE EYER, PH.D.

RODALE

Notice

This book is intended as a reference volume only, not as a medical manual. The information given here is designed to help you make informed decisions about your child's intellectual development and behavior. It is not intended as a substitute for any treatment that may have been prescribed by your child's doctor. If you suspect that your child has a medical or developmental problem, we urge you to seek competent professional help. Mention of specific companies, organizations, or authorities in this book does not imply endorsement by the publisher, nor does mention of specific companies, organizations, or authorities imply that they endorse this book.

Library of Congress Cataloging-in-Publication Data

Hirsh-Pasek, Kathy.
 Einstein never used flash cards : how our children really learn—and why they need to play more and memorize less / Kathy Hirsh-Pasek and Roberta Michnick Golinkoff with Diane Eyer.
  p.   cm.
 ISBN 1–57954–695–1 hardcover
 ISBN 1–59486–068–8 paperback
 1. Child development.   2. Play.   3. Early childhood education—Parent participation.   I. Golinkoff, Roberta Michnick.   II. Eyer, Diane E., date.   III. Title.
LB1115.H56 2003
305.231—dc21   2003013618

Distributed to the trade by Holtzbrinck Publishers

2 4 6 8 10 9 7 5 3   hardcover
22 24 26 28 30 29 27 25 23 21   paperback

 RODALE

CONTENTS

ACKNOWLEDGMENTS

THIS BOOK WAS WRITTEN BY US, it's true, but it was also written by our colleagues in developmental psychology. Were it not for the excellent research that our colleagues have produced, we would not have been in a position to promote the cause of childhood. When we got the idea to write this book, we knew that the research was out there to support the idea that children learn without extra classes and fancy toys, and that socioemotional development is a key aspect of successful adjustment in life. All we had to do was assemble the argument, and we even had help with that! When we would tell our colleagues about this project, it was invariably the case that they volunteered to read it, to endorse it, and to help us in any way that they could. And we took them up on the offer. Each chapter profited from the input we were given by experts in the area we were writing about. We received wonderful feedback on chapter 1 from Joel Gordon and Herman Weiner. For chapter 2, we consulted John Bruer and Sandra Trehub, who quickly answered any of the questions we posed, and Nora Newcombe, who was kind enough to read the entire chapter. Herb Ginsburg, Karen Wynn, Nora Newcombe, James Hiebert, and Nancy Jordan helped with chapter 3, as did wonderful research by Kelly Mix. Richard Venezky read through chapter 5, and Frank Murray and Nancy Lavigne read through chapter 6. Marsha Weinraub,

Julie Hubbard, Carol Dweck, and Kim Cassidy were invaluable for their help in chapters 7 and 8. Ageliki Nicolopoulou alerted us to a wealth of information on play for chapter 9, a chapter that was also inspired by information from Dorothy Singer and Susan Bredekamp. One of the lessons we have learned in writing books for the popular press is that space limitations and "readability" prevent us from acknowledging all the wonderful research that contributed to this volume. We apologize in advance to our colleagues whose research we were unable to include. Finally, thanks to Jeff Pasek, Josh Pasek, Benj Pasek, and Michelle Reimer, who read through some of the material to make sure it was written in an accessible and engaging way.

Funding for some of our research reviewed in the book, and for its writing, came from grants from the National Science Foundation to both of us and from a National Institute of Child Health and Human Development grant to Kathy. We thank these agencies for understanding the importance that we place on disseminating the findings of our research and the research of others in a way that might have beneficial effects on the lives of children. Support of another sort came from our graduate students and laboratory coordinators, who were instrumental in helping us to assemble the relevant literature. They also provided us with much wonderful stimulation. It was a joy to work with Meredith Meyer, Dede Addy, Khara Pence, Mandy Maguire, Diane Delaney, Shannon Pruden, Sara Salkind, and Rachel Pulverman. Maryanne Bowers, Roberta's secretary at the University of Delaware, is excellent at responding with alacrity to our "we need this yesterday" requests. We thank our superlative Honors students—both at Temple University and at the University of Delaware—for their insightful comments.

We also feel lucky to have found a writer who is also a developmental psychologist, Diane Eyer. Although she was literally in Kathy's backyard teaching at Temple University, she is a scholar and writer in her own right and it was a pleasure to work with her. The three of us made a good team, constantly in communication and constantly improving upon each other's writing.

Our agent, Barbara Lowenstein, has been a wonderful skeptic all along, and when we got the green light from Barbara, we knew it meant something! Fortunately for us, she placed us with a marvelous press: Rodale! Lou Cinquino, Amy Kovalski, and Sue Ducharme understood what we were trying to do and gave us the freedom and feedback that facilitated its accomplishment.

And finally, we could not neglect to mention our wonderful families. Kathy's Jeff is our pro bono legal representative and official booster. Her children, Josh, Benj, and Mikey, furnished us with many anecdotes and much support, and her cousin Philissa Cramer is one of the best editors we have ever worked with. Roberta's children, Allison and Jordan, also contributed greatly to her understanding of children and childhood and continue to teach her the virtues of young adulthood.

We are especially fortunate to have mothers (and grandmothers) who serve as our role models. Kathy's grandmother, Helen, understood the value of play. She was the first to teach her how to ride a bike and about ice cream soup. Our mothers, Joan and Anne, are vibrant, involved, and engaged women who gave us as children just enough rope to venture out but not enough to hang ourselves! They served as secure bases for our attachment and continue to be our strongest advocates. So even if no one else likes this book (though we surely hope they do!), at least our mothers will. That's a great feeling!

INTRODUCTION

IT'S NO WONDER that parents and educators are tired and frazzled. We have been caught in a whirlwind of cultural assumptions about how to raise and educate the next generation. We are told that faster is better, that we must push learning along at a rapid pace. We are told that we must make every minute of our children's lives count, that our children are like empty rooms to be filled by the adults who serve as the interior designers of their lives. These assumptions about children and how they learn are at complete odds with the messages coming from the halls of academe, where child development experts have researched how children grow and learn. This book tells the story of development from the scientist's point of view. It thus offers an antidote not only to the hurried child but also to the hurried parent and hurried teacher!

The seeds for this book were first planted back in the mid-1980s, when Professor David Elkind of Tufts University came to Philadelphia to speak about his classic book, *The Hurried Child*. Professor Elkind had his finger on the pulse of the problem long before the "decade of the brain," when parents were told they had to put their children's brain development on their to-do list. He worried about the adultification of children as they began to appear draped in Baby Gap attire while participating in an array of adult-oriented activities revamped for preschoolers—everything from computer science to cooking classes to soccer leagues. His warning signs appeared even before parents could get quick child-rearing advice with just two keystrokes on the Internet. I (Kathy) was a junior professor at Haverford College, doing research on "hurried children," and I was thrilled to host Professor Elkind during his speaking tour. I was also a parent of two young children, Josh, age 4, and Benj, age 2. While I knew that Professor Elkind was theoretically right about finding more down-time with our children and enjoying more playtime, I also felt the pain of hurried parents. Every time my friends would tell me about another art class, or another soccer league for toddlers, I worried that my children would be left behind in the rush toward success.

As a developmental psychologist, I knew that Professor Elkind was correct about the plight of the modern-day parent and child. Yet it took all the knowledge I had to resist the temptation to push my children too far and too fast. Using child development as my guide, I let them play. And 16 years later, I am happy to report that my two oldest sons (I now have three boys) both have gotten into the colleges of their choice and are happy, intelligent, and very creative people.

At the same time, I (Roberta) was raising my two children while a professor at the University of Delaware. Jordy (now Jordan) was 9 and Allison was 5. I remember when my son interviewed to attend a private school and I wondered whether I had failed him by not teaching him to read. But he was 4! The culture had worked its effect on me, despite the fact that I should have known better: I was a developmental psychologist. And yet I resisted because I knew that pushing children can backfire and create children who dread learning. It's not that we sat at home. We did our share of music classes and religious instruction, but we tried to draw the line in the sand at the extras that would have taken away the children's cherished playtime.

When my children were offered coed ballroom dance classes at a country club, I blew the whistle. But it wasn't easy to say "no." The invitations were embossed! And many of my friends' children participated. But, as I have since learned from my children (now 20 and 24), they treasured the time they had to play at home and with their peers. Recently, my daughter shyly told me that as a child, she played a game with the fingers on her hand, imagining that they were a family and each had a role. She loved that game. My son loved the extra staircase we had before we renovated our kitchen because it was such a great place to play hide-and-seek. And they both remember playing inside a box we received with a delivery of an appliance and turning it into their private hideaway. Did they miss out because they didn't take those dance lessons and learn how to interact in mature ways with the opposite sex? Have they suffered socially for lack of the foxtrot or box step? I don't think so. My son graduated from an Ivy League college and is already making a contribution to society through his membership in the Teach for America program. My daughter, still at a fine college, does her share of volunteer work through her involvement with a rape crisis center. Both are caring, happy, and resourceful people.

We tell you these things so that you know that even we, trained to understand how children grow and develop, had our doubts in trying to forge a balance for us and for our children. We tell you these things so that you know that you are not alone when you follow your "gut" and say "no" to that extra activity that all the other kids are doing. We tell you these things so that when your children grow older, they, too, can look back and tell you how important the time they shared with friends and family was to them and their development and how happy it made them.

WHY THIS BOOK NOW?

The pages of this book were written to share the remarkable story of child development with parents, practitioners, and policy makers. The last 4 decades have witnessed an unparalleled burst of scientific study on infants and toddlers, and we have been privileged to be a part of this revolution with our colleagues around the world. As scientists, each with more than 25 years in the research field, and as parents ourselves, we genuinely want to help children and parents get their lives back. We want you to know the story of how children develop so that you can make wise choices based on scientific evidence and then apply your knowledge at home, in the classroom, and in policies for children.

Much of what the media reports about research on child development contains only a grain of scientific truth. News stories and advertisements tell parents that toys build better brains and that infants and toddlers are mathematical geniuses. Here we set the record straight. We chart the terrain of how children really learn as we help you to move from the scientific journals to practical applications of the research. Stocked with "teachable moments" and sections where you can "discover hidden skills" in your children, this book will empower you to resist the temptation to try to create young geniuses and will better equip you to raise happy, healthy, and intelligent children.

WHO ARE WE?

Kathy Hirsh-Pasek earned a Ph.D. from the University of Pennsylvania in Philadelphia. A professor at Temple University in Philadelphia, she is director of the Temple University Infant Lab. Roberta Michnick Golinkoff received her Ph.D. from Cornell University in Ithaca, New York, and directs the Infant Language Project at the University of Delaware in Newark. We both are internationally recognized scholars, and we have worked together on research since 1980. In addition to serving as each other's best listener and child-rearing advisor, we have written and edited a total of 10 books and more than 80 articles in professional journals. With our colleagues in the field, we are discovering the story of human development.

We have shared our views on various aspects of child development at professional meetings across the globe. Funded by your tax dollars through federal grants, we are determined to "give back" and share the fruits of our labors with parents and professionals. Together we study how children learn language—a mysterious feat accomplished by the age of 3! Our earlier book *How Babies Talk* has been translated into four languages, perhaps because our enthusiasm for our topic is contagious.

As we mentioned earlier, we can identify with hassled parents who feel as if they are trying to make the most out of limited, often rushed time. As we were raising our children, we, too, experienced ever-mounting pressure. Sometimes we made mistakes in overscheduling, and we always noticed who suffered as a result: We did. Why? Because our children were cranky and tired and stressed. Parenting is a hard job. It often felt easier to go to work! Even though we never used flash cards with our children, all five of them are toilet trained, know how to read and write, and love learning.

We are also joined by Dr. Diane Eyer, a psychologist who teaches at Temple University and is an acclaimed author of several books on mothering. Her books *Motherguilt* and *Mother-Infant Bonding* were well-reviewed in the *New York Times* book review. Diane's help was instrumental in pulling together some of the research that we wanted to share with you and in making sure that the writing was always readable and engaging.

MOVING BEYOND THE WARNING SIGNS

Professor Elkind and many others have sounded the alarm. Many experts have talked and written about the undue stress on children and parents in today's fast-paced world. This book does more than just sound the alarm: It suggests a remedy. By examining the evidence that scientists have collected on intellectual and social development, you will come to understand why PLAY = LEARNING. You will see your children in a new and exciting way, with a deeper appreciation of their capabilities—and their true needs.

This is not a typical parenting book. It will not tell you when to burp the baby, when to begin toilet training, or how to discipline your preschooler. *It will offer you instead the power to create a more balanced life for you and your family.* Unfiltered through the lens of media hype and professional marketing, the information we bring you in this book comes directly from the lab to your living room and classroom. By understanding better what child development experts are *really* saying, you'll be poised to read future media reports on the topic with a critical eye. Most important, you'll be prepared to move forward with confidence as you parent and teach the next generation.

CHAPTER + 1

THE PLIGHT OF THE MODERN PARENT

ONE SATURDAY MORNING, 6 months into her first pregnancy, Felicia Montana headed to the mall with her friends to shop for the basic gear she'd soon be needing for her baby. What she got instead was a crash course that could be called "The Science of Modern Parenting 101."

Her education began in a store with a rainbow-colored sign, which had seemed like the right place to start shopping. In fact, that was the store's name: The Right Start. "That's exactly what we want for our baby," Felicia thought as she and her friends headed in. But by the time they left, she didn't know what she wanted anymore.

Felicia quickly noticed that the list of "must-have" baby-care equipment these days runs into far more exotic territory than the old standards of diaper bags, strollers, and car seats. Should she buy flash cards with images on the front and words on the back that offered "the best way to communicate new knowledge to your baby"? If so, which flash cards were more effective—the "Baby Dolittle" animal-identification cards or the "Baby Webster" vocabulary cards? Her friends, experienced mothers, all felt strongly about their babies' favorites.

"Jeremy knew all his animals by the time he was 18 months," Anna bragged.

"Alice liked 'Webster' better—she was using some big vocabulary words when she was 17 months," Erica boasted.

Once Felicia made that decision, should she buy the *Baby Einstein*, the *Baby Shakespeare*, or the *Baby Van Gogh* videotape, which offered "a unique introduction to the culture of language, music, literature, and art"? Or would her baby need all three? And what about the *Brainy Baby* video, designed to develop both the left and right sides of her baby's brain "between 6 months and 36 months"?

All of these products seemed to carry lofty promises to improve her baby's development if she bought them—but she also felt an unspoken hint of dire consequences if she didn't. After all, *Babybrain* gives babies the "intellectual edge needed to excel academically and professionally." Isn't parenting all about giving your children every possible advantage?

By the time she emerged back into the mall, her nerves were jangled and her confidence shaken—and she would feel even more unsettled once she got to the bookstore.

Felicia's husband, Steve, had asked her to pick up a few books on parenting. He wanted to be well-read on the subject so he could be an equal partner in raising their child.

Once in the bookstore, she went to the parenting section and picked up the first book her hand fell upon. *Prenatal Parenting* promised to provide guidance for "fetal parenting," including a chapter on "becoming a brain architect." Felicia slid the book back into its slot on the densely packed bookshelf and put her hand to her forehead, pondering her own aching brain.

Fetal parenting? Brain architecture? *This* is what new parents are supposed to worry about now? Felicia found herself becoming increasingly anxious about her baby's intellectual development—before her child was even born!

DOING THE CHILDHOOD HUSTLE

As Felicia now knows, the race to turn children into the most talented kids in their classroom begins even earlier than the crib—it now begins in the womb. Magazine articles coax expectant parents to exercise during pregnancy with the promise that it will enhance their babies' intelligence. Ads on the next page urge them to buy foreign-language CDs to play to the unborn children. Many parents wouldn't flinch at learning that fiber-optic tubes could be used to televise educational courses to "pre-infants" still floating in the womb! Fortunately, we're not at that point—not yet, anyway.

Once these babies are born, the push to move them as quickly as possible toward adult competencies intensifies. They're prodded to pick up reading skills faster, add and subtract sooner, and even master obscure tasks like identifying the faces of long-dead musical composers years before they'll need this information (if they ever will).

The baby-educating industry has found a receptive audience of parents eager to enrich their offspring. One survey shows that 65 percent of parents believe that flash cards are "very effective" in helping 2-year-olds develop their intellectual capacity. And more than a third of the parents surveyed believe that playing Mozart to their infants enhances brain development.

Obviously, parents have been listening to the toy companies' marketing pitches: The baby-educating toy category is now a $1-billion-a-year business. Business is so good, in fact, that companies such as Baby Einstein, which was purchased by Disney in 2001, are extending their product lines, including a "Little Einstein" line aimed at 3- to 5-year-olds.

The pitch has even penetrated into some unlikely audiences. "My grandmother—in an old-age home, mind you—sent me a mobile that plays Mozart and Bach," reports Diane, a San Francisco mother of a 2-year-old and a newborn. "My grandmother said she wanted my baby to be at the top of his class!"

Once these infants get older, many graduate to more extensive—and expensive—learning opportunities, including violin lessons, riding lessons, private grade school, and private tutors.

THE ROADRUNNER SOCIETY: FASTER, BETTER, MORE

In today's world, the prevailing message is that it's no longer sufficient for infants and toddlers to learn independently as they have for millennia, via their own curiosity and a little help from family members when teaching opportunities arise.

However, these little ones are merely the youngest residents of our modern, sped-up, competitive society. Adults are urged to work longer and more productively than their employers' rivals. We eat prepackaged meals nuked in the microwave and schedule our leisure time into blink-and-you-miss-it vacations. Adults hear the message that getting more done faster is better and pass the pace right on down to their kids.

Consider a day in the life of a typical American family—let's call them the Smiths. Marie Smith, a schoolteacher, wakes up at 6 A.M. every day. In the next hour, she'll dress the kids—Gerry, 11, and Jessica, 3—fix breakfast, do housework, and catch a few minutes of TV news before driving Jessica to day care. Her husband, Brian, leaves for McDonnell Douglas at 6:20 A.M., dropping off Gerry at basketball practice on his way to work. Marie picks up Gerry at 7:35 A.M. and they walk to her school, where she teaches kindergarten and he is in the fifth grade.

After work, Marie picks up Gerry at 5 P.M. from his after-school program and Jessica at day care. She buys groceries and often searches for supplies, such as poster board or colored marshmallows, that Gerry needs for homework projects. At 6 P.M., she interrupts her dinner preparation to drive Gerry to soccer, his church youth group, or his guitar lesson. Finally, the pressure ends around 7:30 P.M. when Brian arrives home with Gerry, after a commute of at least an hour, so that they can have dinner together.

Unfortunately, this type of rushed schedule seems to be the norm rather than the exception. One monumental change in family life in recent generations has been the rise in the dual-career family. In 1975, 34 percent of mothers with children under 6 were in the workforce. By 1999, that number had nearly doubled, with 61 percent of mothers in the workforce. A large portion of those working moms were mothers of infants. And of course, we know that most dads have been working outside the home for more than a century. But society is now demanding that both parents not just work, but put in longer hours.

In fact, Americans are now working harder than almost anyone else in the world, including the Japanese. According to a 1997 study by the International Labor Organization, fathers were working an average of 51 hours a week, while mothers were working 41 hours per week.

It's not surprising that a survey of parents found that 25 percent said they had *no time* for their family due to the demands of their jobs. Yet the fact is, time-use studies show that the amount of time mothers spend with each child has barely changed over the last 50 years. What has changed is what parents typically do with their children during that time. Increasingly, it is ferrying them from one "enriching" organized activity to another. They are often in the car, going to activities or playing the role of "soccer moms and dads," cheering and coaching their children from the sidelines.

This gave rise to the idea of "quality time"—a term that originated in the 1970s. Parents quickly picked up on the concept, since "quantity time" is at such a premium. Moms and dads have maximized their quality time with their children by creating the "organized kid"—one whose every moment, it seems, is productively scheduled.

Unfortunately, we're not having much fun at parenting, which should be one of the greatest joys of life. And as we'll see shortly, this vamped-up atmosphere of forced activity and learning isn't good for our children, either. In a recent *Newsweek* magazine article, one mother of four asserted that she spends so much time driving her children to activities that her 1-year-old is practically being raised in the family minivan. "When he's not in the van, he's somewhat disoriented," she explained.

Families are apparently so busy stimulating their children, they increasingly have little time just to enjoy one another. Perhaps it's not surprising that one New Jersey town, Ridgewood, felt compelled to declare one winter evening "Family Night." With the support of school administrators, the town canceled all sports activities, homework assignments, private lessons, and even religious classes so that parents and children could simply spend time together at home.

HOW THE RACE TO IMPROVE BEGAN

To understand how the race to produce smarter children at a younger age began, it's helpful to take a brief look at attitudes toward child-rearing throughout history. Until the early 19th century, there was really no acknowledgment of childhood as a separate period before adulthood. In fact, artwork from that period shows children dressed as miniature adults. The writings of the French philosopher Jean-Jacques Rousseau indelibly altered our view of childhood. In his now classic book *Emile*, Rousseau wrote, "Childhood has its own way of seeing, thinking, and feeling, and nothing is more foolish than to try to substitute ours for theirs." This view, coupled with the movement from field to factory, led to the advent of mass education, which was an effort to prepare youth for the working world.

With the birth of child psychology at the end of the 19th century, the idea that children could be studied and improved began to take hold. In the 1940s, a plethora of scientific journals devoted to studying children appeared. In his famous book *Baby and Child Care*, published in 1946, Dr. Benjamin Spock used his clinical eye and common sense to offer parents a blueprint for how to rear their children. The advice industry was born.

After World War II, when Rosie the Riveter returned to the hearth from the factory, she needed to think of motherhood as valuable work that required special knowledge and training. Parents began to rely on child development experts for information on how to raise their children. In fact, at the White House Conference on Children in 1950, experts were worried that parents had become too dependent on expert advice! Beginning in the 1970s, as the number of dual-career families increased and as information about child development exploded, parents wanted to be certain they were making every moment with their children count. Faced with a sense of dwindling family time, parents turned to child development experts to find out how to best prepare their children for life.

Initial doubts about the effects of accelerating children's development ("early ripe, early rot") gave way to a complete endorsement of the practice. Titles such as *Bring Out the Genius in Your Child* by Ken Adams and *365 Ways to a Smarter Preschooler* by Marilee Robin Burton, Susan G. MacDonald, and Susan Miller became part of the familiar landscape in neighborhood bookstores. The focus on engineering our children's intellectual development had spiraled out of control. We were witnessing an ironic return to our past: taking childhood away from children and treating them like miniature adults.

Warnings about this threat to childhood have been sounded within the halls of academe and beyond. Writers put pen to paper, like David Elkind, professor of child development at Tufts University and author of the now classic 1980 book *The Hurried Child*. More recently, Professor Laura Berk at Illinois State University added to the literature with her stunning book *Awakening Children's Minds*, and author Ralph Schoenstein brought us humorous anecdotes in *My Kid's an Honor Student, Your Kid's a Loser*. But what is a parent or teacher to do in response to the warning signs? How can we change the behavior the experts are worried about? Acknowledging the situation is only the first part of the solution. At the annual meeting of the International Conference for Infancy Studies in the summer of 2000, many urged that, as a group, developmental psychologists respond to the growing crisis. The mountains of research that demonstrated infant capabilities and that revealed newly discovered skills in preschoolers were being misinterpreted and misapplied. Research designed to reveal the inner workings of the human mind for scientific inquiry was being used to market product lines that promise to transform Baby into Super Baby.

THE CULT OF ACHIEVEMENT AND THE LOSS OF CHILDHOOD

Parents who don't want to participate in all of the accelerated opportunities and activities for their children often feel anxiety in this new child-rearing climate. As parenting itself becomes more competitive, many moms and dads worry that their children could be left behind if they don't take advantage of every available opportunity.

One acquaintance of ours will soon be moving to suburban Tucson, Arizona, to run a preschool. Her current school has an "emergent curriculum," meaning that subject areas emerge from *children's* interests and are more experiential than academic. "When I give parents tours at my current school, I say that we're not doing worksheets and direct skill work. They ask if their children will be prepared for school, and I explain that they will, because they will have been given a chance to be curious and explore," she says. "They'll say that this is fine, and then, half the time, they come back later and say, 'Why aren't they using computers? Why aren't the children reading?' As an educator, I know that blocks are truly the building blocks of literacy, math, and other forms of learning. But parents come in and say, 'They're playing. I want my kid to be working!'"

Despite her firm beliefs, our acquaintance is even starting to feel the pressure in how she should raise her own children. "Where I'm going, the parents are really high-powered heavy-hitters who put a lot of pressure on their children," she explains. "I know being low-key is okay, but if everyone else has their children playing the violin by the age of 4, will I doubt the decisions my husband and I have made?"

Another acquaintance, the mother of a 9-year-old boy and a 7-year-old girl, recently moved to a new, affluent development in San Diego and described the level of competitiveness around her. "More than half the children ages 5 to 12 have after-school tutors—not to help them achieve grade level, but to make sure that they're ahead."

Drawing on this parental anxiety, test-prep companies, like Kaplan and Princeton Review, which originally taught courses to help high school juniors and seniors prepare for their college entrance exams, such as the SAT and ACT, are now expanding their offerings to cover children beginning in kindergarten. These materials are aimed at improving students' scores on the annual tests now being used in public schools as part of President George W. Bush's No Child Left Behind Act.

Further, as child development professionals, we—the authors—constantly receive calls from parents who want their children's IQs tested, not because they think anything is wrong, but because they want their children's giftedness certified. The issue of children's intelligence has become just another factor, along with the newest car and the nicest appliances, in the age-old pressure to "keep up with the Joneses."

If parents are being stripped of the emotional satisfactions of ambling along with their little ones through the carefree world of childhood, children are paying their own price. We have entered the world of defensive parenting, which is the unfortunate by-product of the tremendous pressure placed on modern-day parents. We want our sons and daughters to be so intellectually superb that no university would dare turn them down, so good at everything that no employer could possibly afford to let them go.

Whatever happened to play? It has become a four-letter word! In 1981, a typical school-age child had about 40 percent of her time open for play. By 1997, that time for play had diminished to 25 percent. Further, 40 percent of school districts in America have even eliminated recess.

In addition to the pressures brought on by an overbooked schedule, children are also suffering from a new kind of "grade inflation," where skills that were traditionally taught in one grade now have to be learned the year before. For example, reading used to be introduced in the first grade. Now, more and more, it's taught in kindergarten and preschool. And many districts are considering making reading skills a *requirement* to get into kindergarten—even though most child experts agree that time in preschool and kindergarten is better spent on experiential play and building relationships.

Not surprisingly, our children are suffering from excessive depression and anxiety. The American Academy of Child and Adolescent Psychiatry states that "the number of 'significantly' depressed children and adolescents in the United States is 3.4 million, or 5 percent of all youngsters." And sometimes, this depression can become deadly. From 1980 to 1997, the number of 10- to 14-year-olds who committed suicide increased an astounding 109 percent.

Further, children's anxiety levels have increased significantly since the 1950s, with children as young as 9 now experiencing anxiety attacks. Some studies show a growing prevalence of test anxiety in children, possibly due to the increased amount of testing in schools and the high academic expectations of parents. This anxiety, of course, actually interferes with performance and learning. Other anxiety is linked to less-frequent social contact with parents; children gain security through spending time among family. It's also linked to increased environmental threats such as crime, divorce, and violence.

Psychologists are also seeing an increase in phobias, particularly school phobia, and somatic complaints in young children. One psychologist, Dr. Jack Wetter, director of UCLA's department of pediatric psychology, says, "I see small children so programmed they have no leisure time. In mid-March, children get acceptances for private preschools, and you can feel the tension. Little children come into my office and say, 'I got rejected from Carlthorp.'"

Therapists have long known that parental anxiety is communicated to children. As parents devote time and money to enrichment programs, they may expect a return on that "investment." For the children, the experience of learning may be marred by the constant threat of failure. The focus is on the outcome—the test results or recital of a poem—rather than what the child experiences and needs. A child may wonder, "What is wrong with me that I need all this extra help?" Force-feeding academics also gives children the impression that learning is a chore rather than something that derives naturally from curiosity and exploration.

Another problem with this cult of achievement is that it places so much emphasis on developing a child's IQ that an equally crucial aspect is totally eclipsed—what psychologist Daniel Goleman, cofounder of the Collaborative for Social and Emotional Learning at the Yale University Child Study Center, calls "EQ" in his groundbreaking book, *Emotional Intelligence: Why It Can Matter More than IQ*.

Dr. Goleman puts emotions at the center of the aptitude for living life intelligently. He points out that when people of high IQ flounder, and those of modest IQ do surprisingly well, the deciding factor is "emotional intelligence." This includes self-control, zeal and persistence, and the ability to motivate oneself.

This emotional intelligence is also the essence of will and of character. Those who are at the mercy of impulse—who lack self-control—can act in morally reprehensible ways. The other central feature of the emotionally intelligent character is compassion for others, marked by the ability to read emotions, to empathize, and also to get angry in the right amount at the right time for the right reasons.

What this concept of emotional intelligence means for children and parents is that the enjoyment of their *relationship* is fundamental to giving children the very best start in life. Simply taking the time to *enjoy* their children—to play with them and discuss what's going on in their world— is the best thing parents can do for their children's minds and emotional development to guarantee future success.

A BETTER WAY TO GROW SMART KIDS

In his book *The Hurried Child*, Professor David Elkind writes, "The concept of childhood, so vital to the traditional American way of life, is threatened with extinction in the society we have created. Today's child has become the unwilling, unintended victim of overwhelming stress— the stress borne of rapid, bewildering social change and constantly rising expectations."

As child development experts, we are alarmed at how anxiety over the child mind has gripped society. Of course, we all want our children to be primed to learn and thrive at school, but we needn't start infants on mental calisthenics to do so. This pressure to boost children's brainpower is harmful because it threatens to erode aspects of childhood that are crucial to social, emotional, and cognitive development.

By making children dependent on others to schedule and entertain them, we deprive them of the pleasures of creating their own games and the sense of mastery and independence they will need to enjoy running their own lives. The concept of enjoyment, of silliness, of play, is relegated to the back of the bus. The concept of downtime—when we can just do nothing, reflect a little, and have a chance to become ourselves—seems to be a kind of heresy in the current cult of achievement.

Parents also lose out by speeding through a fascinating time in their children's development. The dawning of a child's intelligence is an incredible process. Thinking is so central to being human, and it is amazing to witness its evolution through the child's eyes, yet many parents are missing this unique opportunity because of the intense emphasis on achievement.

The truth is, the key predictors of healthy intellectual and emotional development are "responsive, nurturing relationships with parents and caregivers," according to extensive research by the National Research Council of the Institute of Medicine in its report "From Neurons to Neighborhoods." When you and your children are simply hanging out doing the dishes together, you're interacting in an important way. The casual conversations you share teach your children about the world and about themselves. Parents help children interpret the day's events and sort out little frustrations and confusing emotions. They also serve as "filters"—letting in certain information and blocking out what a young child can't cope with, such as a horror movie or the evening news on TV. As a result, children gain a sense of their own importance and ability.

Our exchanges with our children also promote their intellectual skills, without any conscious effort on our part. In conversation, parents naturally prompt children to tell little narratives about the day. When they do this, parents are helping children to construct and interpret the stories of their lives, a playful game that will turn out to be valuable for what is expected in school. Describing "what happened" also helps train a child's memory and allows him to find the "scripts" in everyday events. And it helps children understand and express their experience—in other words, to think and learn and increase their vocabularies in a playful way.

A study by author Kathy Hirsh-Pasek of children whose parents send them to "academic" preschools versus traditional preschools that emphasize play and discovery found that children in academic preschools had no short-term, let alone long-term, academic advantages. By the time they were in first grade, the research couldn't distinguish between the intellectual skills of the children who had academic training and those who had none. There *was* one difference between the two groups, however: Children who had been in the academic environment were more anxious and less creative than the children in the other group. Another study found that children in preschools that emphasize direct instruction over more child-centered approaches experience greater stress. Why? Perhaps because they've been cheated out of being able to play. Perhaps because they're being pressured to remember random facts. Either way, children are the losers when academics are stressed before children are ready.

With this book, we hope to release caring adults from the cult of achievement. Our goal is to provide parents, teachers, and policy makers with a common vocabulary and set of concepts so they can discuss important issues about a child's learning in a meaningful way and swim against the powerful tide of sensationalized expectations about children's capacities and the need to push children to achieve more at increasingly younger ages. Armed with this knowledge, they can then become attuned to a child's natural learning patterns and abilities and find the teachable moments within each day that help a child build real knowledge, not just memorize isolated facts.

REFLECT, RESIST, AND RE-CENTER: THE NEW PARENTING MANTRA

We understand that parents, educators, and policy makers need a mantra to help guide them through the swirling forces of child-rearing advice. They need a way to achieve the balance we are advocating. We propose that one way to start is with a new "Three R's": Reflect, Resist, and Re-Center. Here's how they work:

The next time you read a sensational headline in a parenting magazine or hear about the latest research on child development at a meeting or on a talk show, stop yourself from frantically grabbing a pencil and scribbling notes about what you need to do differently, go out and buy, or work into your busy schedule or curriculum. Instead, take a moment to:

- *Reflect.* Consider whether jumping to the tune of the media piper is what you should be doing, or whether you will only be perpetuating in your own life the pressures our culture places on parents. Ask yourself, "Is this experience/class/drill/activity worth reducing my child's unstructured playtime further, schlepping to and from in the car, and paying for?" At least some of the time, reflection may well lead you to:

- *Resist.* To resist feels daring and brave and . . . so good! To resist means you stop yourself from joining the frenzy. It means that you allow time to slow down again. It means that you "just say no" (thank you, Nancy Reagan!). And when you do resist, you do so based on the scientific evidence to be presented in this book. This evidence tells us that *less can be more.* It tells us that the "adultification" and acceleration of children is not a positive choice, but one that robs children of their freedom to be. It tells us that to be happy, well-adjusted, and smart, children do not need to attend every class and own each educational toy. Still, we recognize that resisting may at first make you feel guilt. That's why you need to:

- *Re-center.* Re-centering involves reassuring yourself that you have made a good choice, that you have recognized that the true center of childhood is play, not work. After all, play is the primary way children were designed to learn. Although your decision may cause you some guilt or anxiety at first, you'll know you are doing what is best for your child. The best way to re-center is to play with your child. Watch the delight and intensity on your child's face as you join in his play and help him to expand his horizons.

The ability to reflect, resist, and re-center will be the happy outcome of reading this book. The new "Three R's" represent something different from what you often find in books for parents and professionals, something that we call evidence-based parenting. Evidence-based parenting allows you to be in the driver's seat and frees you from running to each and every activity. This approach, which flows from what science has discovered about how children learn, frees you to make your own choices about what is best for you and your children.

The news we have for beleaguered parents is this: Yes, children do need to spend time interacting with their parents (and teachers and child care professionals). But research shows that *a child's intellectual awakening takes place during the normal adult-child interactions that occur in everyday, purposeful activities.* Parents easily foster self-confident learners through activities that gently challenge children to reach to the edge of their developmental level, but not beyond. Playful environments and spontaneous learning opportunities hold the keys for a happy, emotionally healthy, and intelligent child—and for a fulfilled parent.

WHAT YOU'LL FIND IN THESE PAGES

In this book, we offer you usable and practical suggestions that emanate from the scientific findings—such as observations to watch for and games and experiments you can do with your child to see the research principles at work. You may find yourself identifying with the fictional vignettes that we often use, since they are composites of ourselves, our friends, and people whose lives we have observed. So if you think you're reading about your next-door neighbor and find yourself saying, "I know them!" it's only because so many of our lives follow the same patterns.

In the sections called Teachable Moments, we highlight how everyday, mundane experiences can provide opportunities for learning. Other sections, called Discovering Hidden Skills, allow you to become the researcher in your own home, rediscovering amazing capabilities in your children. As we become better observers of our children's behavior, we discover when our children can best profit from our instruction. Each chapter will offer fun and inexpensive activities and hands-on ideas that will foster development while reducing the unnecessary pressure on the already overtaxed parent, teacher, and child. The chapters that describe separate abilities (such as literacy and numbers) can be read out of sequence, when something your child does whets your appetite. But all of the chapters feed into chapter 9, which focuses on play—the central theme in the book. Play equals learning, and through play, we can give childhood back to children. The final chapter sums it all up and gives stressed parents tools in the form of principles to live by.

How will this all work? Let's take an example from the learning of early math skills. Many of the newer teaching techniques encourage you to use videos. There's a shape video for infants and numerous computer games that interactively engage preschoolers in mathematics games while teaching them about the computer. According to numerous research studies, however, the very best way to learn about numbers is to manipulate objects. Adding blocks on top of the stack to see how many you can pile up before it falls is mathematics. And playing a game of cards like War is math at its best. You needn't worry about being "educational." If you follow your children's mathematical interests—which are considerable—your play with them will foster mathematical learning and curiosity.

This book will also help *you* see the world differently. There are learning opportunities everywhere you look. Just as you can find rectangles in buildings and hexagons in stop signs, numbers appear at every juncture of your life. When we evenly divide our French fries with our children and when we make sure there is enough cake for everyone at the table, we are doing mathematics. When we set one napkin out for each of the people at the table, we are using "one-to-one correspondence." When we put books back in their place, we are sorting by sets. We need only to notice the world as our children do, and seize natural opportunities to help them learn.

When we perceive the world as ripe with social and learning opportunities, we will help our children grow. To do more—to use flash cards with infants, to insist on Mozart for the "pre-infant"—is like putting a videocassette on fast-forward instead of play. To put children on fast-forward is to risk turning them off to their natural desire to learn, and instead increases their risk of becoming anxious, depressed, and unhappy.

Childhood is about making discoveries. It is a time when children learn about themselves and their own capabilities. These discoveries do not take place in the context of structured lessons—nor do they come in boxes or on computer screens.

There are thousands of scientists who worked collaboratively to bring you the information that we have captured in this book. These people have devoted their lives to making the world a better place for your children to grow. We speak in one voice when we urge you to celebrate your children more and worry less about creating future Einsteins. We think that you will enjoy learning what we have come to understand. This knowledge will allow you to reclaim childhood for your children, while preparing them to be intelligent, happy, and emotionally healthy adults.

CHAPTER + 2

BRAINCHILD:
HOW BABIES ARE
WIRED TO LEARN

"IT'S A FACT," MARTHA EXPLAINS. "All of the products say so. Classical music increases brain growth." Harold chimes in, "We want to make sure that our children have all of the advantages in life. If we can stimulate their brain growth now and give them a leg up in this complex world, we're going to do so."

Harold and Martha Goodwin learned about the brain-music connection shortly after their daughter Brenda was born. Martha came across a video at Blockbuster called *Baby Genius: Mozart and Friends*, in which two animated baby geniuses explain how they became so smart. In the video, the little boy, Harrison, explains, "Certain types of classical music have been proven to help a baby's brain develop faster. It's a scientific fact. Music can make your baby smarter." The other cartoon child, a little girl named Sasha, tells the viewer that a baby's brain is fully developed by the age of 3 and everything she sees and hears before that age affects the baby's developing brain. The Goodwins have learned that almost from conception, *they* are to be the "architects" of their baby's brain.

When they were expecting their second baby, Harold and Martha would cuddle up on the couch together and place one of the handheld tummy speakers on Martha's belly. They used a CD and 24-page book, *Love Chords, Classical Music, and Creative Exercises to Enhance the Bond with*

Your Unborn Child, compiled by music educator and author Don Campbell. They now use a half dozen of the new classical music CDs marketed to infants and young children, including Campbell's *The Mozart Effect for Children: Relax, Daydream, and Draw*. The Goodwins are concerned about Brenda, who missed out on the pre-infant phase because they had not known about this parenting responsibility when Martha was pregnant with her.

In his book, Campbell asks the reader, "Can music make your child more intelligent?" He answers: "Certainly it can increase the number of neuronal connections in her brain, thereby stimulating her verbal skills. . . ." He also claims, "A recent study found that visual tracking, eye-hand coordination, and other positive behaviors develop more rapidly in babies whose mothers participated in a pilot program of prenatal exposure to music." No wonder the Goodwins believe that playing Mozart is an imperative for building better brains.

But does listening to Mozart really make you more intelligent? Does it prepare you for a life with a higher IQ? The scientific evidence provides a clear answer: No. Early exposure to classical music does not make your brain grow in ways that make you smarter. Why did anyone think this was so? That's an interesting story.

The history of what came to be called the Mozart Effect started with one research study published in 1993 by Professor Francis Rauscher and her colleagues at the University of Wisconsin's Oshkosh campus. The research showed that after listening to 10 minutes of a Mozart sonata, college students did better on one test of intellectual performance. Professor Rauscher got 79 of her college students to sign up for an experiment. She tested them on a small section of the Stanford-Binet intelligence test before and after listening to Mozart. The "spatial reasoning task" they had to complete took a couple of minutes.

Imagine you see the outline of a dollar bill on your test paper. In the second outline, the bill is folded in half so it looks like a square. In the third outline, someone has folded the two bottom corners so it now looks like the end of a man's tie. The test then asks you to imagine what the dollar bill would look like when you fold it again, and you are given five diagrams from which to choose. This paper-folding task is a test of your "visual-spatial abilities." Professor Rauscher found that her students scored 9 to 10 points higher on that task right after listening to 8 minutes and

24 seconds of the Mozart Sonata for Two Pianos in D Major, K 448. The effects lasted only 10 to 15 minutes. But there it was—listening to Mozart had increased spatial reasoning ability on one subtest of an intelligence test for a period of 10 minutes. Professor Rauscher cautioned against distorting the team's modest findings. But the media seized on the results, coining the term the Mozart Effect, and the notion that there was a get-smart-quick formula took flight. Professor Rauscher repeated the experiment several times, and each time, the group that listened to Mozart improved over those who listened to silence.

Sounds intriguing. Yes—but in 1999, the findings of these studies were officially refuted. The authors of reports in two top scientific journals, *Nature* and *Psychological Science*, could not reproduce Professor Rauscher's findings. Listening to Mozart, as opposed to silence or to compositions of Philip Glass (a rather unmelodic, repetitive kind of music) might affect the *mood* of the listeners, but not their overall IQs. In one celebrated paper, Professor Lois Hetland, of Harvard University's Project Zero, examined 67 studies on the Mozart effect with 4,564 adult participants. She noted that there was some short-lived Mozart effect on a very limited set of spatial abilities (the paper-folding task). She concluded, however, that "the existence of a short-lived effect by which music enhances spatio-temporal performance in adults does not lead to the conclusion that exposing children to classical music will raise their intelligence or their academic achievement or even their long-term spatial skills."

How did we get, then, from this modest (at best) Mozart finding to the myth that every infant needs to tune in to classical music to have brain cells turned on? As we will see, the Mozart phenomenon is part of a larger set of myths about how to build better brains—myths that have permeated our society.

WHAT YOU'VE HEARD: WHEN BAD MYTHS HAPPEN TO GOOD PARENTS

Two overarching myths about brain development might actually be *interfering* with the nurture of our children. *The first myth is that parents are brain sculptors, responsible for molding the intelligence and capabilities of their children.* Parents are being told that the development of their children's brains, which, in fact, is programmed by millions of years of evolution, can be altered in just one generation by specific lessons they provide. It is as if the brain were more like some lump of clay than an organ with a master plan authored by nature and the divine. This is the myth that convinces us that we are solely responsible for the way our children turn out intellectually.

The other myth that has the Goodwins in its grip is that *scientific research provides us with a manual for building better brains*. As a culture enthralled with science, we take little bits of evidence about brain function and extrapolate them to explain vast aspects of human behavior. The only problem is that extending our quite limited research findings in this broad way is unjustified.

We have heard some of these brain myths before. Remember the literature on whether you were more left-brained than right-brained or the reverse? A few decades ago, science began to reveal that for some functions, the brain seems to use its right or left side. As scientists looked further, however, they found that even those functions that seemed to occur primarily in one hemisphere of the brain actually depended on interaction with the other side. So, it is unlikely that you are either right-brained or left-brained—you are both, and everything you do utilizes both sides.

How do we know? The most extensive research on the brain's hemispheres has been dedicated to understanding how humans learn language. At birth, the hemispheres have already started to specialize, with newborns showing greater electrical brain activity in the left hemisphere than the right hemisphere when they are listening to speech sounds. However, while speech and grammar seem to be localized to the left hemisphere in most people, the understanding of metaphor and humor involve the right hemisphere. Parents are the beneficiaries of a whole industry of spin doctors who have turned these complicated findings into the claim that the left hemisphere is "logical" and the right hemisphere is "creative."

Being conscientious parents, the Goodwins believe that scientific evidence derived from the latest and most extensive research showed that they should play classical music during the "critical" first years of life, to give their children the best possible start. If they fail to do so, they might forever damage their children's intellectual growth.

Harold and Martha came to these myths honestly. They are good parents. They not only read the packaging in the baby stores but have been living amidst the hype that exists in our accelerated society.

THE ORIGIN OF THE HYPE

It is hard to relax about early childhood when all of our leaders have put so much emphasis on it. Back in 1996, at a White House Conference on Early Childhood Development and Learning, Hillary Clinton linked early learning with a new sense of urgency about the brain: "A child's earliest experiences, their relationships with parents and caregivers, the sights and sounds and smells and feelings they encounter, the challenges they must meet, determine how their brains are wired."

Policy makers needed to bolster their campaigns for education spending, and so they gathered together researchers who were talking about the finite "windows of opportunity" represented by "critical periods" for the rapidly developing brain in infancy. At one White House Conference on Early Experience, researcher Harry Chugani, M.D., of the University of Michigan, who published some of the first research on the developing brain using positron emission tomography (or PET) scans, spoke with urgency. Dr. Chugani stated, "In the earliest years, we have a unique opportunity to decide how the brain will be wired." He described a number of "critical periods," or times during which certain stimulation is crucial for brain growth. "Two years is the critical period for vision. If an infant has very dense cataracts, which are not removed by about the age of 2, it's too late. The visual cortex will be reassigned to other tasks and the child will not see—even if the cataracts are later removed."

Dr. Chugani claimed that "connections that have reached a certain threshold through use will be 'hard-wired.' Less-used connections will be more vulnerable. Thus, in the earliest years we have a unique opportunity to decide how the brain will be wired. . . ." He painted an extreme picture of our ability to sculpt the brain, implying that many skills were hard-wired during critical periods for their development.

But it wasn't just the policy makers, seeking scientific rationales for education spending, who misled parents such as the Goodwins. Marketers of products for babies sensed a breech they could jump into and have eagerly blanketed the parents' world ever since with a kind of running advertisement about the need to manage the baby brain. "Raise a Smart Kid," a recent cover of *Parents* magazine urged, offering—for the busy parent—a "5-minute brain booster every baby needs." The media's motive, of course, is as much to get our attention and make us buy more as it is to accurately inform. When research is described in the popular press, it often makes the urgency of the first years seem even greater so we'll buy more copy. An article in *Newsweek* magazine, for instance, compared the neurons in a baby's brain to computer chips, some of which are hard-wired, but others of which haven't yet been preloaded with software. Of these "empty" neurons, the article then ominously reported, "If the neurons are used, they become integrated into the circuitry of the brain by connecting to other neurons; *if they are not used, they may die.* (Emphasis added—but be sure the parental reader will feel a jolt of anxiety when happening upon this phrase!) It is the experiences of childhood, determining which neurons are used, that wire the circuits of the brain as surely as a programmer at a keyboard reconfigures the circuits in a computer. Which keys are typed—which experiences a child has—determines whether the child grows up to be intelligent or dull. . . ."

This kind of statement puts enormous pressure on parents. Naturally, they feel overwhelmed at discovering they are now to be the programmers of the critical processes occurring in their children's brains. How will they know what to do for this complex and vulnerable system? Not surprisingly, the parenting marketplace is delighted to supply the answers. Almost every product, it seems, is designed (scientifically, of course) to help the baby's brain grow—from toys and games to exercise classes and equipment, from stories to baby food.

Thankfully, a closer look at the evidence suggests that parents might not have to work so hard. As we will see, millions of years of evolution have created children who love to learn on their own—it's how nature has ensured our survival. Humankind has eaten from the tree of knowledge and continues to seek out this delicious fruit from the first moments of life—no force-feeding is necessary. Unless you are living in extreme isolation or poverty, the natural, everyday environments in which families and children find themselves promote strong brain development. Children with loving parents who enjoy them, play with them, and offer guidance and suggestions as they explore their environment will be healthy, emotionally well-adjusted, and psychologically advanced.

Join us in exploring the research findings, and you will come to understand why you can relax and play with your baby while leaving the architecture of the brain to Mother Nature. As our story unfolds, you'll see that you don't have to spend your hard-earned dollars to "educate" your babies.

WHAT REALLY MATTERS FOR BRAIN GROWTH: BASIC PRINCIPLES

The best way to defend yourself against the hype is to empower yourself with knowledge about the brain and the way it functions. The journey takes place in a metaphorical sense, as we imagine ourselves flying around the brain as if we are in a space shuttle orbiting the earth. If we could do this, we would be able to observe key structures that are related to various aspects of the ways we think. We will be especially interested in the large continent covering most of our globe—the cerebral cortex—which makes up about 80 percent of the brain's volume. Most of the research on early learning focuses on this outer layer of the brain, which is essentially our gray matter. It is like a continent divided into four countries: the frontal lobe, which is involved in voluntary movement and thinking; the occipital lobe, in vision; the temporal lobe, in hearing; and the parietal lobe, in processing information about body sensations such as touch.

The Brain and Its Lobes

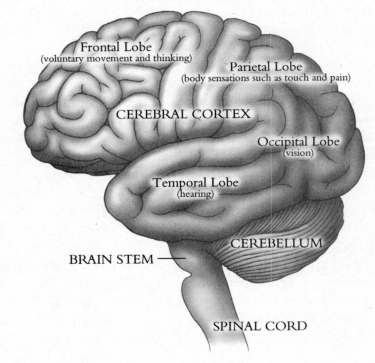

Frontal Lobe
(voluntary movement and thinking)

Parietal Lobe
(body sensations such as touch and pain)

CEREBRAL CORTEX

Occipital Lobe
(vision)

Temporal Lobe
(hearing)

CEREBELLUM

BRAIN STEM

SPINAL CORD

Just as the Earth is divided into Eastern and Western Hemispheres, the cerebral cortex is divided into left and right hemispheres. The term lateralization is used to describe the specialization in the brain's two halves. For example, in most people, speech and grammar tend to be localized in the left hemisphere.

Flying into the brain for a close-up look, we make a smooth landing in a neuron, one of the 80 billion nerve cells that serve as the hard-wiring of the nervous system and handle information processing. Neurons are serviced by 100 billion *glial* cells that nourish and modulate their activity. The neurons are a little bit like the rivers that flow over continents, allowing people to transport themselves and cargo from one region to another. In the brain, however, each neuron transports information. Each

Information Processing in a Neuron

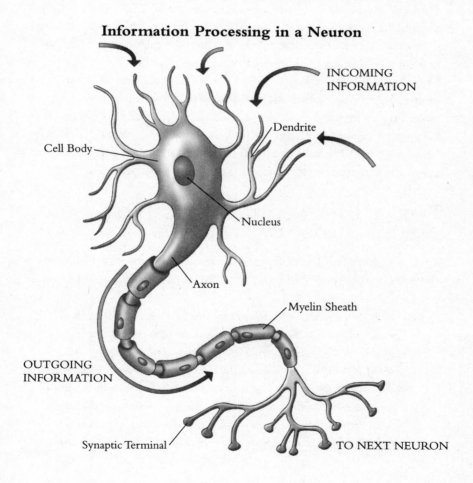

INCOMING INFORMATION

Dendrite

Cell Body

Nucleus

Axon

Myelin Sheath

OUTGOING INFORMATION

Synaptic Terminal

TO NEXT NEURON

one begins out of a little wellspring, or cell nucleus, surrounded by a cell body. Out of that cell body two kinds of branches emerge, and wouldn't you know, our landing gear seems to be tangled up in some of these branches, called *dendrites*. It's their function to receive incoming information, and they seem to want to make sure they have a good grasp on whatever we're carrying before sending us out through the long tail of the *axon* and out the synaptic gap, to the next thicket of dendrites. It's as if we're passing through a security check.

Suppose, for a moment, that we are carrying the nursery rhyme "Rock-a-bye baby, in the treetops . . ." as cargo. We clear security and shoot out along an axon at lightning speed. A *myelin sheath* consisting of fat cells encases the axon and acts like a riverbank, keeping us on course until we are popped out of a synaptic terminal. Then we are helped through the portage area, called the *synapse*. Various neurotransmitter chemicals carry us over that region and into the thatch of the next set of dendrites, and so on throughout the region. Like the early explorers, we have now established the first trail in the brain for this nursery rhyme. The next time we make our passage through the brain's pathways with the same nursery rhyme, our rocket ship seems to navigate a little more easily because we've already blazed the trail; the brain remembers "Rock-a-bye baby." Victory! But how does that happen? And can we learn anything about the functions of the brain as we continue on our journey?

FOR A BRAIN, BIGGER IS NOT NECESSARILY BETTER

Carla Shatz, a neurobiology professor at the University of California at Berkeley, compares the neurology of the brain to a complex phone system.

> . . . It communicates with other brain cells by a combination of chemical and electrical signaling. So when you make a connection, one phone may ring, or 10,000 may ring. In all, the brain has to create a network of more than a hundred trillion connections; what's more, the hook-ups have to be very precise so that when you phone home, you reach your house and not a wrong number. Just to illustrate the complexity, there are about a million connections from each eye, and there are about 2 million possible destinations that each one of these con-

*nections could reach. And yet, fewer than 100 connections are selected
from this vast number of addresses, in a process called "synaptogenesis."*

So what about this *synaptogenesis?* The spin doctors have us thinking
that since the synapses are developing fast and furiously in infancy, we
want to keep as many of them as possible. More is better. Bigger is better.
Right? Then why does nature prune the brain by eliminating some of
these precious synaptic connections? Because having 500 connections
making the decision whether to turn left or right is not going to be efficient. The brain *wants* to be pruned in order to be quick and precise.

Connections form so quickly that by the time children are 3, their
brains have twice as many synapses as they will need as adults. These trillions of synapses are competing for space in a brain that is still far from its
adult size. By the age of 3, a young child's brain is apt to be more than
twice as active as that of her pediatrician. If children have more synapses
than they will have as adults, what happens to the trillions of excess connections? The answer is that they are shed as children grow, much like the
way a snake sheds its skin in order to accommodate a bigger body. Brains
downsize for the same reasons so many other "organizations" do: With
streamlined networks, they can function more efficiently. Pruning is a natural development. This refinement is good. In fact, in a genetic abnormality
called Fragile X Syndrome, the resulting mental retardation, learning disabilities, and short attention span are related to a *lack* of pruning.

It is estimated that about 40 percent of the cortical synapses present in
infancy are eliminated by adulthood. Because pruning is necessary for the
normal, healthy growth of the brain and body, the extent of synaptic
elimination has been carefully studied to determine "normal" levels of
synapse loss.

How does the brain "decide" which connections to shed and which
to keep? Each time synapses fire, beginning with the early months and
years of life, they become sturdier and more resilient. Those that are used
often enough tend to survive; those that are not used often enough are
history. In this way, a child's experiences in the first years of life do indeed
affect her brain's permanent circuitry. However, scientists report that
throughout the developmental process, the brain is producing new
synapses, strengthening existing ones, and eliminating ones that aren't used
often enough. In fact, if all this research on the brain shows any consis-

tent pattern, it's that throughout life, the brain is always growing and changing.

One of the first researchers to show that there is a pattern to this process of synaptogenesis was Professor Peter Huttenlocher, a pediatric neurologist at the University of Chicago. He showed that the human cerebral cortex is characterized by the rapid proliferation and overproduction of synapses, followed by a phase of synapse pruning that eventually brings the overall number of synapses down to their adult levels. Professor Huttenlocher made this discovery by painstakingly counting the number of cells. He found that different brain regions with different functions appear to develop on different timetables. What's of special interest for the concerned parent is that synapses grow in many areas of the brain—even without stimulation from the environment. Before the eyes of rats open, for instance, synaptic growth proceeds according to its own biological timetable.

Moreover, extra stimulation is not always good. An example of "more is not always better" comes to us from the neonatal nursery. On the increasingly prevalent cultural assumption that more stimulation is better and that it is never too early to start, neonatal units used to be filled with bright lights and soothing but stimulating sounds. Scientists later found, however, that the sounds and lights of the neonatal care units were actually contributing to problems of attention deficit and hyperactivity. So now the units are darkened and softened to resemble the environment nature had intended these babies to experience—that dark and muffled place called the womb.

ENRICHED ENVIRONMENTS AND BRAIN GROWTH

If synaptic growth and pruning are proceeding nicely on their own in infancy, then where did the emphasis on making the brain better come from? What is the intellectual underpinning that the marketers draw upon to push us to "enrich" our babies' lives with all these educational products? Research on the brains of animals, primarily rats, shows that enriched environments produce bigger, better brains. Yet, as we shall see, this research has been misinterpreted to make the case that enrichment is essential for human brain growth.

How to Make Rats Smarter: Does the Logic Work for Children?

The best way to understand the concept of an enriched environment is to consider the work of the late Professor Donald Hebb of McGill University in Montreal, Canada. About 50 years ago, Professor Hebb brought some rats home to his children to raise as pets. It was a free-spirited household, and so the rats had the run of the house. Professor Hebb took them back to his laboratory for some visits, though, and discovered that they learned to run mazes more quickly and made fewer errors while learning than did their lab-reared cousins. The rats that had been raised as pets were considered to have been raised in "enriched environments."

In the 1960s, Mark R. Rosenzweig, a professor of psychology at the University of California at Berkeley, began to publish findings showing that rats raised in enriched environments had heavier brains and thicker cortexes in certain brain regions than did rats raised alone in a cage. In the 1970s, Professor William Greenough, of the psychology department at the University of Illinois in Urbana-Champaign, continued the study of how different aspects of rats' environments affect their behavior and brain development. Typically, he would set up three different conditions: One rat living in solitary confinement in a small cage; a rat living in a large cage with several other rats; and a rat living with other rats in a kind of Disneyland, with toys and slides and running wheels. As you might guess, the Disneyland rats had more synapses in their brains (20 to 25 percent higher synapse-to-neuron ratios than the isolated rats), and so they learned to run mazes more quickly and effectively.

The Rosenzweig research is one of the key pieces of evidence that spurred the new frenzy toward creating bigger brains in children. People assumed that if rats in enriched environments did better than rats in impoverished environments, then surely humans in enriched environments would outperform humans in *normal* environments. But there are two ways in which this analogy breaks down. First, the rats raised in solitary confinement in small and boring cages have no equivalent in children's lives (except in cases of the very worst deprivation). That is, people do not raise their children in closets, but in the natural world replete with other people and toys and houses. The second flaw in the analogy is that the leap from impoverished environments to enriched environments with rats is not the same as the leap from normal environments to enriched environments. In fact, infants might profit *more* from natural environments than from enriched environments. In fact, though it received much less press coverage than his other discoveries, Professor Rosenweig made one more useful observation: The rats that remained in nature had the best brains of all. They were stimulated by the sights, sounds, and smells of the world around them. They met up with termites, spiders, and cats. They socialized in packs, chose their leaders and mates, dealt with lice and fleas, and probably even frolicked from time to time. In other words, their *natural* environment was the best thing in the world for their rat brains—even better than the Disneyland the researchers created in the rats' cages.

Professor Greenough and his colleagues point out that a great deal of brain development actually occurs *independently* of experience. As we mentioned earlier, research on rats shows that rapid synapse formation, for instance, begins in the rat visual cortex about 2 days after birth and increases rapidly until the rat is around 3 weeks old. This rapid synapse formation begins *before* the animals have any sensory stimulation from their environments. Why are the synapses for sight growing rapidly even before the newborn opens his eyes?

The answer takes us right to the heart of the early learning debate. The critical growth of the brain that takes place early in life is programmed by nature to unfold. Our eyesight, our speech, and probably our athletic abilities, too, are functions that Mother Nature has pretty much covered. Professor Greenough calls these *experience-expectant* behaviors. A result of millions of years of evolution, the brain expects to have the experiences of seeing things, hearing language, and moving limbs, so it just goes on its merry way, growing normally as it encounters these experiences in its environment. Unless it is severely deprived of these experiences, the brain will build itself. It doesn't rely on parental architects who put each experience in place for the young rat or the young child.

Of course, not all things you can learn about fall into the category of experience-expectant. Your brain cannot assume that it will encounter reading, chess playing, or computer games. Such cultural acquisitions are designed to be picked up by the brain *throughout* our lives—and are called "experience-*dependent*." Clearly, humans can survive without these skills, though they can't survive as well without developing experience-expectant skills. Unlike experience-expectant skills, however, experience-dependent skills don't depend at all on early learning. They depend on our unique cultural experiences. Experience-dependent learning continues throughout life, fosters new brain growth, and refines existing brain structures that vary for every individual.

Ordinary, everyday, run-of-the-mill experiences, or doing what comes naturally, are all that is necessary for experience-expectant brain development. Of course, as a parent or educator, you aren't as concerned about your role in developing experience-expectant behaviors like vision or walking, but you do wonder about the experience-dependent behaviors like reading and chess. Fortunately, most experience-dependent behaviors have a very wide window of opportunity for their development. That is, you needn't learn them in the first 3 years or even in the first 5 years of life. Even in those cases where there may be an optimal window of opportunity for learning, the window extends well beyond early childhood. Professor Huttenlocher writes, "Second-language teaching and musical training are likely to be more effective if started early, during the period of high plasticity, which includes the early school years (ages 5 to 10 years)." Thus, we needn't rush music and language training into the crib.

A more potent argument against rushing early learning comes from the potential problem of neurological "crowding." What's crowding? Crowding is when information competes for synaptic connections in the brain. Imagine that you're waiting for tickets at a movie theater and there are two lines. Now imagine that the manager comes out and closes one of the lines. Your line becomes more crowded, and it takes longer to buy your ticket. So, too, with neurological crowding. As Professor Huttenlocher says, "One has to consider the possibility that very ambitious early enrichment and teaching programs may lead to crowding effects and to an early decrease in the size and number of brain regions that are largely unspecified and that may be necessary for creativity in the adolescent and adult." Too much early learning may actually be an impediment rather than a boon to later intelligence. As Professor Huttenlocher acknowledges, "It may be no accident that Albert Einstein was a rather average student in his early years," allowing his brain to avoid early crowding effects.

By now, we hope we've convinced you that you are unlikely to create an abundance of synaptic connections that build a bigger brain by exposing your children to early enrichment and mind-building toys. Surely, however, you've heard that the first years of life are critical for brain development. Even if your children won't have more synaptic connections and bigger brains, you don't want to miss out on the window of opportunity that presents itself in the first 3 years of life, do you? The "critical period" assumption is perhaps the most frequent argument the marketplace waves in front of our faces. As professor of psychology Edward Zigler and his colleagues at Yale University point out, " . . . The implications of media portrayals of critical or sensitive periods for learning lead parents to worry that they need to implement musical instruction, math games, or foreign-language lessons in the playpen or even in the crib."

THE FIRST 3 YEARS AND THE "CRITICAL PERIOD" THEORY

"Critical period" is a concept that comes to us from biology. It is a window of time in which some important aspect of development occurs, and it has a definite beginning and end. To illustrate this concept, let's consider the tragic case of women who used a tranquilizer called thalidomide, which was prescribed in the early 1960s to pregnant women to help them with morning sickness. If a pregnant woman took the drug on the 26th day after conception, the developing arms of the embryo were interfered with, and the child would be born with very truncated arms. If she took the drug 2 days later, the embryo's arms might grow—but not past the elbow. There would be no way for the child to recover that period of growth later on—the period was *critical*. In human beings, damage at a critical period needs to be extreme—like consuming medicines that damage the fetus—to have an effect on the child from which he or she cannot recover.

Critical periods definitely exist in biological development. Many argue, however, that they exert their effects on psychological development as well. Witness the shocking case of Genie. "Girl 13, Prisoner since Infancy" was the headline in the *Los Angeles Times* on November 17, 1970. It was a horrible story about a 13-year-old child who had been kept in a small bedroom since she was 20 months of age. She was bound to a potty chair in her small room; the door was opened only when the parents fed the child. She was small, frail, and malnourished when her almost blind mother walked into a social service agency by mistake. Even after extensive intervention, 4 years later Genie's language skills were still quite limited. She had amassed the vocabulary of a 5-year-old, but was never really able to use grammar effectively. Genie represents an extreme case of deprivation. Her case seems to suggest that if you miss exposure to language within the period when you are particularly receptive to learning it, you can never catch up and develop adequate language skills. (Of course, not all cases that illustrate the critical period concept involve deprivation this extreme.)

Professor Elissa Newport of the University of Rochester in New York studied the competence of speakers of American Sign Language. Some of these speakers learned the language as infants from their parents. Others weren't exposed to the language until they were 12 or 13 years of age and in school. Professor Newport found that those children who weren't exposed to the language until after early childhood never did as well as those who learned it early—even if they had used the language for 30 years.

Professor Newport's study is buttressed by another interesting study of second-language learning conducted by Professors Kenji Hakuta of Stanford University and Professors Ellen Bialystok and Edward Wiley, both of York University in Toronto, Canada. Soliciting responses from 2.3 million immigrants from Spanish or Chinese backgrounds, they asked whether the age of immigration made any difference in the ability to master the English language. They found that across all ages, immigrants who arrived in the United States earlier had better language proficiency than those who arrived later. Yet they report that there is no "critical" age after which the new language *cannot* be learned. Put more positively, if you moved to Romania today, you could still learn the new language, even if you never had one day's prior exposure to Romanian.

Taken together, these studies point to three main conclusions. First, there appear to be more and less receptive periods for learning certain behaviors, like language. The behaviors that have these receptive periods are almost always experience-expectant behaviors that the species cannot live without. Thus, language learning and visual learning are good candidates for behaviors with "critical periods."

Second, and importantly, while 3-year-olds do better than 30-year-olds, there does not appear to be a "critical period" that is suddenly over at a certain point in time for learning these behaviors. That is, the window for language learning doesn't snap shut after the first 3 years of life. It seems to stay open at least until puberty and under some scenarios for a lifetime. As Professor Ross Thompson from the University of Nebraska and Professor Charles Nelson of the University of Minnesota write, "Windows of opportunity for early stimulation better characterize basic sensory and motor capacities than higher mental and personality processes, and even so, most such windows close very slowly with development."

Third, and finally, responsive periods do not seem to exist at all for experience-dependent behaviors like chess and gymnastics. There is simply no reason at all to generalize that if there are responsive periods for learning evolutionarily primed behaviors, then there must be a critical period for everything the child could possibly learn. In fact, nothing could be further from the truth. When we rush learning, we often try to teach things that make little sense to the child and that would better be learned at a later age.

As Dr. Irving Sigel, senior scientist at the Educational Testing Service in Princeton, New Jersey, has written, " . . . The teaching of concepts and skills at this very early period is very time-consuming, even for rote learning, because learning is more difficult when understanding does not accompany the learning experience." In other words, memorizing composers' faces and names (yes, there are flash cards like this) is a useless experience for a toddler or preschooler who cannot connect this information to anything meaningful in her world. Even flash cards with color names or numbers don't build competencies if they are not part of a child's everyday experiences. Furthermore, there is no evidence that these early learning experiences improve the brain.

So, are the first 3 years the golden age for learning? Do they represent a critical period of rapid brain growth that will prepare children for lives as future geniuses? The simple answer to this question is no. If children are growing up in normal, everyday environments filled with objects and buildings, with people who love them and talk to them, their brains will grow all by themselves. Parents are not the *sculptors* of their children's brains, nor do they have the responsibility for deciding which *particular* sorts of experiences to provide to make synaptic connections happen within a critical period of time.

Relax! Even basic behaviors like learning language can be acquired over a long span of time without your child losing even a moment's advantage in the international marketplace. If you hire that Spanish-speaking nanny when your child is 2 or when he's 5, your child will still learn to speak Spanish. In fact, he probably won't be at a future disadvantage if his first exposure to the language arrives at age 8 or 9.

The assumption that all has to be learned in the first 3 years is simply untrue. Indeed, it is what Dr. John Bruer, president of the James Mc-Donnell Foundation in St. Louis, Missouri, called The Myth of the First Three Years. In his now-classic book by the same name, he argued that we don't need to overenrich the environment for young brains to develop.

He goes on to suggest that critical periods cannot be used to justify constructing better environments for better brains. We are not the architects of our children's brains, so we do not have to agonize over what inputs to provide. Thankfully, millions of years of evolution have taken care of brain development for us, and we are unlikely to change the course of this development in a single generation.

BRINGING THE LESSONS HOME

Now that we know the scientific data about how children's brains develop, several lessons emerge. One is a cautionary note, and the others offer ways in which you can see the world differently and stimulate your child's brain growth in a more natural way.

Let the buyer beware! Don't let yourself be taken in by the messages about enhancing your baby's brain development that appear on flashy product lines. Just as sex is used in advertising to sell products to adults, marketers have figured out that brain development sells to parents. *There is no evidence, however, that particular educational programs, methods, or techniques are effective for brain development.*

For example, listening to Mozart is not bad for your child. That is, if you like Mozart, there is no harm in playing it and exposing your child to music. But you could just as well sing lullabies, play Simon and Garfunkel, the Indigo Girls, or any other band you like. Music is wonderful. There is no doubt about it. But the evidence from research says that listening to Mozart, Madonna, or Mama Cass will *not* make your child a math genius or budding architect, or even increase his general intelligence.

Think outside the box—literally. Your child will learn more when you play with him than when you buy him fancy boxes containing self-proclaimed "state-of-the-art" devices with exorbitant claims to build his brain. So what is an appropriate way to use playtime? Take your cues from your children. By taking the time to notice what they are interested in, you can begin to see the environment in a whole new way, as a series of natural opportunities that are stimulating your children at all times. You can then build on these opportunities to make them even more enriching.

Switch from *Sesame Street* to *Barney* and *Teletubbies*. We love *Sesame Street*, but there are also lessons in slow-moving, repetitive programs like *Barney* and *Teletubbies* that children enjoy. The developers of the famous show *Blue's Clues*, for example, actually studied what children prefer in order to make their episodes maximally appealing. They found that children love repetition. Indeed, although it may be deadly for us (how many of us have fallen asleep midsentence?), children love to hear the same stories night after night—they get something new each time and enjoy finding predictable patterns. Furthermore, recent research suggests that limited (1 hour a day) educational television actually has advantages for our children, and these advantages show up in later reading and number skills when our children enter school.

Here's your assignment: Watch an educational program with your children and see what they enjoy. Research indicates that children get more out of television when their parents watch alongside them. What does your child find exciting in the show? Use it to build on your child's interests. Perhaps take out some children's library books on those topics. These interests can also yield conversational material your child will love to talk about.

Move from memorizing to learning in context. If we really want to promote learning and brain growth in babies, toddlers, and preschoolers, we must help them learn in context and *not* through flash cards. Memorizing just does not do the trick and often is mistakenly thought to be true learning. One example of toddler "genius" comes to mind. This child was touted by his mother as an extreme intellect—a child who could already read many words just after his third birthday. He was asked to visit the neighborhood psychologist, who happened to be me, Kathy Hirsh-Pasek, to show off his academic talents. When he arrived, he showed me his *Speak* *and Spell*, and the mother proceeded to have him read each word (book, shoe, cup . . . the list went on). After the performance, I applauded and asked the child to go to my television, on which the familiar words "color, volume, channel" were written in large letters. I politely asked him to read these. After all, a child who truly knows how to read should be able to read any new word. You can read the nonsense word "thurld" because you know the sounds of the letters and how to combine them. However, the child got so flustered after looking at the words on the set that he fled, and the performance was over. He had learned how to memorize words, perhaps from their shape (for example, "ball" has two tall letters), but he had not really learned to read.

There is no pressing need to have our children read before they go to school. But if we read to them and for them when they ask us what is written on that cereal box or street sign, we are implicitly teaching that reading is fun and has utility. This is what we mean by learning something *in context*. The other "reading" is simply memorization and has little merit beyond the performance. Thus, some of the gadgets and gizmos on the market offer wonderful opportunities for performing, but fail to create genuine learning. Learning is always more powerful and lasting when it occurs in context.

Plan a field trip—to your own backyard. It's great to travel to exotic locations or expensive theme parks, but we don't have to go there to build brains. We can get a tremendous amount of stimulation in our own backyards, where we can witness the miracle of blades of grass blowing in the wind, of ants building homes, of all that teaming life that lives right down in the dirt. The film *Honey, I Shrunk the Kids* illustrates the wonderful hidden life that goes on beyond our notice. For children, the yard is a world of bustling activity, science lessons, physics lessons, and lessons about nature and color.

While you're in the backyard, you can stimulate creativity in your 4- and 5-year-olds by asking them to imagine what it would be like to be the size of an ant. What would look different? What could you hear? What would you be afraid of? Children often love to imagine the fears others may have, so they know they're not alone.

And along these lines, ask them if they can hear the music of the backyard. Are there instruments to be made from sticks and stones? Whistles from leaves and rhythms from the raindrops? Bring out a blanket and lie down with your eyes closed. What can you hear? Do you hear the leaves rustling in the wind? A bee buzzing? A car grinding? The timpani of thunder? The chickadees' chatter and the mockingbirds' trills? Even 2-year-olds love these games.

Where do the animals and insects in your yard live? Discover each creature's home. In a wonderful book, *A House Is a House for Me* by Mary Anne Hoberman, the author asks us to think about a house for a bee and a house for a bird. How do the animals build their homes? Can our 4- and 5-year-olds build nests, too? Would they like to tell us about something they saw that we could write for them? Children love to tell stories as we type them into the computer. "Can we make up stories together about Irving the Ant and how he finds his friend Libby on the forest floor?" There are hours and hours of fun and games in each patch of backyard, no matter how small. And if you can find this much in your backyard, imagine the stimulating environment you'd encounter at the zoo. Or at a children's museum.

Move from city malls to tennis balls. Sure the malls are fun for us, but they are a buzzing and blooming confusion for our children. Imagine what it must be like to be in a world where all of the people tower over you, where the sounds and the colors rush by, and where adults are more interested in their friends than they are in you. There is no reason to exclude the mall, but we often fail to realize what we can do with everyday objects that surround us all the time. Furthermore, what do you do in the car as you travel to the mall? This is a wonderful time to play children's music on your tape or CD player and sing along. When your child is a little older, you can play the "I Spy" game. "I spy a . . . dog!" "I spy a . . . policeman!" Oops, mommy better slow down.

At home, an activity as simple as rolling a ball back and forth on the living room carpet can be fascinating to your young child. How do you roll it so that it lands near the other person? How hard do you have to push? What is the angle you have to use? Will the ball hit other objects along its trajectory? This is experience-expectant learning at its best, with physics and math concepts thrown in for free. And it costs no more than the price of a ball.

And before you spend $25 on that educational toy at the mall, think of all the things you have around the house that baby will find very stimulating indeed. Pots and pans and plastic containers are a blast in the kitchen and make a great symphony with a wooden spoon (we never said this would be restful). Laundry baskets on their sides are great for climbing in and out of, as are the large boxes that appliances arrive in. For some reason, children love hiding in and under things and climbing in and out. Blanket forts made by spreading a blanket over a few chairs can be fun for hours if you join in the make-believe and make it grandma's house. Adding a pillow and a few stuffed animals and books inside can make it a friend's house or a room at preschool. And why do babies always like to pull things out of drawers? To see what's inside! Take one low drawer and fill it with surprising and fun things (stuffed animals, books, cars, pictures of family members, and so on) that you change periodically, and let baby have a ball unloading it all. Never underestimate the power of ordinary objects when examined with a child's eye. For children, they are not ordinary at all. And these experiences—free and fun and unfettered with concerns about doing something educational—all build better brains.

CHAPTER +3

PLAYING THE NUMBERS:
HOW CHILDREN
LEARN ABOUT
QUANTITY

AMY, MOTHER OF 2-YEAR-OLD JESS, was devastated when she opened the newspaper and discovered the headline "Infants can perform addition and subtraction." Jess could count to 10, and Amy thought *that* was a real accomplishment. But if tiny 5-month-old babies can add and subtract, Jess must be behind!

That very day, Amy ran out to the mall and bought flash cards with dot patterns to help Jess learn to add and subtract. The pressure was on! What if Jess got to nursery school and was the only one who couldn't do math?

The headline Amy read bears a grain of truth. It evolved from a now-classic study whose interpretation spiraled out of hand and became the foundation for media hype and infant marketers. No doubt you've seen the toys available in the marketplace to foster mathematical development in young children. Indeed, parents have been led to believe that toddlers can and should learn arithmetic. As you will discover in this chapter, however, there is a significant difference between truly doing math and simply understanding differences in quantity or being able to memorize the numbers from 1 to 10.

The truth is that while children seem innately primed to be interested in basic math concepts, their understanding develops according to a set sequence of milestones, and trying to "skip ahead" is not only a waste of time, but a frustrating experience for the child. Before children can learn addition and subtraction, they must first learn the basic principles of counting and understand the concept of a number line. And the best way to learn these concepts is to let them slowly unfold as your children play with and investigate the objects in their world.

TWO STUDIES, TWO DIFFERENT OUTCOMES

The study that inspired the misperception that infants can add and subtract was conducted in the 1990s by Karen Wynn, professor of psychology at Yale University. She was interested in discovering what babies know about what could be called the basics of addition and subtraction.

In the experiment, Professor Wynn first showed a 5-month-old baby a Mickey Mouse doll sitting on a mini-stage. When the baby's interest in the doll started to wane, a student would raise a screen from the bottom of the stage that completely hid the doll. Next, the baby would see an outstretched arm place a second Mickey Mouse behind the screen, so that logically there should now have been two dolls there. The question Professor Wynn was exploring was whether or not the baby would realize this. Did babies understand that $1 + 1 = 2$?

When the screen was lowered, it revealed only one doll. This is known as the *impossible condition*. Professor Wynn studied babies' reactions when they saw two dolls revealed, or the *expected condition*. Judging from the longer amount of time they looked at the impossible condition and their looks of surprise when they saw it, the researchers concluded that babies could "add."

To study whether babies could "subtract," the study was done in reverse, with two dolls shown to begin with and one then taken away. Again, babies expressed surprise at the impossible condition, indicating a rudimentary understanding of subtraction.

You can see why the researchers and the news headlines capitalized on the idea that infants could add and subtract. The babies clearly knew something about number, or at least about the amount of "stuff" that they were shown. They even understood how the amount could be changed. Before we get too excited, however, consider that rhesus monkeys demonstrated the same abilities when they were shown similar impossible conditions with eggplants (something monkeys find much more interesting than Mickey Mouse dolls). Further, we must ask whether this is *truly* addition and subtraction as we understand addition and subtraction. It turns out that the answer to that question is more complicated.

Enter Professor Janellen Huttenlocher, of the University of Chicago department of psychology. She and her colleagues study toddlers, 2 to 4 years of age, to see how well they can "add" and "subtract." The researchers are not using flash cards with formulas, of course. They use what children are able to literally grasp—three-dimensional objects that they can hold and manipulate. One researcher observes whether Amanda, a 2½-year-old, can add "3 plus 1." Amanda sits across from the researcher, who shows her three red blocks. Amanda watches intently as the researcher then covers up the blocks with a large box. To make sure Amanda understands the game, she is then asked to show the researcher, using another set of blocks, how many the researcher has hidden under the box. Amanda is happy to oblige. She lines up three blocks on her side of the table. With the original blocks still hidden, the researcher now adds another block underneath the box while asking Amanda, "Can you make yours look like mine?" All Amanda has to do is pick up one more block and place it in the pile to make a total of four blocks. Does she succeed? Not this time. She picks up two more blocks instead of just one. At 2½, she still doesn't get all the answers right to problems like these. In another year, she'll be able to work with small numbers like $1 + 1 = 2$ or $3 - 1 = 2$. And by the end of her third year, she'll even be able to do the task correctly with larger numbers like $2 + 2 = 4$.

A little confused? You should be. Why should 5-month-olds "pass" the Mickey Mouse test in Professor Wynn's lab only to later fail a similar task in Professor Huttenlocher's lab at 2½ years? The answer is that babies have only rudimentary number skills—a sensitivity to quantity—but not awareness of the kind of math that we think of when we talk about addition and subtraction. Derrick's responses at 5 months are very impressive. But some scientists believe that what Derrick is really doing is recognizing *amounts*, like *more* or *less*, instead of specific quantities, like two of something or four of something. The latter ability must come with development.

NUMBER SENSITIVITY
IS NOT THE SAME AS MATH

The "education president" George W. Bush mandated that all children in the United States need to be "ready to learn" by the time they enter elementary school. But what does this really mean? Many believe that it means children enrolled in our Head Start programs and preschools must develop number skills. What exactly *are* children supposed to know? Current standards hold that 3- and 4-year-olds should be able to count to 10 and know the names of the numbers. While these are important skills, they represent only the tip of the mathematical iceberg and fail to account for children's naturally maturing computational abilities. Does a child who can count know math?

A turn-of-the-century story about the numerical "genius" Clever Hans helps to explain the problem. Clever Hans was a horse whose trainer claimed he could add, subtract, multiply, and divide. When given a math problem, such as "Hans, what is two plus two?" the horse would tap out the correct answer with his foreleg. It wasn't until psychologist Oskar Pfungst blindfolded Hans that the truth was revealed. When he was unable to see his owner, Hans failed to get the right answer. Pfungst figured out that while Hans wasn't doing math, he *was* reading the nonverbal signals emitted by his owner. The owner would lean forward when he asked the question and gradually become upright as the horse tapped out the answer. When Hans reached the correct number, his owner stood straight up, as if to say, "That's it!" Hans's truly amazing ability to read unconscious nonverbal cues was not appreciated by his owner. He committed suicide, fearing he had perpetuated a hoax on the public. Clever Hans was clever all right—in the social domain. But he knew virtually nothing about mathematics.

What does the Clever Hans story teach us about children's abilities? It teaches us that children may not approach a task as we would, regardless of whether they come up with the right answer. Children are even better than Clever Hans at finding ways to solve the problems we present them with. They are often excellent, for example, at memorizing strings of things—car names, body parts, letters of the alphabet ("LMNOP" is often one letter), and yes, even numbers. For this reason, being able to recite the numbers in a row does not necessarily mean that a child understands anything about math. In fact, even knowing that there are three items underneath the box does not tell you that children have any idea that three is more than two but less than four. Perhaps a child memorizes that three is the "name" for three things in the same way that "blue" is the name for a certain color. Flash cards work like this. Children learn to bark out the appropriate answer to two dots on a card, but it's not at all clear that they understand what "two" means.

From this discussion, you might conclude that children's math abilities are shallow and superficial. While this is true when children are artificially pushed to respond on command, there is actually more to the story. Scientists know quite a bit about children's early number skills—even before they enter school. One of their most important findings is that the foundation for all mathematical learning takes place in infancy and early childhood, constructed by children around the world, regardless of their parentage. In fact, we believe that nature has programmed children to learn about numbers.

After all, it is hard to imagine how you would ever stumble upon numbers in the world if you didn't have some priming by Mother Nature. Numbers are everywhere, yet found nowhere. They are abstract and embodied in the physical, but not physically present. Given the importance of recognizing quantity of food, of attackers, and of suitors, it is a good thing that evolution has equipped us to pick up cues for quantity and number in our everyday world.

NUMBER VERSUS AMOUNT OF "STUFF"

While babies (and monkeys) can at least distinguish between different small amounts, just what they *understand* about number is currently under debate. There are researchers who argue that infants don't pay attention to number at all but, instead, to the *amount* of "stuff" they see. The following experiment attempted to distinguish between these alternative stories of infant number ability.

In experiments conducted by Professors Melissa W. Clearfield of Whitman College in Walla Walla, Washington, and Kelly Mix of Indiana University in Bloomington, 7-month-olds were tested using the "habituation" method. In this type of study, the child—let's call her baby Carla—will be shown something over and over again until she gets bored. A hidden researcher watching Carla presses a button connected to a computer to record her looking time. When her looking time falls below a certain level, Carla is shown something new. If she can distinguish the new from the old, she will start looking again. If she can't distinguish the new from the old, she will just continue to be bored.

What do the researchers show Carla to figure out if she is responding to number or amount of stuff? Two medium-size squares. The squares are placed on a board and, over the repeating trials, moved to different places on the board. Carla is at first fascinated and looks for a long time. Gradually, her time looking at the two peripatetic squares drops off as if Carla is saying, "Enough already—I get it." The question is what did Carla *get*? One way to find out is to show Carla two different scenes: *two larger* squares (the same number but *different amount*), or *three little* squares (a different number, but the *same total amount*). If Carla thinks that number of objects is the key, she should look longer at the scene containing three squares. If she thinks that amount of stuff is key, she should respond by looking longer at the two-square scene, since the amount has increased.

The winner? Amount of stuff. Carla looked a long time at the scene in which two larger squares appeared, but seemed uninterested when three smaller squares, with the same original quantity, were seen. Carla seemed to be solving this task based on amount and not number per se.

What should we make of this finding? One conclusion is that infants are capable only of noticing amount of stuff and are not really tuned in to number at all. Being tuned in to amount of stuff, however, is not a minor skill. It is a critical ability, despite the fact that it falls far short of claiming that infants add and subtract in a more numerical way. Perhaps what all infants possess is a basic conception of *more* and *less*. Some argue that this basic level of quantitative understanding is hard-wired in the brain and might be exactly what we share with animals foraging for food. We shall have to wait for further data on this. In any event, it is clear that infants are not doing addition and subtraction in any way resembling what we do, or even what preschoolers are capable of.

NUMBER AWARENESS: DOWN FOR THE COUNT

As children get older, the story of number development continues. By age 2½, most children can say a small string of numbers like "one, two, three, four." If they are shown a set of three balls, they can produce a like set of three balls. At 3 years of age, children can begin to count a medium-size set of objects—even going beyond sets of three and four items. Children of this age, however, can't tell if another person is counting correctly or incorrectly. They might also say a number more than once as they enumerate the objects. For example, they might count "one, two, two, three, two."

By age 4, children really start to put their number skills together. They are able to count sets of objects, tell us when a puppet or person miscounts, and join the Count on *Sesame Street* when he counts objects on the screen. At this age, they can even compare sets. They can realize that one set of items is larger than another and smaller than a third set. For example, they know that a set of four cookies is bigger than a set of three cookies and smaller than a set of five cookies.

Finally, by age 5, children develop the ability to both count and compare quantity at a level that becomes the hallmark of preschool number achievement. It is at this point, some argue, that children can place a number in its proper location in a counting series, relative to other numbers. It is also when children begin to use "counting on" when they have to add two sets of objects together. This strategy is late developing but a lot of fun to watch. Give a child three dolls to count. He will say, "one, two, three." Now give him two more dolls and ask, "How many do we have now?" You and I would count, "four, five," and quickly generate the final answer. Watch what children who are 3 or 4 do. They restart the counting with the first three dolls, "one, two, three, four, five," to arrive at the same answer. By age 5, these children realize that they already had three dolls and just "count on" from there like we did.

Discovering Hidden Skills | Counting On

Ages: 4 years to 6 years

See if your child uses "counting on." Get five toys and let your child play with them. Then separate them so that they form two distinct sets of three items and two items. Ask your child to first count the three-item set and tell you how many toys there are. Then give your child the two-item set and ask, "How many are there now?" What does your child do? Does she "count on"? If she doesn't, try this experiment again in a month and see if your child has now developed this ability. It will usually come in around age 5.

WHAT DO CHILDREN REALLY KNOW ABOUT COUNTING?

When children do something as simple as counting a small set of objects, do they really understand what they're doing? Jean Piaget, the late world-renowned Swiss developmental psychologist, doubted that children knew very much about numbers at all. Piaget loved to do mini-experiments with his own and other children to understand how they reason about the world.

To test what is known as a number conservation problem, for example, Piaget might place a row of five blue disks in front of 5-year-old Francoise. Then he would lay out another row of disks for himself. The rows would be only about 3 inches apart, and the disks would be lined up parallel to each other. He would then say, "Francoise, these are your circles here (pointing) and these are my circles here (pointing). Do you have more circles, or do I have more circles, or do we both have the same amount?" Francoise, looking a little uncertain, moves her head around the two rows of disks as if she is trying to get a better perspective. Interestingly, although Francoise can count, she seems just a tad hesitant to respond to the question. "We both have the same amount," she finally concludes.

Next, in full view of Francoise, Piaget would then spread out his row so that the disks in the two rows were no longer lined up with each other and his row took up more space. He would then ask Francoise the exact same question: "Francoise, do you have more circles now, or do I have more circles, or do we both have the same amount?" Francoise is certain this time and concludes cheerily, "Why, you have more now. Look how spread out your row is!"

To adults, such a response seems shocking. How could the child respond in this way? In fact, even other psychologists had a hard time believing the study's findings. Yet this finding is observed all over the world. Maybe if we ask the questions differently, or allow children to manipulate the displays themselves, the psychologists reasoned, we can get children to solve what seems like an incredibly simple task.

After many, many studies, Rutgers University professor Rochel Gelman's work made clear that children know more about number than Piaget and his followers gave them credit for. This does not mean that you can't get your own young children to fail a conservation task—or eat the stimuli first if you use M&M's! But Professor Gelman reasoned that children were unclear about which dimension to pay attention to in that conservation task. It is as if the child asks herself, "What matters here? Should I rely on the number of items in each row? Or should I rely on how much space they take up? Or should I rely on how squished together they seem?"

It turns out that you can train children to pay attention to the relevant dimension—number—and get them to respond correctly. Professor Gelman did this using "magical" mice. She presented children, one at a time, with a number of problems where she changed the number of mice and/or the density or spaces between the mice. Sometimes she showed two mice far apart opposite from three mice very close together. Sometimes she showed the mice with rows of the same length. She would ask children to pick the plate with more mice—the "winner." The plate with three mice was always the winner—no matter how it was arranged—and the plate with two mice was always the "loser." When children got it right, she rewarded them. She essentially taught them that number was the dimension that mattered in this task. Then she tricked children (one of psychologists' favorite tasks!) into showing her what they had learned about number. She surreptitiously ("magically") removed one mouse from the end of a row of mice or from the center, making the rows equal in length or density but now the *same* in terms of number. Children showed surprise and, in their verbal responses, clearly showed that they had figured out that number was what mattered here. Some asked where the missing mouse was or looked for it. Others offered explanations for the mouse's disappearance, like "Jesus took it."

What is important about Professor Gelman's work is twofold. First, it shows that young children can learn to pay attention to number as a relevant dimension and pass Piaget's conservation task. Second, it shows that young children approach simple tasks like this one in very different ways from adults. They need time and experience to figure out that number is what matters in the conservation task. In fact, as other researchers have shown, children who fail the standard conservation task act as if their answer *must* be correct. Francoise responded with great certainty, based on her belief that the way things look is more important than how many there are. But, as Professor Gelman's dissertation showed, there are ways to induce children to notice that number is really what matters. Ironically, this is just the sort of knowledge that we don't need to teach our children. They come to understand this on their own from their ordinary world experience.

There may be ways, however, in which conversations with parents about number help children reach these understandings sooner. For example, one of the skills that contribute to an understanding of number is demonstrated when children line up two parallel sets of things. The fancy name for this is one-to-one correspondence, and it helps children to compare sets. It also comes naturally to children. At 3 years of age, one of our children (Josh) thought there was simply nothing better in the world than lining up all of his many toy cars. After meticulously placing each car in a long row, he took his little plastic stand-up dolls and put one doll beside each of the cars. Children can play this "game" with anything—shoes and socks or books and animals. You may be surprised to notice how often your child sorts objects and then creates one-to-one correspondences with them.

| Discovering Hidden Skills | Conservation Problems |

Ages: 3 years to 6 years

Do your own conservation experiment with your child, imitating what Piaget did with Francoise above. Every conservation problem has three components: First, the child must agree when asked that the two sets of identical items before her (whatever they are) have the same number of items. Second, as the child observes, the adult manipulates the set, either squishing the objects within it together or separating them. Finally, the adult again asks whether the sets are the same or different.

It is truly shocking to see your child be fooled by how the sets look. After all, you haven't added anything or taken anything away. But children will often fall into this trap. Furthermore, if you put the items back into alignment, they will then agree that you both have the same again! No wonder siblings fight over who got more goodies: If the goodies look different—regardless of whether they have the same number in the set—children will insist that someone has been cheated. Three- to 5-year-olds will most likely fail this conservation experiment, while children around age 6 will begin to "pass" the experiment.

COUNTING PRINCIPLES: WHAT CHILDREN CAN DO WHEN

Professor Gelman went on, collaborating with her husband, Professor Randy Gallistel, also of Rutgers University in New Jersey, to separate out the abilities necessary for children to pass the conservation task. They asked crucial questions about what children know about number and when they know it. The results of their many studies yielded five principles that govern counting. These principles are things that children work out on their own from simply playing with objects in the world and talking with people about number. This knowledge is based on things that children like to do on their own, unsupervised, with whatever objects they can lay their hands on. In other words, children come to these principles through that magical activity we call *play*.

The One-to-One Principle, or One Item Gets Only One Number "Tag"

Let's think about what is involved in counting a set of objects. If we counted items more than once, we'd get the wrong answer. But when do young children know this? This is the one-to-one principle, and Professor Gelman found that children assign only one number "tag" to an item—even if they can't count correctly yet—by the time they are 2½ years old. If shown a set of four objects and asked to count them, they might say "one, two, four, six," assigning only one number (even if it's the wrong number) to each item. This is pretty impressive. Somehow they have figured out that each item gets counted only once.

The Stable-Order Principle, or Numbers Occur in a Fixed Order

Again, whether or not children have the number list correct yet, they seem to appreciate that the numbers they have learned occur in a stable order. In other words, when counting a set, you shouldn't say "one, two, three" one time and "two, one, three" the next time. Ask a 2-year-old to count a set of objects, and you may be surprised at what she does. She definitely knows that number words are to be used—that is, she won't answer you by saying, for example, "blue, red, green. . . ." But she might not use the number words in the order you expect. She might say "one, two, three, four, seven." Yet, when you give her two different sets to count, she may keep those numbers (her personal number list) in the *same order*. Again, this is pretty impressive, because no one sits down and teaches children this principle; they induce it on their own from watching people count and counting on their own.

Discovering Hidden Skills	The One-to-One and Stable-Order Principles

Ages: 2 years to 4 years

Does your child use the one-to-one principle and the stable-order principle yet? Collect some objects to make up three small sets, with maybe three or four objects in each set. Ask your child to count one of the sets and see if she assigns only one number tag to each item, thereby using the one-to-one principle. Try this again in a few months if she doesn't. This would be wonderful to try with children of different ages, too, to see what a difference a year or two can make. Also, listen as your child counts the objects to hear whether she uses her (possibly idiosyncratic) number list in the same order each time, thereby observing the stable-order principle.

The Cardinal Principle,
or The Number of Items in a Set Is
the Same as the Last Number Tag

Once children grasp the stable-order principle, they are set for using the crucial principle of cardinality—the idea that the final number counted represents the size of the set. What does that mean? If I have counted three cups, then the last number that I counted—three—represents the number of cups in that set of objects. This is fun to observe in our children, because when they get to the end of counting a set, they will often look up and raise their voices in finality and with pride and say, "Six!" It doesn't matter, either, if they used their idiosyncratic counting list. You know they understand this principle when they tell you the last number they counted is "how many" there are.

The Abstraction Principle,
or I Can Count Anything!

The character of the Count on *Sesame Street* speaks to our next principle, which is that of abstraction. Anything can be counted—anything. We can count our shoes, cars going by our window, and even the number of times since lunch that we received telephone calls from telemarketers. Numbers are universals that apply anywhere to anything. And thankfully—even though the words change across language (*un, deux, trois*—or one, two, three)—these principles are the same around the world.

The Order-Irrelevance Principle,
or It Doesn't Matter Where You Start Counting

Piaget tells us about a friend who turned out to be a mathematician and remembered how he had a great epiphany as a child. He was playing with some stones and arranged them in a circle. He started counting on one stone and got the answer "six." Then he selected another stone to be number "one" and still got the answer "six." Amazing. It didn't matter which stone he started counting; he always got the same answer. Piaget's friend had discovered the order-irrelevance principle all on his own, as the rest of our children do it. This principle says that not only can we count anything we wish, we can count these items in any order, starting with any item.

Discovering Hidden Skills	The Cardinal Principle, Abstraction Principle, and Order-Irrelevance Principle

Ages: 2 years to 4 years

You can tell whether your child is using the number principles by giving him sets of objects. See, for example, whether your child uses the cardinal principle. When you ask "How many dogs, birds, toys . . . are there?" does your child know that the answer is the highest number that he counted in the set? And is your child willing to count *anything*, showing you that he follows the abstraction principle? Ask your child to count one of the sets of tangible objects, and then ask your child to count the number of clouds in the sky or the number of times you called grandma last week. Does he object? Or is he willing to consider counting anything you ask, even if it is far away and out of reach?

Finally, see if your child operates with the order-irrelevance principle. Point to one object in a five-item set and ask her to count how many there are. Then have her do it again while you point to a new starting object. Does she come up with the same answer both times? Is she willing to do this? Ask your child why it always comes out the same way. Don't expect her to be able to say something that makes sense, but it is fun to see what kind of rationalization a child comes up with.

By the age of 3, most children seem to operate according to these five principles most of the time. They emerge in the normal course of development and are currently being implemented in early mathematical curricula and assessments. Should we run out to buy materials to teach our children counting principles? No. First of all, we cannot teach counting principles to a 2-year-old even if we want to (and we are not sure why you would want to). How would you explain to a 2-year-old that the order in which you count the items in a set is irrelevant? Children will figure this out on their own and in due course. Talking about these principles is too abstract for children to grasp. That's why they need physical experience with the objects around them to work these principles out for themselves.

You can play "math" games with toy cars, teacups, and any other everyday item you have in your home; you don't need to buy anything special. As the principle of abstraction teaches us, children can find the elusive "number" everywhere they look, and if we look with them, we can have fun counting worms, slugs, and French fries (although hopefully the latter are not in the same set!). To learn addition and subtraction, you do need to learn more than just numbers. That brings us to the next step in the figurative equation—the number line.

THE NUMBER LINE CONCEPT

Numbers do not just float around in space. They are determined by their relationship to one another. To fully master skills like addition and subtraction, children must understand that, for example, five is greater than four by one unit and greater than three by even more—two units. Further, they will have to understand that five is one unit bigger than four, but at the same time, it's one unit *smaller* than six. Research suggests that this is a more difficult concept to master and that children learn it first between 2½ and 3 years of age.

Even at 3 years of age, it is easier to see a number in relationship to much smaller and much larger numbers than to understand how a number stands in relation to other numbers when it differs from them by only a little bit. For example, toddlers are more likely to note where five is in relation to one and to eight than to where five is in relation to four and to six. Perhaps the reason children (and adults) are better with differences of greater magnitude relates to what we talked about above with babies. Since research suggests that we start out thinking in terms of amount of stuff, it stands to reason that when the stuff is very different in magnitude, we have an easier time making that judgment than when we really have to use our knowledge of the number line to make judgments about small differences. This ability takes some time to develop. It was not until one of our children (Benj) was 5 that he could truly understand why his parents got more ice cream than his older brother, his older brother got more than he did, and he got more than his younger brother, Mike. The strategy all made sense when he viewed the family by age on the number line and justified ice cream portions relative to that line.

The Number Line

This one is for you: Is 56 + 75 closer to 125 or 150? Is 56 + 75 closer to 130 or 136? Professor Stanislas Dehaene of the National Institute of Health in France suggests that the first of these should be easier than the second because you, like your children, approximate better with numbers that are further apart than you do with numbers that require more exact mathematical reasoning.

This one is for your 3- to 6-year-old child: Take three sets of objects (one with three objects, one with five objects, and one with seven objects) and ask your child which set is the biggest and which set is the smallest. Can your child do this? Since this is a comparison between two sets that differ in magnitude a lot, it shouldn't be that hard. Then ask your child about the middle set. Now things might get trickier, since the middle set differs from each set by a smaller magnitude. Is it bigger than this set (point to the smallest one)? Is it bigger than this set (point to the biggest one)? See how your child responds to this task.

THE CROWNING ACHIEVEMENT: COUNTING AND COMPARING

In order to truly learn addition and subtraction, your child has to be able to use the principles of counting together with knowledge of the number line. This means that your child needs to know not only that a set he has counted has three balls, but that three balls is more than two balls but less than four balls. This final step in preschool mathematics seems to happen at around 5 or 6 years of age in most children.

The discovery of the number line allows children to add sets and to know that when they get a set of three items and add it to a set of four items, they move up the number line to seven items. Then and only then has the child learned the distance in magnitude of the difference between three and seven. Then and only then does the child implicitly realize that *adding* and *taking away* are operations that take place on the same continuum—the number line. Children couldn't begin to explain the number line; it's unconscious knowledge, but knowledge nonetheless. The development of the number line and all that it implies is the preschool child's crowning mathematical achievement. And the best, most seamless way for your child to reach this pinnacle is both through play and by working through simple addition and subtraction word problems you make up as part of your daily living.

Teachable Moments	A Homemade Number Line Game

Many board games have the number line at their core. The goal of these games is to get from the start line to the finish—and to be the first one there. The spaces on the board are a kind of number line, and we move through them with the roll of the dice. When the die has six dots, we move six spaces and are immediately ahead of the player who moved only three. Not only do children learn one-to-one correspondence here (one space for every dot on the die), but they also learn principles of the number line. They move forward toward the goal (which we could even set as a specified number of spaces, say 50).

If you want to get very fancy, you could even make your own game. By cutting strips of paper and making lines on them to represent the numbers zero to 50, children can watch pieces move up the number line toward the numerical goal. The sophisticated parent can even add write-in spaces that say "Go back two spaces" so that children can learn the relationships between adding and subtracting on this two-way street.

As you play, you can challenge your child: Who is farther ahead? Why? And by how much? You can see that as you play this game, you begin to look at number development in a whole new way.

WHAT THE RESEARCH MEANS FOR YOUR CHILD

Research shows that at a minimum, even neonates are able to pick up information about quantities like *more* and *less*, and in the latter half of the first year, infants have some sense of equivalence. Some researchers suggest that this early period represents one in which babies rely on amount of stuff rather than on knowledge about number. But some researchers believe that infants possess a kind of rudimentary knowledge of number—for very small sets—that will later result in the ability to reason about numbers.

Over time, infants become toddlers who begin to count and to compare. For a period of about 3½ years, the child's counting ability and comparing abilities develop as if on separate planes. Then magically, our preschoolers develop ways of integrating these two systems: of counting on and comparing numbers on a number line and of thinking in truly mathematical ways.

As we move into an era when all children may well be attending preschool, educators and researchers are looking seriously at the natural course of preschool number development, and curricula are appearing that capitalize on children's natural abilities to think in terms of counting and comparing. Researchers are busy developing games that will illuminate the *processes* that children bring to the table during preschool. And it is the processes that are important, not the *products*. A 2-year-old who has memorized her number facts is not necessarily as far "ahead" as a child who understands the counting principles, for example. The first child is simply a parrot. The second child is a budding mathematician.

One example of a fabulous preschool mathematical program is called *Big Math for Little People*. This curriculum is built upon the discoveries that we mentioned above. It also capitalizes on the fact that 4- and 5-year-old children spend much of their day playing in ways that use number skills. The developer of *Big Math*, Professor Herbert Ginsberg, an educator at Teachers College of Columbia University in New York, studied 80 children to see whether they naturally played in ways that used mathematical abilities. He found that in their free play, 46 percent of the time children were either sorting objects into sets (spoons here and forks over there) or counting objects or exploring patterns and forms. Would you ever have imagined that our children were spending this much time engaged in mathematical thinking? This is one of the reasons why we needn't fear that we must provide our children with explicit mathematical instruction. Our children are doing mathematics all the time!

Planning a Picnic

One of the games used in *Big Math for Little People* is Bag It. Present your 4- and 5-year-olds with five plastic bags, each of which has a number written on the front (1, 2, 3, 4, and 5). Then get out a bag of peanuts, or any object that comes in multiples. You can incorporate the child's stuffed animals and pretend to be going on a picnic. Ask your child how many peanuts each animal deserves. The game is simply to insert the correct number of items in the bag. There are also variations on the game in which children can dump out the contents of two bags and compare which has more or less, and so on.

We've talked about number skills that children achieve on their own and have said very little thus far about the constructive role that parents might play. And yet, parents do play a significant role in their children's achievement of the principles and knowledge we have discussed. Professor Geoffrey Saxe and his colleagues at the University of California at Berkeley have studied how 2- to 4-year-olds interact at home with their mothers over simple math problems the researchers gave them to do. They videotaped the natural interaction children and moms had when they were asked to count the number of objects in a set or match sets by number. What they found is reassuring for any parent who worries about her own ability to nurture a child's innate desire to learn basic math concepts.

The researchers discovered that mothers were naturally sensitive to their children's skill levels, giving, for example, more explicit help to 2-year-olds than to 4-year-olds. When the researchers assessed children's ability within an age group with a separate test, they found that mothers were again responsive to their children's levels, giving more guidance to the less competent children. Helping children in ways sensitive to their level is what the brilliant Russian psychologist Lev Vygotsky called "scaffolding." By this he meant that adults often help a child reach a higher level by supporting their efforts in ways that will not be necessary later on. And this is exactly what the researchers found: Children could accomplish mathematical tasks with help (scaffolding) that they could not accomplish on their own.

But what happens outside of the time that researchers are asking mothers and children to solve math problems? Is there any evidence that mothers and their children interact in mathematical ways when the researchers go home? The researchers found evidence from interviewing the mothers that there were plenty of times when mothers and children talked about number and played little spontaneous math games. And as children understood more about number, the complexity of the games and conversations about number advanced as well. Furthermore, other research on such social interactions between a child and an adult indicates that the child's independent performance improves after interacting with a supportive adult. If this is true for mathematical interactions—and there is every reason to believe that it would be—then interacting at home in a natural way with a parent or with a sensitive caregiver who has the time to respond to children's queries should help children achieve the mathematical insights that will serve as the basis for math achievements in school.

But do not take this as a message that you have to buy fancy cards and games. You need only do what comes naturally. There are some principles that can guide you in your everyday, ordinary, and spontaneous mathematical interactions with your children.

BRINGING THE LESSONS HOME

Think blocks, not videos. Many of the newer teaching techniques come by way of video. There's a shape video for infants and numerous computer games that interactively engage preschoolers in mathematics games while teaching them about the computer. Yet the very best way to learn about numbers is to manipulate objects, line them up, compare sets, and so on. There is simply no substitution for playing with objects, and these actions speak louder than words. Plus, this type of play is something children love to do without being told!

Find the numbers everywhere. Just as you can find rectangles in buildings and hexagons in stop signs, numbers appear wherever you turn. When we deal the same number of cards to each player and when we count up how many party favors we need for our guests, we are doing mathematics. When we use a different paintbrush for each new color, and put one napkin out for each of our friends, we are using one-to-one correspondence and beginning to compare set sizes. And when we add more ice cream for the additional person, we are adding quantity. When we then eat the ice cream, we are doing subtraction.

Taking older children shopping (once they're past the throwing-everything-in-the-cart stage) presents a virtual gold mine for learning about comparing and contrasting based on number and amount. Which box is bigger, smaller? Which costs more? Less? When children get to the age of 5 or so, they can also buy a little something at the store and get change—that's addition and subtraction.

Now that you know where to look, you'll discover that numbers are found in every corner of our lives. You need only notice these—as your children do—and seize the natural opportunities for learning.

Playing = Learning. We have always marveled at the way children learn so much better through play. Elementary school children who have trouble with fractions seem to have no difficulty at all computing the batting averages of their favorite players in complicated decimals. Brazilian street children fail on school math problems but are whizzes at calculating the costs needed for their street transactions. Playing the card game of War is math at its best. Money offers wonderful opportunities not only for counting but for creating sets. Can your child match the set you have created? If you put out three pennies, can he? If you take away one penny, can he? Which is worth more—three pennies or one nickel?

We need not be concerned about being "educational" with our children; all we need to do is *follow their lead* and play games they love that foster mathematical curiosity.

Encourage your child to learn in context. We all learn better when we learn something meaningful. A 5-year-old learns more about the power of money when he has to earn his own dollar at a lemonade stand (and see how much it buys him) than he will ever learn from flash cards. Children will learn much more at a supermarket looking for big and small apples than they will from computer games. At around 3 or 4, children love to play board games. Candy Land is one that has been forever popular among the young set. When you and your child roll the dice and move your pieces, you are using one-to-one correspondence, and the outcome really matters to the child! Our job as teachers and parents, then, is to seize the opportunities that live around us and to allow children to learn in context.

Remember: If you just do what comes naturally in your day, you will build number skills in your home. You need not buy anything extra or worry about getting the edge over others. One of our sons, Josh, taught us this lesson when he discovered the foundations for multiplication at age 4. When baking muffins in the muffin pan, he remarked, "Mom, did you realize that having two rows of three muffins is exactly the same thing as having three rows of two muffins?" With experience and play, mathematical skills blossom. Our job is simply to recognize the teachable moments in every day.

CHAPTER + 4

LANGUAGE: THE POWER OF BABBLE

LINDA CAPLOW IS SITTING ON THE FLOOR with her 20-month-old son, Jason. She holds a set of flash cards in her hands designed to expand Jason's vocabulary. She bobs up and down as she attempts to get him to focus on the card pictures as they recite the accompanying words together. "Giraffe," Linda says, pointing to the picture of a giraffe. "Where ball?" Jason says, scanning the hardwood floor for his big ball with the jingle bell inside. Linda considers the problem of her baby's wandering attention and decides to switch activities. She takes the box marked "Little Linguist" off a shelf and pulls out the interactive toy, which promises to build Jason's vocabulary in English and Spanish. Her next door neighbor's daughter, the same age as Jason, can already say a number of Spanish *and* French words. Linda fears that she will be failing Jason if she doesn't teach him during this critical time in his development.

Though she has Jason's best interests at heart, Linda has clearly succumbed to the popular belief that parents must become teachers when it comes to language development. She frets that without structured lessons, Jason will be left behind his peers, who she believes are not only developing an extensive vocabulary, but learning a second language as well.

GETTING THE CONVERSATION GOING

Despite Linda's fears, developmental science provides clear evidence that parents are nurturing their children's language abilities even when they aren't using vocabulary flash cards, linguistics computer programs, or any other expensive teaching devices. Think about it a moment, and you will realize that children around the world, whether they are reared in a hovel, a hut, or a high-rise, all learn to talk. Research shows that your common, ordinary, mundane daily interactions with your child are all you need to promote excellent language development. When you talk to your children as you go about your daily routine, when you listen to your children and respond by building on what they say, and when you read and interact with them over picture books, you are providing all the help with language skills they could possibly need. And the language that you provide for your children is richer than anything that a computer can give them.

But wait! You want your child to be accelerated—not just to *learn* language, but to *master* it. After all, language is the medium of school instruction, and language skills are related to children's reading and mathematical skills. What's the best way to master language? Years of research provide the answer: It's not with drills or computer programs, but with daily conversation that gives the child motivation and allows time to respond. When children interact with real people in a social context, they are motivated to express their needs, thoughts, and feelings. Nature has programmed us to learn language through social relationships. Computer screens, while modestly interactive, do not adapt to our children's interests. With live conversations, we have the ability to follow up on the themes our children want to talk about. Since children are maximally engaged when we interact with them over what grabs their attention, it is experiences like these that provide the foundations for language growth. Consider the following "dialogue."

Jordan: (Vocalizes repeatedly until his mother turns around)
Mother: (Turns around to look at child)
Jordan: (Points to one of the objects on the counter)
Mother: Do you want this jelly? (holds up jelly jar)
Jordan: (Shakes head "no")
Mother: Do you want this spoon? (holds up spoon)

Jordan: (Shakes head "no" and jumps in frustration in his high chair)

Mother: How about this? (shows him cheese) Is it the cheese you want?

Jordan: (Shakes head "no," leans forward as if pointing with his whole body)

Mother: This sponge? (said incredulously as she picks up sponge)

Jordan: (Leans back in high chair and puts arm down; tension leaves body)

Mother: (Hands child sponge)

Through observing episodes just like this one in research settings, one of us (Roberta) found that babies *who don't even talk yet* can hang in there for an enormous number of conversational turns if they want their moms or dads to understand their "message." Given that we think of babies as having short attention spans, this is startling. Babies will persevere with a parent who is dense enough (how outrageous!) to be unable to quickly decipher pointing and grunts.

Roberta discovered by filming at mealtime that babies as young as 11 months will go back and forth through an average of seven conversational turns to establish, for example, that it's a grape they want, not a cookie. Or that it's the clock on the wall they want to hear a name for and *not* the cow in the picture below the clock. As you might imagine, such episodes provide ripe ground for word learning while parents or caregivers struggle to supply just the word the baby wants to hear. And as parents cycle through the names of alternatives to zero in on what it is the baby wants, babies hear many words over and over again. Would you learn a word for "grape" if it took you seven attempts to get one? Motivation for word learning is high in such episodes. These are just the kinds of experiences that television programs, toys, and computers can never provide. Babies are in charge when we allow them to direct the interaction based on their interests. Such interactions provide the best environment for language learning.

Discovering Hidden Skills | The Negotiation Process

Ages: 9 months to 18 months

You'll need a child who isn't talking much yet to try this. Once your child can speak in sentences, it's unlikely that you'll be able to observe the negotiation process. It may be easier to observe this, too, if you ask someone else to do this experiment. Have the adult you choose take an interesting object and show it to your child until she finds it interesting, too. Then have the adult place it on a high shelf or table just out of the child's reach, but in sight. Instruct the person to feign ignorance about what the baby wants so you can observe how the baby and the person respond to each other. Notice how the child communicates her desire for the object. Does she grunt? Point? Does she try to say something? And how does the adult respond to the child? Does he name alternatives present in the vicinity? For how many back and forths (turns) does the child stay focused on obtaining the object? Of course, we are not promoting torture here—after some turns, allow the person to name the object and give it to the baby.

The persistence your child shows in communicating her desires for an object by nonverbal means is nothing compared with the persistence with which your child works in unseen ways, on her own, to learn language. In this chapter, we will take apart the myth that you have to "teach" your child language. Instead, we'll dazzle you with what babies will figure out on their own—as long as we provide them with the resources. And what are those resources? The interactions in which you and your children are focused on play or food or reading books or anything else that is a part of their ordinary, daily lives. Interactions in which language is front and center.

Most importantly, we will describe the wide range of individual differences that exists in early language development. Some children say no words at all at 16 months, and some say as many as 100. Some children talk in short sentences at 18 months, and some don't use sentences until 28 months. Realizing the wide variability in early language development should help to reassure parents like Linda Caplow, parents who are eager to accelerate their children's abilities but don't yet appreciate the astonishing skills their children's imperfect language already reveals. *The irony is that each child is born to be a linguistic genius.* Children are better at learning languages than we are. We big, smart adults who drive and operate dangerous equipment (like the lawn mower and the car) aren't as good at language learning as 3-year-old children who don't tie their own shoes or know which fork to use in a restaurant.

So, you may be thinking, why not invest in those computer programs and tapes that teach other languages to our children, who are, after all, just ripe for the experience? Because as this chapter will reveal, languages don't get learned from computer programs or tapes—regardless of the promises that appear on the product boxes. Language gets learned in the context of *interaction*—in the context of eating and playing and asking for the names of things, not passively looking at a computer monitor. And that's where parents and caregivers come in: We make the interactions possible.

THE LANGUAGE INSTINCT

Some researchers have argued that humans are born to learn language just as spiders are born to spin webs. In fact, we are the only species for whom language is an "instinct." We are the only species that has language, despite many experiments with our closest relatives, the primates, and even dolphins. With language, we pass on cultural knowledge and teach others, so that every generation need not "reinvent the wheel." Language allows us to talk about the future and to remember the past. Language can also be a tool for good or evil. Churchill's words provided a beacon for nations during the Second World War, while Hitler's words drove people to do the unthinkable. Thousands of years of evolution of our brains as well as our language-producing instruments, such as our mouths and throats, allow the achievement of language.

As important as we are to our children and to their language learning, language development is not solely the responsibility of parents. Noam Chomsky, the world's most famous living linguist and a professor at MIT in Cambridge, raised this possibility when he suggested that babies are born with a "language acquisition device," a metaphorical organ that is responsible for language learning. Just as the heart is designed to pump blood, he argued, this language acquisition device is preprogrammed to learn language, whatever the language community children find themselves in. No particular language is any more difficult for a child to learn. How do we know this? Because when a baby is born, it's not predetermined whether she'll end up in Germany or China. Babies must be ready to learn whatever language they find themselves surrounded by; otherwise, international adoptions would fail. This means that even though languages seem very different on the surface, they must have more in common than it first appears. Chinese sounds very different from English. But babies learn Chinese as well and as rapidly as they learn English. Professor Chomsky argued that there must be some important and deep commonalities shared by all languages. He referred to these deep commonalities, the core that all languages share, as Universal Grammar.

Professor Chomsky's theory is still hotly debated. See how you would evaluate the data that have been assembled in favor of humans being endowed with the ability to learn language. The first piece of evidence comes from a recent study published in the prestigious journal *Science*. The study shows that by 5 months of age, babies are already specializing by using the left side of their brains for language sounds and the right side for expressing emotion. Professor Laura-Ann Petitto, a psychologist at Dartmouth College in Hanover, New Hampshire, and her colleagues used a simple test to discover this fact. It turns out that we all speak out of the *right* side of our mouths. Take a close look at a friend or a TV personality. You'll see that they ever so slightly favor the right side of their mouths when they talk. Why? Because language resides in the *left* side of the brain, and the connections in the brain are "contralateral," or crossed. The right side of the body is controlled by the left side of the brain, and vice versa. If babies use the right side of their mouths for babbling, then babbling is a language function being controlled by the left hemisphere— even at 5 months of age. That would suggest that we arrive on the scene prepared to learn language. If babies showed no preference for the right side when babbling, that might indicate a lack of brain specialization for language at this age.

What do babies do? Studies show they babble out of the right side of their mouths! When they smile, however, they use the left side of their mouths. The researchers concluded that from the get-go, the left side of the brain is specialized for language. We are biologically primed to learn language.

The babbling study is only one in a series of experiments that make the case for innate language abilities in young children. Research on deaf children with hearing parents also adds fuel to the argument. Professor Susan Goldin-Meadow and her colleagues at the University of Chicago studied deaf children with hearing parents who wanted their children to learn lip-reading and speech. To make sure that they did not use the "crutch" of sign language (from their perspective), these parents were careful not to expose their children to any signs. In fact, these parents *withheld* sign language training and didn't learn any signs themselves because they wanted to enroll their children in oral language schools for the deaf.

What happens when children don't have a first language until they are 6 or 7? The answer to the question was stunning. On their own—without any outside help from parents or teachers—these young children invented a gestural language. While it was not as rich a signing system as the one used by deaf children who are exposed to formal sign language, it was as if children could not suppress language from emerging.

There are other cases in which children invent language. Professor Derek Bickerton, a linguist at the University of Hawaii in Honolulu, tells the story of what happened when Japanese, Korean, and Filipino immigrants came to Hawaii to work on sugar plantations. To trade with one another and to be able to communicate, the immigrants created a very impoverished language (called a "pidgin") made up of various pieces from the different languages. What the children born into this community did with the pidgin language is fascinating. They naturally heard and learned the impoverished pidgin language. Yet they expanded and refined it beyond what the grownups had developed and turned it into a full language, called "creole." A creole language contains all the structures of existing languages—nouns, verbs, inflectional markers, and so on. How did the children add language grammatical structures that they had never heard? How did they know just what pieces to add so that the resulting creole language resembled all other languages in the world? Like Professor Chomsky, Professor Bickerton proposes that these languages emerge because humans are endowed with a language "bio-program"—a core grammar that will emerge in all people. In other words, Professor Bickerton argues that the capacity to learn—or, on some cases, invent—a human language is innate.

One additional piece of evidence for the universality of language is the fact that children around the world experience the milestones of language development at roughly the same time. It doesn't matter if a child is born in Kalamazoo or Kathmandu; the timetable for language learning appears to be the same. That is, all children start out with single words at around 1 year of age, and they all communicate like members of their native tribes—whatever language is spoken—by the time they are 3.

As you can see, young children are language geniuses. Yet there is still much that we can do to facilitate their language growth. To appreciate what we can do (and to accept that we need not sit down and carefully teach each noun and verb or model diagramming sentences), let's explore the development of language itself. Here science has a very coherent story to offer.

How Babies Learn to Talk

When does language development begin? We all know that we don't hear a word from our children until they are in the vicinity of a year of age. What we are about to share with you, however, will make you look at your baby in a new way. Language development begins way before the baby's first birthday. In fact, it begins in the womb.

Seven months into pregnancy, babies are already eavesdropping on their mothers' conversations. Research by Professor William Fifer, a developmental psychobiologist, and his colleagues at Columbia University in New York City indicates that babies remember stories and songs that they heard in the womb. And they prefer to hear their mothers' voices over other female voices. How could we possibly know this? Several methods allow scientists to figuratively peer into the womb.

In some of these studies, for example, scientists had mothers lie down (not one complained) while they recorded fetal heart rates. It turns out that babies will have fairly steady heart rates until they hear something that piques their interest. Professor Fifer and his colleagues asked mothers to repeat a sentence like "Hello, baby. How are you today?" The minute the baby heard the mom, the fetus's heart rate changed. As expected, the heart rate actually went down. Then it went back to normal. How do we know it was actually mom's *voice* and not something about her muscular contractions when she spoke? Because babies' heart rates did not go down when the mothers were silent or when they *whispered* the same words. A baby actually tunes in when mother talks. Since mother talks quite a bit, over the course of a day the baby gets much exposure to language.

Heart rate is not the only way in which scientists discover what babies can learn about language while in the womb. Sucking offers another clue to what little minds are processing while they float in their amniotic cocoon. In Professor Jacques Mehler's laboratory at the Recherches au CNRS laboratory in Paris, France, babies' sucking patterns were monitored to discover that at just 2 days of age, babies already prefer their own language over a foreign language. In his studies, two groups of newborns (tested individually) happily sucked away on pacifiers. One group heard a recording of French over and over. Eventually they got a bit bored, and their sucking slowed down. At just that moment, the researchers changed the language to Russian (using the same voice) to see what the babies would do. Another group first heard Russian and then heard French. In the first group, the French babies seemed nonchalant when they encountered Russian. Their sucking rate remained low as they looked around the room. The second group, however, sucked wildly when the language changed from Russian to French, as if to say, *Vive la France!* The conclusion? Babies can distinguish between two languages and prefer their native tongue—chauvinists at just 48 hours old.

This finding is not unique to French babies. It also happened across the Atlantic when investigators tested American babies, who heard English and Italian. These babies preferred English. Babies' preference for their native tongues comes from the time they spent eavesdropping on their mothers while in the womb. While they are floating in a pool of warm water, hearing a percussion of heartbeats and gurgles in the background, fetuses are listening to the melodies of speech. Babies are natural pattern seekers, even in the womb. They don't have to be schooled to listen to the rhythms of language.

Discovering Hidden Skills | Listening In While in the Womb

Ages: The 7th month of pregnancy until birth

If you are pregnant or know someone who is, you can try proving to yourself that from about the 7th month on, babies can hear in the womb. Ask the pregnant woman to lie down, and get a pot and a big spoon. What does the baby do when you strike the pot several times? Can you see the baby jump in the mom's uterus? Does the mother report movement if you can't see it? Now try having the mother talk. What effect does this have on the baby? Try having her whisper, too, and see if anything happens. You can do this several times and can even compare reactions to a stranger's voice if you like.

If babies are "tuned in" at just 2 days old, it should come as no surprise that they pay close attention to our language as the weeks and months pass. They have so much to learn. Imagine what it must be like to be a baby learning a language. Consider the analogy (imperfect though it is) of being transferred by your company without notice to a foreign country, surrounded by well-meaning people who don't speak a word of your language. People in your new country seem to talk a mile a minute. Could you learn the new language in just 2 or 3 years and sound like a native? That is exactly what babies do. And if they are lucky enough to be exposed to multiple languages, they will master all of them, as long as the languages are presented in a natural context, such as when dad speaks Spanish and mom speaks English or the live-in nanny speaks French. How? Babies are primed to analyze the language stream coming at them, just as they are primed to walk. Nature has given them tools to absorb the jumble of language and find a way to break apart its never-ending flow. To understand how they do this, come into the lab and see what scientists have found.

Finding the Units
That Make Up Language: Sentences

One trick babies learn is to divide language melodies into sentences. If they can just find the boundaries of the sentences, they will have something akin to the borders of a puzzle. Then they can start looking within the puzzle (the sentences) to discover the units therein—the words. It turns out that by just 4½ months, babies can do this. They know where one sentence ends and another begins. This ability was tested in experiments using a new, revolutionary method called the Headturn Preference procedure. Imagine that Rebecca brings 4-month-old baby Jason to a university laboratory. They are asked to enter a small room. Rebecca holds Jason on her lap while she sits in the middle of a three-sided enclosure about 10 feet across. Straight ahead they see a green light and a small hole for an observer. Ninety degrees to Rebecca and Jason's right and left are two additional lights and two speakers, one on each side. Rebecca is given a pair of earphones to wear that play music so that she cannot inadvertently influence Jason when he shows off his skills.

Now for the experiment. Jason is about to hear samples of speech from a mom talking to her child. In one set—from the left side—Jason hears talk that is broken into natural sentences, with 1-second pauses placed where they naturally occur—at the ends of clauses and sentences. Please read the following passage aloud, consciously pausing where the slashes appear to see how natural it sounds.

> *Cinderella lived in a great big house / but it was sort of dark because she had this mean, mean stepmother. / And oh, she had two stepsisters that were so ugly. / They were mean, too.*

When the sample is done, a center light comes on, and Jason then hears samples of speech from the same voice from the right side. This next set is read in a different way, so that the pauses actually *disrupt* how language works. Please read the following passage aloud, too, placing pauses where the slashes are now.

> *Cinderella lived in a / great big house but it was sort of dark because she / had this mean, mean stepmother. / And oh, she had two /stepsisters that were so ugly. They were mean, too.*

Sounds bumpy, doesn't it? Jason will hear a number of these samples so that he can indicate which he prefers. No one expects Jason to understand the meaning of the passage. The investigators simply want to know if he is sensitive to the cues that indicate when sentences begin and end, because this would be like discovering the border of the puzzle. Will Jason prefer to listen to the normal sample (the first one) or to the sample where the pauses come in the wrong places (the second one)? Will he show us indirectly by his looking that he already has a sense of when sentences begin and end? Each passage has the same number of words. Each has three pauses, so how could he tell?

Amazingly, when one of us (Kathy) conducted this experiment with her colleagues, we found that 4-month-olds could tell the difference between the two sets. At this young age, babies already preferred to listen to the more natural samples. With a simple head turn to each side, Jason and other babies of his age show us that they are finding ways to separate the never-ending speech stream into "chunks." And this is progress! Finding the cues that signal where sentences begin and end is a kind of pattern analysis, and babies were born to find the patterns.

Finding the Units That Make Up Language: The Word That Is My Name

Once children are aware of the puzzle boundaries for language, we can look to see what they know about the words inside. The next clue in the story comes from the fact that babies at just 4 months of age not only know about the melodies of speech, but also recognize a few words. They know their own names.

It turns out that recognizing your own name is a big deal. When you hear language coming at you, it helps to recognize one or two very frequent words. Then you can use your name as a *wedge* into the language stream, recognizing that new things come before or after your name.

Let's go back to the Headturn Preference procedure and watch another mother, Sheila, with her baby, Morris. Here, the observer hiding behind the apparatus sees Morris looking at the light and starts the tape recorder and the blinking light on Morris's right side. Morris turns to the right and hears a pleasant voice saying, "Harry. Harry. Harry . . ." over and over again until he turns away. Why *Harry* instead of *Morris*? Because the researchers are comparing Morris's attention to his *own* name and his attention to *another* name that also has two syllables, with the same heavy stress on the first syllable—"HARry" versus "MORris." Once Morris turns away, the center light blinks again. Morris looks at it; the hidden researcher turns it off, and turns on the light on Morris's left side. That speaker now begins, and the same pleasant female voice says, "Morris. Morris. Morris . . ." until Morris turns away. Trials like this go on for another 4 minutes or so, with the left or right side playing in random order. Will Morris look longer at the side playing "Morris" than at the side playing "Harry?" If he does, then he must at least recognize the difference in the two names. The answer—yes! Morris prefers his own name. He may not know that *he* is Morris, but he recognizes his own name.

But does such knowledge come in handy for Morris? You bet.

Research conducted at Brown University with one of us (Golinkoff) contributes to this part of the story line. At 6 months, babies like Morris can learn to recognize a new word that follows their own name in a passage. They don't learn a word that follows someone else's name. In other words, something that follows their own name is treated as something worth remembering. This finding tells us that knowing your own name is not just good for being called to dinner! It helps babies recognize the building blocks of language—the words—and remember them. And just by talking to babies, we give them grist for their language mill. As natural pattern seekers, our babies are discovering language each time we talk to them. It is no accident that we repeat their names often and exaggerate the beginnings and ends of sentences. These are things we do quite naturally when we communicate with our children, and they are the keys to early language development.

Discovering Hidden Skills	Knowing Your Name

Ages: 4 months to 8 months

To see if your baby knows her own name, think of a name with the same stress pattern and number of syllables. Then sneak up on your baby when he or she is awake and alert. Stand to one side and a little behind so that the baby has to turn to see you. Say her name. For example, "COrey!" Did the baby turn to look at you? If she did, it is still not evidence that she recognizes that her name is Corey. Follow with "JAson," and then try Corey once more. Did the baby turn to you for Corey but not for Jason? At what age did she do this?

The hidden treasures we have mentioned thus far let you know that well before your baby talks, she is working hard to find patterns in the language stream. At first, babies need a familiar word to serve as an "anchor" to help them remember words they hear. But by 7½ months, they don't need their name to remember words. Tested in the Headturn Preference procedure, babies of this age can remember words presented in little passages when no familiar name is used at all. First, they hear a short passage that contains a particular word: perhaps "hat." Then they are tested in the Headturn Preference procedure to see if they listen more to that word (hat) than to one that they didn't hear, such as "cup." By preferring to listen more to a word they have heard in the passage, they show us their ability to remember speech.

This is pretty snazzy work for a baby who won't say anything for another 5 or 6 more months. But that is just our point: Months before spoken language comes on the scene, babies are working out how to find the sentences and words, and they're remembering frequently heard items.

By 8 months, babies are even more sophisticated at detecting patterns. In one study, babies heard a monotone series of nonsense syllables like "bedagolagadapityga" for 2 minutes. Try saying this without any intonation but perfectly flat and you'll have it. In the Headturn Preference procedure, babies then heard three-syllable sequences from one side that had familiar patterns (such as "pityga") or three-syllable sequences from the other side that had not occurred in the list, such as "bepida." Babies shocked the scientific world by showing that they could remember which syllables followed which other syllables. This makes 8-month-old babies little statisticians! What we have seen, then, is that from the earliest time we can test them, babies are carving language into smaller units in an effort to learn their native tongues. They break sound passages into sentences, they find familiar words, they use these words to learn new words, and they calculate patterns of sounds that can become words. They don't need us to teach them these things. They do this because as their language partners, we provide the patterns and they create the solutions.

Gazing and Pointing: Communicating without Language

We have given you a glimpse into what babies know that you cannot observe, but some of their learning in the 1st year is also visible to the naked eye. Did you know, for example, that infants can follow our eye gazes to an interesting toy at 6 months and can follow a pointing finger by 9 or 10 months? Following our gazes to an interesting object or scene precedes babies' ability to check whether we are following *their* gazes to an object. The same is true for pointing: Before they can point to direct our attention, they have to learn to follow our pointing fingers.

Research shows that babies who are better at following a parent's eye gaze at 6 months have larger vocabularies at 18 and 24 months. In other words, if you can look where your mom is looking when you're little, perhaps you are more likely to figure out what she is talking about when she uses words. While we cannot say that being able to follow a gaze *causes* a bigger vocabulary, we can say that being able to follow mom's gaze allows babies to check on what *we* think is important. That they might learn from following our gazes, which are ordinarily accompanied by talk when we are in the company of our babies, makes sense. This is another capability for language that babies are primed to learn, another place where conversations with parents and caregivers make a difference for development. You might not have noticed the development of either pointing or gaze following before, but we hope you look for them now. Babies are amazing.

Discovering Hidden Skills | Following a Gaze or Point

Ages: 6 months to 12 months

Can your baby follow your gaze to an interesting display? You can try this experiment yourself or direct someone else so that you can more easily observe the baby's reaction. Move the baby's high chair to a new place in the house. After the baby is happily ensconced (this might take a little food), look at something interesting that faces the baby and call his name and then look at it. For example, say, "Irving!" and then look in the direction of the interesting object. Does Irving follow your gaze to it? Don't say more than the baby's name to get his attention. See if he can rely on just your gaze to know where to look. If your baby can't do this right away, try it about once a month and you'll be pleased to see when he can do it.

You can try the same thing with pointing. When your baby is in the high chair, point at something interesting in the distance. You can even say, "Look, Irving!" Try this starting at about 8 months. Don't be at all surprised if your baby looks at the end of your finger when you point! Try it again if he does, about a month later. By 9 or 10 months, what does he do? You should see a shift in this emerging ability as he learns that points indicate what speakers want him to see.

The Benefits of Babbling

Infants are good communicators, and as we all know, they have more in their repertoire than just gestures like pointing. From the first months of life, we hear coos, cries, and laughs. (It is somehow heartening to know that the peak of crying comes at around 2 months of age and then decreases from there.) The first belly laughs occur at around the same time—nature's way of making up for the piercing bursts of sadness. And throughout the early months, we hear cooing that consists of a series of back-of-the-throat vowel sounds ("aaa," "eee," and so on). It is interesting that American parents respond to all of these, indeed to any bodily emission(!), as if they were contributions to the "conversation." We have even convinced ourselves, contrary to the evidence, that they are all meaningful contributions and that each different cry stands for some different bodily state (such as hunger or wetness) in our offspring.

At about 7 months, infants reach the next milestone—they start to babble. The first consonant sounds (ba, ga, ma) occur when babies close their lips and decide to make sounds at the same time. Parents notice that this sounds much more like speech. Babies now sound like Barney Rubble's son, Bam Bam, sometimes carrying on conversations that only they can understand (e.g., "ba ga ga ga ba ba?"). And by the end of the first year, our children seem to be babbling away. While babbling in itself is meaningless, it is an important step on the way to controlling one's voice box (larynx) and volume. That's why babies often scream and whisper with abandon; they're figuring out how their parts work.

What we see, then, is a child who has attained some sophisticated strategies for making his needs known. Jordan, from the beginning of the chapter, was able to make his desire for the sponge known, even though he had no word for it or for other objects he was offered. Obviously, he wouldn't get anywhere if he didn't have parents and caregivers who were eager to honor his communicative attempts. We play a role here, too, by honoring our children's "messages" as if they were clear and easily understandable, which they are not.

Our journey thus far has taken us up to about the time the first word is produced. This milestone is the one that language development is ordinarily associated with. All the wonderful things babies do before that first word are ordinarily ignored or not mentioned. Yet we have demonstrated in this review of just a few of the existing studies how much work children are indeed doing to analyze language prior to the first word.

THE LANGUAGE ORCHESTRA

One way to think about what babies are achieving in the 1st year is to compare language development to an orchestra. Language is composed of many parts that work together intricately to provide a unified sound. Just as there are sections in the orchestra (strings, brass, wind instruments, and percussion), there are individual components of language, such as sounds, meanings, words, and grammar, and rules for how you use language in culturally appropriate ways. When we speak of language acquisition, then, we are really speaking of the development of many pieces of a language system that must evolve and work in tandem to perform the "score" of human talk. With this analogy in mind, we can see that much of language learning in the 1st year is concentrated on the sounds of the instruments in the orchestra.

Babies don't really understand what the words they discover *mean* until at least the last quarter of the 1st year. Up to that time, they are focused on the sound patterns in their language. They are working to figure out, for example, what sound sequences are acceptable in their language. What should strike you is that many of the real accomplishments they make in the 1st year, they achieve on their own. We don't ordinarily notice the things they are working on, so it is unlikely that we would know how to teach them the right stuff.

THE 2ND YEAR: WORKING ON THE MEANING SECTION OF THE LANGUAGE ORCHESTRA

Most parents find that true language emerges with the first words at around 13 months. There is an admittedly fuzzy line between recognizable sounds and first words. Oh, happy is the day when the baby first says "mama" and "papa." Naturally, parents believe these to be the baby's first words. Are they? Well, they might be—or they might just be babbles. Words for mother sound like "mama" in most of the world's languages. Why?

Take a moment to say the words "mama," "papa," and "baby." Where are these words pronounced? Right—all at the front of the mouth with the lips. Now try "kaka," or "nana." You will notice that our near universal adoption of "mama" has a rationale. Sounds made at the front of the mouth are easy to produce and visible to the baby when see others produce them. Lip readers tell us, for example, that it is far easier to tell what someone is saying when they use their lips than when they form sounds in the deep recesses of the mouth.

Now back to our story. How would we know whether "mama" and "papa" or "dada" actually function as words? Researchers generally hold out for three criteria to be met before they are willing to grant that a child is using a word as a word—even if the child pronounces it correctly. First, to qualify as a real word, the word must have the same meaning each time it is used. So if "dada" refers to daddy one day but to the dog the next, baby hasn't figured out what dada means. On the other hand, if dada is used for dear old dad and for other men (which could be embarrassing for mama) and to label daddy's possessions, baby is getting closer! Second, for it to be a real word, baby must use it with the intention to communicate. If she just likes saying "dada" over and over again, but doesn't do it when dad is present, we shouldn't write it in the baby book just yet. Finally, real words allow baby to name pictures of daddy as well as the real McCoy. They are flexible in their use across contexts. Being able to use a word in a variety of instances is further evidence that the baby is using a word as a real word.

| Discovering Hidden Skills | Baby's First Words |

Ages: 9 months to 18 months

See if you can catch your baby's first couple of words. Write them as a list in the baby book, with the date when they were first used added under each one. Across the top create three columns: "consistent meaning," "attempt to communicate," and "variety of instances." Then look for whether your baby is doing these things with those words. Enter the date when you think you have observed these things with each word. How long did it take from the first appearance of the word for your child to meet all of these criteria for a real word? It would really be interesting, too, to record the circumstances under which the first words were used. In a few years, it will be great fun to look back and remember how you watched your child's real words emerge.

Baby Signs as Word Boosters?

Some people have proposed a jump-start for word learning through "baby signs"—hand configurations (such as patting the head for "hat") that resemble the signs used in sign languages. Since signs are more readily visible than tongue and mouth, perhaps babies could learn faster if we just signed a little bit with them. This is an interesting recent claim and one that has a grain of truth.

According to research conducted by Professors Linda Acredolo and Susan Goodwyn at the University of California at Davis, learning signs is a little easier than learning words. When you use signs with your baby, you are finding new ways to communicate. Fostering communication can only help language growth. So, should you sign with your baby? It couldn't hurt, and it might offer interesting ways to introduce new words in a fun and engaging way.

Discovering Hidden Skills	"Baby Signs"

Ages: 10 months to 18 months

If you are serious about teaching your baby signs, take a look at Professors Acredolo and Goodwyn's book, *Baby Signs: How to Talk with Your Baby Before Your Baby Can Talk*. When your baby is about 10 months of age, start by introducing a small number of signs, preferably built on gestures your child makes, like pointing into the sky for an airplane. If you and your child do this a few times, the point will now become the sign for airplane. Then you might add a couple more signs, like these.

Hat—pat the top of your head with your hand open and palm down
Flower—make a sniffing gesture with a wrinkled nose as if smelling
More—tap the index finger of one hand into the opposite palm

Remember that as in spoken language, the more you use a sign, the more likely it is that your baby will learn it. The researchers claim that children who learn baby signs actually become advanced linguistically relative to children who have not used signs. Why should this be? Perhaps because every time a parent uses a sign, they also say the word. And perhaps toddlers have more energy available to learn the word because they are not frustrated about getting their point across.

Bigger Meanings in Longer Sentences: The Grammatical Section of the Language Orchestra

Whether they use some baby signs or spoken words, babies talk about the same things. First words are often body parts or proper names (like the name of the family pet), and they seem to be learned laboriously, one at a time. By 18 months, most children say about 50 words, which are mostly names for objects and people in their environment (words like dog, daddy, ear, apple, juice, bottle). After children's vocabularies reach a kind of critical mass of 50 words, something seems to happen inside them that leads to a "naming explosion." Words seem to spurt forth in profusion. This is the time when our inquisitive children start to ask for the names of things: "Whas sat?" Some researchers have suggested that at around this time, typical 18- to 20-month-olds can learn as many as nine new words a day. Imagine that—63 new words a week! And children need only hear a word used once, at this stage, to begin to use it themselves in a reasonably appropriate way. The consequence is usually good, but it also means that you have to watch what you say. A reporter once asked us, "Why do children start swearing?" We had a ready reply: "What goes in is what comes out!"

The 50-word watershed is important for another reason: After children achieve this critical mass of words, they begin to combine words for the first time, making two-word sentences. Before this time they were capable only of uttering one word at a time—sometimes rapidly and in succession, as "Dog." "House." Each word is spoken as separate and distinct. Suddenly, at about 18 months, children start expanding on the meanings they express and begin working on the grammatical part of the language orchestra. Now they can say "doghouse" in one smooth utterance to convey that the dog just came into the house. But notice what is omitted.

The verb "is" and the preposition "in" were not used in the sentence. This is completely characteristic of the first word combinations children produce. English-speaking babies omit small words like "the" and "an," prepositions such as "to" and "from," and grammatical markers like the plural "s" or the "ing" we put on verbs. Their speech is what scientists call "telegraphic" because it sounds like an old-fashioned telegram: "Arrive Saturday. Bringing six trunks. Be at dock. Have car waiting. Aunt Martha."

Everywhere in the world, children's first word combinations are expressing the same meanings in just this manner. Children ask for more of something by saying things like "More milk"; they reject things, as in "No bottle!" They notice things, as in "Look kitty"; or comment on the fact that something has disappeared, as in "All gone milk." Using these limited sentences and omitting many elements, children nonetheless express complete meanings with their short utterances. And think for a moment about the fact that they have no models for speaking this way. No adults around them speak in telegraphic speech. So why do babies do it? Children are *pattern seekers*. They don't have the capacity yet to use whole sentences, but they are driven by a need to communicate. They analyze the speech they hear, pulling out the heavily stressed, meaning-bearing main words, and use them effectively, and mostly in the right order, too. No one teaches babies how to do this; they just use their analytic skills and march on ahead.

Discovering Hidden Skills	Word Combinations

Ages: 18 months to 30 months

Listen for your child's first word combinations and write them down. They will be fun to look at in years to come. Also write down what you think your child was trying to say, because she will leave out much important linguistic information from her early combinations. Watch, too, for these omissions. Did she include articles like "the" or "a"? Did she add "ing" or "ed" to the end of the verb? Did she use prepositions, like "in" or "under"? Noticing your child's early language makes these months so much richer! Usually, this process just takes off and we wonder how it all happened so fast. Recording these things and being sensitive to what is omitted—and later to what is included—makes the whole language development epoch seem much less mysterious and much more enthralling.

THE 3RD AND 4TH YEARS: FANCIER SENTENCES

Once children produce word combinations, their sentences continue to increase in length. They are now working on the grammar part of the language orchestra: How do I put sentences together to express my thoughts? Starting with single-word sentences like "Ball" for when they want their ball, which is currently under the couch, they progress to "Want ball!" and then on to the more complicated "Want Jason ball!" to "Want Jason's ball under couch" to the pièce de résistance, a two-sentence expression: "I want my ball. It under the couch!"

Notice that many of the grammatical niceties originally omitted are, bit by bit, now included in their verbal telegrams. This incremental progress is very significant. Still limited by how much they can literally spit out, however, children might say "No eat" or "No lunch" instead of telling us that they "do not want to eat lunch now." It is interesting that sometimes their minds race faster than their mouths. They have so much to tell us, but they can't get it all out smoothly, which sometimes leads to stuttering. This is not real stuttering, however, and it's nothing to be concerned about or call attention to. It's just a mind working faster than a mouth. Real stuttering is a very different phenomenon. Real stutterers will stutter at multiple places within the sentence—not just at the beginning. Often real stutterers are male and have some genetic propensity (dad or Uncle Peter stutters).

By this point, children are becoming sophisticated language users. But you might notice something odd that a very observant and concerned mother, Jane, pointed out to us in a phone call. She noticed something strange about 3-year-old Allison's language. Allison had just said, "I goed to the bathroom." Jane was concerned because she knows that Allison used to say "went." Could she have a language problem? Is something very wrong?

The short answer is no. Not only is nothing wrong, but Allison is actually demonstrating her brilliance. If you want to say the past tense of walk, you say "walked." If you want to say the past tense of "jump," you say "jumped." If you want to say the past tense of a made-up verb, "blix," you would know to say "blixed." Allison is showing us that she has learned this rule. No one taught it to her; no one sat Allison down and said, "Listen. Most of the time when we talk in the past tense, we put 'ed' on the verb." Having discovered this rule, Allison might unconsciously assume, "I must have had it wrong before. I'll just use the general rule." That will straighten itself out over time. No need to worry. This is a process that has fascinated many researchers for years.

The fact that Allison figured out how the past tense of most verbs is formed without any formal instruction from her parents cuts against the grain of popular perceptions for how language learning takes place. It seems counterintuitive to credit our unskilled, occasionally bumbling children with such intellectual powers. Yet no parent says "goed." So where did that come from if imitation is the answer? The fact that children come up with this on their own helps us to debunk the biggest myth that we carry about language learning. Parents who believe that they are completely responsible for giving their children language lessons need to know that children take the language they hear and run to the end zone unassisted. Not that they don't have to hear language. They do. But parents are not charged with being their children's personal Berlitz tutors on a 24/7 basis. Children work out much of language on their own.

Discovering Hidden Skills | Language Rules

Ages: 24 months to 36 months

In 1958, a psychologist came up with the "wug" test. By cutting out a few things from a magazine, you can give your own child this test to prove to yourself that she has figured out some of the rules that language uses. You can try doing this every 4 months or so to see your child's progress.

Assemble the following pictures: someone doing something active, say running; a picture of one object and another of two or more of the same object, say one apple and two apples; and a picture in which an activity is being performed on a substance (perhaps a woman kneading dough).

You'll also need a stuffed animal or a doll. Tell your child that the animal (give it a name, say Brighty) needs help knowing how to talk. Looking at the running picture, you can say, "Brighty says, 'The boy is blixing.' How should Brighty say, 'Yesterday the boy _____'" and leave a blank for the child to verbally fill in. This way you can see if the child uses the past tense. For the single apple picture, you can say, "Brighty calls this a wug." Then pull out the plural picture and say, "What would Brighty say here? Now there are two _____." This obviously gets at whether the child uses the plural. For the picture of the activity on a substance, you can ask three different questions. To get at whether the child can find the verb, say, "Brighty says this lady is daxing. Can you point to where she's daxing?" Look for the child to point to the hands. Next you can ask, "Where's the modi?" and see if the child points at the bowl, knowing that you are using a new noun. Or if you ask, "Where's some roltan?" you can see if the child points to the mushy stuff, recognizing that it doesn't get an article before its name as a mass noun.

THE 4TH YEAR: CHILDREN WORK ON THE PRAGMATICS PART OF THE LANGUAGE ORCHESTRA

Having mastered the sound system of language, learned the meanings of many words, and discovered how to structure sentences, children at around 3 or 4 years of age turn their attention to the way language is used in social situations. This is "pragmatics": Distinguishing when and how to say something, depending on whom you are talking to. Training in how to use language appropriately starts early in America. Babies who can't yet speak are urged to say "please" and "thank you" as they are carried about to homes for their first Halloween. And once language emerges, the child who says "More milk" is cajoled by parents to "use the magic word—please." Knowing what to say and when to say it is as important as being able to put sentences together. None of us wants to raise a child who has his proverbial foot in his mouth all the time. But even here, we can relax a bit. Pattern seekers that they are, children observe us to figure out how to use language on their own. You know that this is happening when you catch your child using a stock social phrase when you least expect it. When 4-year-old Amanda gushes at your guests as they are leaving, "It was so nice to see you!" it makes you cringe a bit because you know where she picked that up!

Discovering Hidden Skills | Pragmatics

Ages: 12 months to 24 months

Try to notice how you train your child—and others train their children of different ages—to use words, such as "please" and "thank you," that grease social interactions. Even parents of tiny babies will teach this, and it's fun if you notice it. Also, once your child can say these words, try to notice if he uses them appropriately. Or does he use "thank you" to mean "please" or vice versa? Do you notice parents telling older children how to say things and why? Do you notice yourself giving pragmatics lectures about saying hello ("Say hello, Tara") and telling about where you went yesterday ("Tell Mr. Jones where we went yesterday")? This is how many of us teach children how to enter a conversation and that they have something to contribute.

We all give pragmatics lessons at one time or another to our children. The social skills we attempt to teach our children will be important for knowing how to talk to the teacher at school. Our talkative youngsters look to us as models of how to be polite and to tell stories. And since each culture does these things differently, when we encourage our children to do it this way or that, we are teaching them how social discourse occurs in our culture. For example, in middle-class Anglo society, we look into people's eyes when we talk to them and not at their feet—or ours. So you might catch yourself saying, "Please look at Mrs. Robinson when you talk to her." But if you are Chicano and live in Texas, you will be saying just the opposite. "Please don't look at Mrs. Robinson when you talk to her." Why? Because in that culture, it is considered impolite and a sign of disrespect to make eye contact with your elders. Each culture has its own rules for how people should be spoken to.

An important aspect of learning how to use language appropriately is understanding what people *really* mean to say. Imagine where we would be if we interpreted everything people said to us *literally*.

Woman on the street: Do you have the time?
You: Yes. (And you keep walking!)

The woman was not interested in whether you were in *possession* of the time. She wanted you to *tell her* the time. She asked for this information very indirectly, not even mentioning the action she wished you to take on her behalf, since it is more polite in our culture to do it that way.

Clearly, knowing the words and the grammatical structures that hold sentences together is only part of the story of language development. In the 4th and 5th years, children are working to harness their language in service to communication. They need to be able to express their wishes and their needs even when they talk to people they don't know very well, like new teachers or babysitters. They also need to unearth the more re-fined meanings in our social chatter. Four-year-olds are notorious for in-terpreting everything literally.

Mom's friend Samantha talking to 4-year-old Jane on the phone:

Samantha: Hi, Jane! Is your mother home?
Jane: Yes. (This is followed by a long silence as Jane, remaining on the phone, imagines that Samantha has really called to acquire just this tidbit of information.)
Samantha: Jane? Are you still there? Would you get her for me?
Jane: (Puts down the phone without a response and goes off to get mom)

Jane answered the literal question. But the literal question was but the surface question. The *real* question was Samantha's polite request to have Jane put her mother on the phone. Jane also does not yet realize that we must respond orally to someone's question on the phone, even if we are fine with carrying it out. How strange it would be to talk to an adult who just put down the phone and went off to find the person we wanted without any verbal acknowledgment. We would think it quite rude.

Not only are children learning about literal and nonliteral meanings at this age, but they are also learning about stories and how they work. Re-searchers have done extensive studies of story development, some of which we will review in the next chapter, which discusses reading. For now, though, simply bear in mind that children at this age *love* stories. They love to hear about you when you were a child, to look at photo albums of trips that the family took, and even just to hear bedtime stories that you either invent or read from books. Researchers find that storytelling has become somewhat of a lost art in homes, even though it provides the bedrock for later literacy skills. When we tell a story, we set a context, put in the characters, set them on a journey where there will be some conflict, and offer a resolution. Our children don't know about all of these parts yet, but the analysts within them will discover story grammar if we tell them stories and construct stories with them.

Teachable Moments	## Storytelling

Children tell lots and lots of stories, but sometimes we don't recognize that that is what they're doing. Little snippets seem to come out of nowhere, and we listen without taking the chance to help them build their tale. So, the next time 3-year-old Marissa says "dinosaur," follow up with a conversation.

Mom: Ah yes, the dinosaur . . . once upon a time there was a dinosaur and the dinosaur was green?

Marissa: No, blue.

Mom: Right. Once upon a time there was a blue dinosaur and it was very hungry . . .

Marissa: And it was going from forest to forest to find food . . .

We need only start the exchange and it seems to generate its own momentum. When we become active and engaged listeners, we coconstruct stories with our children and learn more about their thoughts in the process.

CHATTERBOXES AND THE STRONG, SILENT TYPE: NOT ALL CHILDREN ARE THE SAME

The picture we have presented so far is of the average child. But none of us have average children. We have children like Joe and Samantha, and Martha and Peter. Despite the wide variation in their language development, all of them are perfectly normal. Joe didn't start speaking until he was 17 months old because he had many ear infections. Plus, he had two older siblings, and they hardly let him get a word in edgewise. There is some truth—though only a grain—to the idea that later-born children speak a little later. They don't get as much of our attention, and probably not as much data to work on, as do the first-borns. Let there be some solace, however, in the fact that by age 3 or 4, you would never know which of the many children in a class uttered her first word early or late.

Then there is Samantha. At 16 months, she's a talker, but she doesn't like to go around labeling things like her older brother, Matt. He drives the family crazy learning the name for each and every object he can see—at home, in a museum, on the road. Sammy likes to meet and greet. She says "hi" and "bye" to everyone she meets, and while she has some words, she also knows some social expressions such as "pease" and "tank you."

Martha is off the charts. At age 2 she is the class orator who seems to talk in paragraphs. And then there is Peter, who is slow getting language off the ground. As Jessica, mother of 18-month-old Peter, remarked, "I feel insecure every time I go to my playgroup. Sixteen-month-old Allison and 17-month-old Jake are all spouting words. Peter only knows two." Phyllis, experienced mother of another playgroup member, actually noticed remarkable differences in her own two older children. "I keep a diary for each one. Suzie had 61 words at 18 months, while Arlene only had about 5." Phyllis is more relaxed about the slow pace of her third offspring because she knows Arlene later learned language just as well as Suzie.

If children's language development does vary widely, then how do we know when to worry? Several markers are key. If a child has no words at all by 24 months of age and is still not putting together two words in a sentence by 2½ years of age, it is worth checking out whether there is a problem. Also, if a child does not look you in the eye when you talk and seems to be distant, there might be cause for concern. *If there is a problem, the earlier the intervention, the better.* The first line of defense is to have your child's hearing tested and to talk with your pediatrician.

The Parent's Role as Language Partner

Now you understand a large part of the language development story as researchers see it. Children bring a lot to the table in language learning, and a lot is going on behind the scenes. But what is the role that parents and teachers play? If children know so much, then what is left for us to do? We have illustrated why you DON'T need to *teach* them. But you DO need to *partner* with them and keep the communication going. The more opportunities we take to talk with children, the more data they have to analyze, and the better their foundation for language. A large body of data tells us this is so.

Keep the Conversation Going

Scientists like Professor Erika Hoff at Florida Atlantic University in Davie have spent many hours looking at the relationship between how parents talk with children at mealtimes and playtimes and the children's subsequent language sophistication. Parents who encourage more conversation, ask more questions, and build on conversations that their children start have children with more advanced language. How do you do this? Compare two mothers—Mary and Jamie—who are very similar in terms of education and income, each with 3-year-old at dinner.

> **Child:** I want bread.
> **Mary:** (Handing over bread) Here.
> **Child:** Mmmm.
> **Mary:** You want more?
> **Child:** Yes.
> **Mary:** (Handing over bread) Here.

> **Child:** I want bread.
> **Jamie:** The bread is good, isn't it? Do you want one piece or two?
> **Child:** One, please.
> **Jamie:** (Handing over bread) Did you like the bread on your sandwich at school today?
> **Child:** Yeah, it was good.
> **Jamie:** The bread I used for your school lunch was called pumpernickel. Pumpernickel is a black bread. Did you ever have black bread before?

Mary complied with her child's request, but did not take the opportunity to expand on the conversation. Once a child has expressed an interest, a conversation can go in a host of directions. Jamie realized this and took the teachable moment to partner with her child. She reinforced her child's sense of number, gave her child a restricted choice so that she was empowered with a decision, and expanded on her request in ways that built language skills. She even introduced a new name for a kind of bread.

When parents build upon the child's interest and use it as a basis for conversations, they stimulate language growth. A large body of data tells us that this pays off in a big way. In fact, research shows that even children as young as 18 months have larger vocabularies than their peers if their parents talk with them about objects and actions that the children are interested in. These are the same children who have larger vocabularies at the beginning of school and higher reading and mathematical levels in kindergarten and first grade.

But don't think we are recommending that you carry this to extremes. You needn't wake your child up in the middle of the night to have a conversation about death and taxes! And you don't have to respond to each and every conversational bid your child makes. Just keep in mind that much important information is conveyed—about language and other things—when you have true conversations with your child that build on what he says and thinks.

Size Matters! Talk to Your Children a Lot

One dramatic study of parents' role in language learning comes from Professors Betty Hart and Todd Risley, senior scientists at the Schiefelbusch Institute for Life Span Studies at the University of Kansas in Lawrence. They talk of partnering as a kind of social dance that parents and children engage in as children learn language. In their magnificent study of 42 families over 3 years, they demonstrated the enormous importance of our contribution to children's language learning. They looked at families who differed in their social backgrounds, studying language interaction in professional families, working-class families, and families on welfare. Their findings were literally headline news—and cause for concern. Welfare parents talk less to their children than do either working-class parents or professional parents. According to their data, the average welfare child heard only 616 words per hour, while the working-class child heard about

1,251 words, and the professional children heard an average of 2,153 words per hour. Extrapolating from these figures, over the course of a year, the numbers become overwhelming: 3 million words of language experience for the welfare child, 6 million for the working-class child, and 11 million for the child of professionals.

The study looked not only at the amount of speech, but at the *type* of language parents use with their children. Some parents speak to children using what the researchers term "disapprovals," while others use more "affirmations." Disapprovals are negative statements such as "No," or "Don't do that," or "Stop that!" They close off conversation rather than engage children in talk. On the other hand, affirmations include praise, as in "Good job!" and encouragement, "Let's try that again," and compliments, "You really did that well!" Look at this example from Inge's mother when Inge is 23 months old.

Inge says, "Ball," and her mother repeats, "Ball." When Inge throws the ball over the TV as she repeats words from a commercial, her mother responds, "You know better. Why you do that?" Inge sits on the couch with the ball, gets down, and falls. Her mother initiates, "Now when you hurt yourself, then what?" Inge gets back on the couch, stands, and then climbs over the back of the couch. Her mother initiates, "Hey, quit climbing over my couch."

While we all need to be in control to be sure that our children will not hurt themselves, there are ways to reprimand children while keeping the conversation going: "Let's not throw the ball inside, okay? Wanna go outside to play?" or "Can I help you find something else to play with?"

When the researchers looked at the differences in the sheer number of disapprovals and affirmations, their findings were shocking. The average child from a professional family heard 32 affirmations and 5 disapprovals per hour— a ratio of 6 to 1. Those from the working class heard roughly 12 affirmations and 7 disapprovals—a ratio of 2 to 1. In stark contrast, this pattern flipped for children from welfare homes. They received 5 affirmations and 11 disapprovals per hour, for a ratio of 1 to 2. The effect of these differences and the messages they send to language-learning children cannot be underscored enough. The professional children are being rewarded for talking—the welfare children are not. They are being taught to follow commands. The professional and working-class children are being encouraged and praised, while the welfare children are being told things that cannot help their self-esteem.

Professors Hart and Risley suggest that the social dance metaphor best describes the parent–child interaction that takes place during language learning. They wrote: "Beyond encouraging practice and providing language experience, conversation contributes to a parent–child relationship. . . . The important concern for parents is the amount of dancing. . . . The first three years of experience put in place a trajectory of vocabulary growth. . . . That will make a lasting difference in how children perform in later years. During these first three years, children are almost entirely dependent on adults for dance partners. With their rudimentary skills, 2-year-olds have less need for language experts than for willing dance partners. What children need from adults is time, not tricks."

In other words, the key to how children learn to talk—and whether they will have a large vocabulary—is talking with them. Talk contributes not just to language development, but to children's expanding knowledge about the world and to their willingness to engage in dialogue with others. The parenting differences just discussed were highly related not only to the size of their children's vocabularies, but also to their later IQ scores. The challenge to parents and caregivers, then, is to do the "communication dance."

It's not hard to do and there are no intricate steps to be wary of. You just have to follow your child's lead and dance around what she is interested in. Even at the dinner table, significant things take place that contribute to language learning. The old "Tell mommy what we did today" prompt offered by dad and the help he provides in filling in the blanks is a lovely dance. Children who are present for extended mealtime conversations and therefore watch others dance, especially around descriptions of past events and explanations, have a larger vocabulary than children who do not get to dance over dinner.

| Teachable Moments | ## Vocabulary Development |

Virtually every exchange can become a rich opportunity for asking a question or for adding new vocabulary. For example, while children are cleaning up toys (wishful thinking?), we can move from demanding

"Please pick it up now" to asking "Can you think of another way to pick up that toy?" Then surprise your child by saying and doing something unexpected, such as "I'm going to put this one away with my toes!" Children generally chime right in, and they'll have a blast not only discovering silly ways to put their toys away but also brainstorming ever crazier ideas—all the while chatting a mile a minute, and unknowingly getting some practice stretching their vocabulary.

Provide Stimulating Language Environments

As you can see, what we say and do with our children as language partners is critical to their later language growth. Research on the role of language stimulation and language intervention in child care and preschool settings suggests that the same formulas for success at home are also optimal for language learning in these other contexts. The National Institutes for Children's Health and Human Development, for example, recently mounted a large study of 1,300 children across 10 different cities in the United States. Author Kathy Hirsh-Pasek is a member of the research team that followed these children from birth, looking extensively at how the various contexts in which they live promote or hinder later development. Since language is so central for development, this study investigated the role of language stimulation on later school-readiness skills. The study showed that when teachers and caregivers talk more to children and ask many questions, they create more stimulating language environments for the children in their charge. The result? Children who are involved in conversation know more letters, colors, and shapes at age 3 than children who are not addressed so frequently. This result parallels many in the literature. It is a fact that language stimulation is one of the best predictors of later vocabulary, reading, and mathematical skills.

Intervention studies find the same results. Here, researchers literally "intervene" in unstimulating environments to help raise language levels in the children. They, too, find that when you introduce language and reading stimulation into impoverished environments, children benefit tremendously.

The conclusion from these research efforts leaves no doubt that increasing the amount of language in school and child care settings is central to later academic success. With so many of our 4- and 5-year-olds now in some sort of preschool setting, it is imperative that we provide stimulating language environments there. The same language stimulation and responsiveness levels that informed parents use is what we must insist upon in our preschools. Teachers and caregivers need to talk a lot with children—narrating activities, asking questions, and reading books.

BRINGING THE LESSONS HOME

The main message in this chapter is that the pressure is off. Parents don't have to be teachers of language to their children, but they do need to be *partners*. We give our children the opportunity to hear language and to become little statisticians, computing the "how often" and "under what circumstances" various aspects of language occur. This is what allows them to discover the rules. We also invite them to engage in conversation, allowing them to offer their insights and tell *us* new things. Sometimes their contribution will be only a burp or a babble. Sometimes it will be a story. We need to make space for their contributions and slow down enough in our lives to hear what they have to say.

Talk about what your child is observing and doing. When we have a captive audience, they will take in every word. Sometimes we violate this principle by failing to recognize when we do have a captive audience. In other words, we don't capitalize on those teachable moments. Here is an observation one of us made at the renowned Please Touch Museum in Philadelphia.

> **Child:** (Fully engaged while looking at the big elephant made of gadgets at the front of the museum)
> **Mother:** Let's go—oh, look. Look at that Alice in Wonderland exhibit.
> **Child:** (Still looking at elephant)
> **Mother:** (Getting frustrated; grabs child's hand) Let's go look at all the wonderful things they have here. . . .
> **Child:** (Looking back at elephant while being dragged to next exhibit)

Many of us recognize ourselves in this vignette. We just paid all of that money to go to a museum and our children only want to look at the

elephant? But we could make conversation about the elephant, be partners with our children, and then move on. Whose agenda is it? Do children really have to see everything in the museum? We need to remember
that our children's rhythm is slower than ours. It takes them longer to
absorb the information that we process very quickly. For them, everything is new. Whenever our children become enraptured with something, we should view it as a teachable moment and build on their focus
of attention.

Build on what your child says. Scientists call this "expansion," and
it seems to make a big difference for our children, probably because we
are implicitly showing them that there are other, more complete ways to
say what they just said. It also adds information to the dialogue that they
can retrieve and use at another time. Here's an example of how dad
(without even thinking about it) expanded on what Joel (age 2½) said to
keep the conversation going.

> **Joel:** See dat big cow!
> **Dad:** I see an animal, but it's not a cow. It's a horse. It goes "neigh"
> (demonstration). Can you do that?
> **Joel:** (Attempts neighing)
> **Dad:** Good! A horse lives in a barn and may have a cow for its friend.
> Would you like to go for a ride on a horse?
> **Joel:** No! Dat too big. I fall!
> **Dad:** Oh, you think he's too big? That you'd fall off? No, I'd hold on
> to you. I wouldn't let you fall!

The point is that conversations with parents help children hear multiple ways of conveying their meaning and subtly teach them new vocabulary and information.

Be a conversation elicitor, not a conversation closer. Find ways
to engage with your child so that you can keep the conversation going.
The social dance requires that we ask questions and probe for answers.
We want not only to build on their answers, but to scaffold and support
their talk to us. Ask specific questions rather than broad ones. When you
ask, "What happened at school today?" you might get "Nothing!" If you
ask, "What did you do at circle time today?" or "Was Jenny in school
today?" you open up opportunities to dance together.

Don't be afraid to use baby talk. Parents are often worried that they need to be somewhat sophisticated in speaking with their children. They are worried that if they use baby talk in the 1st year or so, their children will talk that way. But the research shows that it's fine to use baby talk (even if you do feel a bit foolish). With its exaggerated singsong intonation and high pitch, accompanied by your exaggerated facial expressions, baby talk is just the thing to get your child interested in the dance. And don't be concerned that you'll still be talking baby talk when your child goes off to college. Parents unconsciously decrease their baby talk by the time children are about 3 years of age and talking themselves.

Research suggests that baby talk may even have some real advantages for children. The high-pitched talk seems to act as a signal that this language is for them. Not surprisingly, then, babies prefer to listen to baby talk over adult talk. Baby talk also conveys emotions to children, so it is highly communicative. And because baby talk exaggerates language's properties, it helps babies figure things out about the way language works. Professor Anne Fernald, of the psychology department at Stanford University in Palo Alto, California, did a marvelous demonstration of this with 6-month-old babies. If you say something nice but in a gruff tone, babies may get upset. But if you say something not so nice in baby talk, babies answer with smiles and coos. So fear not: There is no evidence that baby talk stunts language growth. To the contrary, there is evidence that baby talk heightens infants' attention to language and its properties.

Limit TV time to small doses. We also need to trust our instincts when it comes to toys and television. Science tells us that children need active, adaptive language partners, not passive or even interactive toys. Television and computer games are not optimal language learning devices. For example, television programs don't build on children's talk or ask questions. They do, however, capture their attention and then comment on what they see. Research on television viewing and language is still in its infancy. Yet the latest studies tell us that educational television does teach children some vocabulary. Shows like *Sesame Street*, *Blue's Clues*, *Barney*, and *Teletubbies* are not harmful for children. It's always best (though not always practical), however, to watch with children so you can discuss what they see. And, of course, time should be limited to no more than 30 minutes a day below 18 months and no more than an hour a day above that. Trust your instincts here and be assured that a little high-quality TV isn't bad for children.

Evaluate your child's language environment at child care. Silence is not golden when it comes to child care environments. Children should be engaged and talkative. Take some time to observe your son's or daughter's child care setting, paying special attention to the following five markers of a solid language environment.

1. Responsiveness: Does the caregiver or teacher respond when the child addresses her?
2. Positive emotion: Does she respond with a smile and a positive disposition?
3. Does the teacher have the attention of the children? Is she talking about things the children are interested in?
4. Expansions: Is the teacher asking questions and building on the children's talk?
5. Reading: Is the room filled with written material and books? Does the teacher read to the children?

If you'd like to introduce a second language, do so in a real-world situation. In our increasingly small world, it is an advantage to speak two or more languages. Leave the toys that label items in French or Spanish behind. When you are looking for a child care center or school, or even an in-home nanny, you have an excellent opportunity to genuinely expose your child to a new language. Give it a try. You'll be surprised by what you will see. Research shows that children who are learning two languages do best when the languages are kept somewhat separate, so that dad speaks one language and mom another, or one language is in use at school and one at home. With these optimal conditions, though, you'll find that baby geniuses learn two languages and use them appropriately from the time they are 2 or 2½. One language or two? If you really want to do something great for your children, give them another language early when they are ripe for learning.

The key is to enjoy the language game. Talk with your children and make them your conversational partners from the beginning. There's no need to correct your children's speech; they'll master that thing they do incorrectly if given enough time and language exposure. After all, your children bring great skills, honed through thousands of years of evolution, to language learning. To become champion talkers, all they need is for you to talk to them.

CHAPTER + 5

LITERACY: READING BETWEEN THE LINES

CONSIDER THE FOLLOWING INSTANCES of two different approaches to introducing books to toddlers—something we like to call A Tale of Two Readers. Which of these two families do you think is better preparing their child to learn to read?

Rachel is a very active 2-year-old who lives with her single mother, Anne. Anne has every intention of providing her daughter with the home experiences she needs to become a good reader once school starts. Anne reads to Rachel nearly every night before she goes to bed. But because Rachel is so active, it's sometimes very frustrating for Anne to read to her. When she does get the reading in, Anne tries to minimize interruptions. Anne ignores Rachel when she asks questions, points, or tries to engage her mom about the print on the page. Instead she plows on so that she and Rachel can finish at least one book each night. Anne also comes equipped with a few secret weapons. After they read, Anne helps Rachel learn the alphabet with a set of flash cards with big, brightly colored letters. Rachel's room is also a gold mine of learning opportunities. She has the new robot toy that teaches reading and math readiness (as well as thinking, problem solving, and manners, according to the box). She also has the latest Smart Books, which make alphabetic learning "fun." With a rich environment like this, Anne is certain that Rachel will read before she goes to school.

Two-year-old Nate lives with his parents and his older sister, Kristen. He often climbs up into his parents' laps or his sister's lap with a book and demands, "Read! Read!" They have been reading to Nate practically since he was born, and his little room is strewn with books and crayons and paper. Nate makes storybook reading a challenge. He seems determined to hear every book he owns every time a session begins. He asks a million questions about the pictures ("Whas dat?"), pointing with his little index finger as he looks up into the face of his reader. Still, his parents and sister don't mind. They continue to answer his questions, to point out things on the page themselves that he might not have noticed, and to ask him questions about the story: "Why do you think Mr. Owens (the character in the book) wants to find his kitty?" And "How do you think Mr. Owens will feel when he finds his kitty?" Nate can't always answer these questions, but they sure get him thinking. Despite the fact that Nate's parents see his love of literature, they worry periodically about whether they should be doing more. There are so many teaching products when they go to the store, and they are receiving flyers from Web sites like Bright Horizons, which "nurtures children's potential." Maybe they should be teaching Nate his letter names with flash cards like some of their friends are doing.

What You've Heard: Learning to Read

Despite their different approaches, both sets of parents believe that they need to teach their children to read before school starts. They have heard this on television shows and in parent magazines. They have witnessed the newfound emphasis on reading in preschool, and they even feel the push toward reading every time they go to the toy store. By the end of this chapter, you will be able to make a well-grounded prediction about whether Rachel or Nate will have more success in reading once school starts. Rachel's mother is determined to have her child know the names of the letters and even read before she enters kindergarten. Nate's parents have so far resisted doing formal instruction with him, but they worry about it and have doubts all the time about whether they are doing enough. Both sets of parents worry that if they don't provide explicit instruction, their children will fall behind. After all, reading is such a fundamental skill for school success that they both think it can't be left up to the schools. And even if the children don't learn how to read before school, maybe at least they should be drilled on the names of the letters.

But is that true? Is learning the names of the letters critical for success in reading in school? Are flash card drills more important than reading aloud to your child? Should book reading be a quiet time with no interruptions so the child can concentrate (like Rachel's reading sessions) or a raucous time with lots of conversation (like Nate's sessions)? What can parents do to instill a love of reading in their children? And how do children get started reading in the first place?

The answer to all of these questions is the same reassuring one: The most important thing you can do for your child is to make reading fun— not work. As you begin to understand the true building blocks for reading—vocabulary, storytelling, phonological awareness, and deciphering the written code—you'll see how children gradually discover important aspects of literacy as they reach certain milestones on their reading journey. These milestones include distinguishing between pictures in a book and real objects, identifying letters from squiggles and designs, and learning how to sound out printed words. While each of these is critical to children's literacy development, none of them should be rushed in an attempt to get children to master reading before they are ready and able. Efforts to do so are, at best, a waste of time and, at worst, a serious impediment to helping children develop the most important aspects of literacy: a love of reading and imaginative storytelling.

In the following pages, we'll tell you how parents in ordinary, loving, and nurturing homes are providing children with the activities and skills that are known antecedents for learning to read. We'll also point out things you can do that perhaps you've overlooked that can help your child accumulate these prerequisites. What you'll *not* find in this chapter are exhortations to go out and buy flash cards, or robots, or reading/writing toys and computer programs. Rather, we'll explain why environments rich in "old-fashioned" reading and storytelling promote emergent literacy in a way that naturally unfolds with your child's own developing abilities and awareness. By the end of this chapter, you'll come to understand why the

National Academy of Education Commission on Reading declared that reading aloud to children is the "single most important activity" for ensuring success in learning to read. And even though you might feel lured by the national push to increase phonics in preschool, we'll show you how to maintain balance and to create environments that stimulate language and literacy development without overspending your credit limit.

We will explain why children who learn to read at age 2 or 3 are generally not on the genius track. (In fact, a number of studies indicate that children who have been taught to memorize printed words might be ahead in first grade, but by third and fourth grades many of the other children have caught up or even surpassed them.) Further, we'll show why the time you spend in drill and practice would be much better spent cuddling up and reading to your child and discussing what is on the printed page. After all, reading is about *making meaning* from squiggles on a page. And emergent literacy activities should be fun and pleasurable so children learn that "books are friends."

WHAT REALLY MATTERS FOR LEARNING TO READ

How did we get to the point where many parents believe they must formally teach reading to their children before they begin school? Professor Hollis Scarborough of Rutgers University in New Jersey, an expert on reading and reading failure, gives us some perspective when she writes, "As recently as 20 years ago, learning to read was not thought to commence until *formal instruction was provided in school.* Accordingly, reading disabilities were largely considered to be an educational problem with *no known antecedents* at earlier ages. It is now abundantly clear that reading acquisition is a process that *begins early in the preschool period,* such that children arrive at school having acquired vastly differing degrees of knowledge and skill pertaining to literacy (our italics)."

Other experts in the field, such as Susan Newman, Ph.D., former assistant secretary for elementary and secondary education, and David Dickinson, Ph.D., senior research scientist at the Education Development Center in Newton, Massachusetts, add that ". . . the emergent literacy perspective, the understanding that literacy development begins long before children start formal instruction, is now largely taken for granted.

Today, there is consensus . . . that children are doing critical cognitive work in literacy development from birth through age 6."

No wonder we are crazed! We are now told—based on research evidence—that pre-reading skills start in infancy. But precisely what does this mean—and what can we do to help our children develop these skills?

The answer can be found in a careful examination of the concept *emergent literacy*. The term emergent literacy arrived on the educational scene about 20 years ago. It is the belief—backed by solid research studies—that reading doesn't happen with a bang once school begins, but that many, many literacy experiences prime the child to emerge as a reader. Even the phrase conveys a sense of something occurring gradually and not abruptly. The emphasis on "prerequisites" to reading is good, since it can only help us provide the right sorts of experiences for our children. And it is not a trivial goal to provide the "right sorts of experiences." Estimates are that 88 percent of children who have reading problems in first grade will likely continue to have problems in fourth grade. But before you panic, only 20 percent of children have reading problems. Unfortunately, these children tend to come from environments where poverty predominates and in which they are rarely exposed to books. One of the reasons these children have reading problems is that parents don't read to them at all or often enough.

According to National Household Education Surveys conducted in 1993, 78 percent of the parents surveyed said that they read to their preschoolers three or more times in the week prior to the survey. That means that 22 percent of children did not hear books read that often. There was also a relationship found between a mother's level of education and how often she read to her child. If mothers had at least a high school degree, they were more than 20 percentage points *more* likely to read aloud to their children than mothers who had not completed high school. Paradoxically, a lower level of education was associated with *more* explicit teaching of letters, words, or numbers. Mothers who were more educated offered less direct teaching of letters and more reading than mothers who were less educated.

In other studies, researchers have tried to close the gap between rich and poor to see whether offering extensive language and literacy experiences to children in poverty would help them learn to read. Their findings showed that when teachers provide a model to children for using language to communicate and be understood, and when teachers and parents read to children and discuss the contents of the book, they offer a recipe for later reading success. For example, the Abecedarian project in North Carolina followed children from ages 5 to 21. Some of the children received language and reading enrichment, while others did not. Did researchers find differences between these groups of children? Yes. Not only did the children who participated in the enrichment programs do better in reading when they entered school, they also continued to show gains in reading relative to their peers through high school. They also stayed in school longer, and they even got married later than their friends who did not receive the benefit of enrichment. Talk about long-term benefits! Barring extreme circumstances such as these, however, most children are exposed to emergent literacy events every day in their homes and preschools.

THE BUILDING BLOCKS OF READING

Before they can begin to read, children need to develop four basic abilities. Central to these abilities is a strong command of language. If you've ever tried to read in a foreign language, you immediately understand the importance of knowing a language for learning how to read. In many traditional Hebrew school programs, Jewish children learn to "sound out" the letters that appear on the page. To many, this suggests that they *read* Hebrew. But are they really *reading* Hebrew? No, actually they are just connecting sounds with the letters, and quite often they have no idea what the words or phrases mean. To go from print to meaning—*the goal of real reading*—you first need a strong command of the language. This involves having a good vocabulary, being able to tell a story, and understanding how sounds make up words ("phonological awareness"). But even this isn't enough. To learn to read, children also need to know about the "written code," the letters that make up the words, and how words tell stories through books.

Vocabulary

Reading piggybacks on the language system that children already have. This means that it is easier for an American baby to learn to read English than Romanian. It also means that a child who has strong language abilities will have a real advantage when it comes to reading. Why? Because when you translate the written words, you form coherent ideas that take you far beyond the pages of the book.

Children who have larger vocabularies are the ones who generally get more out of early reading. In fact, vocabulary is the strongest predictor of later reading and literacy ability. And the best way to build vocabulary is through talk, talk, and more talk. There's no need for parents to consciously introduce big words when they talk with their children, however. This happens automatically as parents converse with their children. Research has found that without even realizing it, parents adjust how they speak to their children. They seem to be always slightly ahead of their children's capabilities. So if a child is speaking mostly in three-word sentences, parents tend to add another word or two to their sentences, but not to speak in paragraphs as they would to another adult.

Storytelling

Barking out individual words when we see a printed page is not reading. A robot can do that. Vocabulary knowledge is important, too, but it's not enough. The second language skill that is critical to later reading is storytelling. It turns out that storytelling is one of the bridges that move children from language to reading.

A number of researchers have looked at the relationship between storytelling and reading. First, we know that the language we use in stories (known as narrative discourse) is something that children develop over time. In her magnificent book, *The Stories Children Tell*, Professor Susan Engel of Williams College, in Williamstown, Massachusetts, treats us to the lost art of storytelling and shows us how children develop this skill. She reports one story from a 2-year-old, who tells his mother, "We went trick and treating. I got candy, a big red lollipop, and I lost my hat."

In contrast, she shares the following story told by a 5-year-old, an example of a much more developed story.

> *Ya know what? Ya know what? We had a raccoon on our porch. A big, huge raccoon. It was in the tree and he was trying to eat the bird food. And we wanted to scare it away, but my Mom didn't want our Dad to scare it. But he scared it anyway by throwing a stone at it and it ran away! Maybe it went to get its friends and now they'll all come back to eat the bird food!*

A number of scientists have focused on exactly what changes in what they call narrative or story grammar. For example, as children get older, they add more to the narrative structure. The story the 2-year-old above tells has a beginning and an end, but it lacks the kind of detail that the 5-year-old's story includes. Good stories contain an introduction that has a setting and some characters, some statement of a problem, some goal, a plot through which the actors move purposively toward the goal, and an ending in which the character obtains the goal. By 9 years of age—around third grade—children have all of the parts down pat. At age 2, when children are just beginning to tell stories, we have to work at interpreting their stories to figure out what our children are trying to tell us.

As children get older, not only does the structure of their stories become more sophisticated, but the language does too. Stories from 2-year-olds are often centered on the "I," while older children can tell stories about others or about fictional characters. Older children of 4 or 5 also use connector language like "and," "but," and even "if-then."

What does all of this have to do with reading? Several studies find that the ability to tell stories is directly related to the ability to learn how to read. The fancy name for what goes on in storytelling is "decontextualized" language. That is, when you tell a good story, you set up the listener with all of the structure and language he needs to interpret what you are saying. The listener should be able to follow the story and "get it." This is very different from the kind of "contextualized" language that we often use with our friends and children. When we talk to people we know well and with whom we share gobs of experiences and information, we can leave out all the niceties involved in setting the scene and providing a structure. We can just talk and know we will be understood.

Discovering Hidden Skills | Storytelling

Ages: 3 years to 5 years

See how your child does in telling stories. Some researchers study children's storytelling by having them look at picture books that stimulate their imagination without words. Get a new picture book. One that is particularly popular in this kind of research is *The Frog Story* by Mercer Mayer. Any book with pictures that tells a story will do; after all, your children become the authors of the tale the pictures seem to tell. Read the book with your child and see how elaborate a story she makes up. Does she describe the setting? The characters? Does she set up a problem and describe a goal and a resolution? You can try this about every 6 months and watch how your child's ability to tell a coherent story continues to grow. Keep a record of how she told the same story over time. This will be fun to look at later, when she's *writing* stories!

Another way to assess storytelling is to give a prompt to your 3-, 4-, and 5-year-olds. You can easily generate what is called a personal narrative. Start them off with something like "The funniest thing that happened to me today was . . ." Or try "The best thing that happened in school today was . . ." Then let them go off on their own and see what they come up with.

Fortunately, children naturally enjoy telling stories, and there is much we can do to foster their storytelling abilities. Professor Engel offers a number of practical strategies. First, she reminds us to listen attentively. Much of what children say has value and needs to be treated that way. Often we half-listen and fail to hear the personal stories and important moments that children are trying to share. She also suggests that we respond substantively. Ask questions and listen with an ear toward understanding, not correcting. Finally, collaborate—the very best stories come when we work with our children to expand upon what they say. By doing so, you are modeling the style that will help your children master the decontextualized language we use when we are in story mode.

Phonological Awareness, or "You Mean That Words Are Made Up of Sounds?"

We have established two aspects of language that form a base for early literacy and later reading: vocabulary and storytelling. The third piece is called *phonological awareness*. You use phonological awareness when you can isolate the sound of the "b" in "bat" or the sound of the "l" in "follow." This is actually a very difficult task for young children.

Our words are made up of sounds, sounds even smaller than syllables, called *phonemes*. And these phonemes are the bits of sounds that connect with the letters of the alphabet. (To complicate matters, there are 40 phonemes in our language, including the "ch" and "sh," and only 26 letters. Ah, well.) Children spend a lot of time trying to play with language and to isolate these phonemes. But they are not very good at it until they are 4 or 5 years of age. They might start with appreciating rhymes that vary initial phonemes, as in "The *cat* in the *hat* found a *bat* with a *vat*." Sometimes by age 4 or 5 they even enjoy phonemes in bad jokes: "Did he wash his face? Let's soap so." (We did say BAD jokes.) In these examples, children are looking at the language and pulling it apart, trying to understand how it works.

But how does a child ever become aware of the fact that the word "cat" is composed of three different sounds? Think about this for a moment. Oral language is transparent to us; we pay no attention to the sounds that compose speech. When someone talks to us, we focus on the meaning of what he is saying. The only time we notice the sounds of language is when we're conversing with someone with a foreign accent (or a child) and we're forced to figure out how she uses her sounds so we can understand them. ("Oh, she's using the 'r' sound as an 'l'!") If oral language is transparent to us, then how would a child ever figure out that words are composed of pieces? Learning to talk is just a start. When a child learns to talk, she has to combine the separate sounds, or phonemes, that make up words to pronounce them. But she's not conscious of what she's doing when she says a word. Reading requires that the child become conscious of the fact that written words are made up of pieces of sound (phonemes). It requires a deeper level of awareness of language—phonological awareness.

Since phonological awareness is a prerequisite for learning to read, figuring out when children typically develop this awareness is an important key to understanding what we can do to guide them. But how do we know if a child has developed phonological awareness? Some researchers ask young children to manipulate a word or analyze its sounds. For example, a child might be asked to "Say 'top.' Now say it again and leave out the 't' sound." Or "Say 'ball.' Now say it again and take away the 'buh' and put in a 'kuh' sound instead." One of the most fascinating approaches, however, was devised by the late Dr. Isabelle Liberman of the Haskins Laboratory in New Haven, Connecticut, who studied phonological awareness in the 1970s.

In Dr. Liberman's experiments, 4-year-old children were given a dowel rod and asked to tap it on the table for the number of sounds in a particular word. Each child was then individually read 42 one-syllable words, each with between one and three phonemes. Next, Dr. Liberman individually tested a different group of 4-year-olds, asking each to do the same task with syllables. This time, the children were read a list of 42 words with between one and three syllables. For example, Dr. Liberman would ask a child to tap out "How many parts do you hear in the word 'rocket'?" Dr. Liberman decided that children could achieve either task if they could tap out six correct responses in a row.

What were the results? The 4-year-olds tested in the phoneme task got none of the items correct. In contrast, roughly half of the 4-year-olds achieved the 6-item-correct criterion in the syllable task. The fact that the children did much better on the syllable than on the phoneme task shows two things. First, it means that preschoolers can play the game—when the unit of analysis (the syllable) is big enough for them to notice. Second, it shows that preschoolers are not yet sensitive to the individual sounds (phonemes) that make up words.

How did kindergarten children do? On syllables, roughly half of them succeeded; on phonemes, only 17 percent of them succeeded. Surely, you may be thinking, once reading instruction begins in the first grade, we would expect all the children to pass the phoneme and the syllable test. And almost all first-graders did pass the syllable test. Surprisingly, though, only 70 percent of the first-graders could pass the phoneme-tapping test. Even reading instruction had not yet made 30 percent of the children aware of the fact that words are composed of separate sounds.

Dr. Liberman waited until the next fall to see if the children's performance on her phoneme-tapping task related to how well they were doing in reading. She found that of the children who were in the top third of the class in reading, none failed the phoneme test. And of the children who had failed the phoneme test, half were in the bottom third of the class in reading. Not one was in the top third. This was a powerful indicator that phonological awareness is important for reading success.

Many, many other studies by now have supported these findings. It is now clear that lack of phonological awareness is one of the causes of reading failure. We also know that children who have this knowledge are better readers. While we're not quite sure how this realization begins to dawn in children, we know from much research how to help children become phonologically aware. Basically, it's child's play! You can't explain the concept in a way that will make sense to a preschooler, but you can sure play games that illustrate the concept.

| Teachable Moments | Playing with Words |

Play with language by singing songs or reading children's poetry that rhymes. Simple verses like "The cat in the hat that sat on the mat" help to make children aware that the initial sounds in words can continually be replaced by other sounds. Read Dr. Seuss, a genius at using rhyme to tell stories. And remember a popular song that involved fooling around with the sounds in someone's name? It went something like "Rory rory fo fory banana fanna fo fory: Rory." Play it with your child with her name and the names of family members. Notice what the song does: It replaces the initial sound of the name, implicitly teaching that words have parts that can be moved around. Change initial letters to make new names out of old. Remember that old standard, the alphabet song (A-b-c-d-e-f-g, etc.)? Sing it with gusto! That way children will get to hear the letter names and maybe even notice some of their sounds.

Play word games in the car, too. When driving, you can look for objects that start with different sounds. "Can you find something whose name starts with an 'm'? Oh, I see something. There's a MAN!" These games may even reduce the frequency of that perennial question "Are we there yet?" Say a familiar word and ask the child to say it without one of its parts. "I'm going to say 'baseball'! Can you say it without the 'ball'?" And there are always tapes to play that recite rhymes and sing songs for your child.

In short, reading builds upon language. A strong language foundation in vocabulary, storytelling, and phonological awareness is central to emergent literacy. Of course, reading isn't *just* about language; it is also about knowledge of the print itself.

Reading the Small Print

The next part of our story turns from what children know in language to what they know about the written code. We call it a code because, just as oral language is composed of sounds that are by themselves meaningless, writing is composed of squiggles on a page that alone are meaningless. It is only when a child cracks the code and discovers that these squiggles have meaning that she has learned to read. How do children crack the written language code? How do they come to learn that written language maps to meanings?

Before we look at learning to read from your children's vantage point, we first need to ask, what does it take to learn to read? Imagine picking up a book written in a language you are not familiar with, such as Greek or Chinese. What would it take to learn to read those squiggles?

First, you'd need to be able to *tell the letters apart*. If you can't distinguish one squiggle from the next, how could you read the words? Second, you'd need to learn what *sounds* each letter or letter group made. Reading is, after all, the translation of print to speech—even if this occurs silently in your head as an adult. Once we get good at it, we are rarely conscious of sounding words out. Third, you'd need to know how to combine the letters and their sounds into words, to *blend* them together. Although this step also seems so effortless for us as adults in English, it might not be so easy for us in Greek, and it is certainly something that our children have to learn.

There's another piece to the puzzle. Even before you identify the letters or characters, you need to know in which direction the foreign text flows. You might assume that it works like English, from left to right. But perhaps it goes up and down on the page (which is how Chinese is read) or from right to left (like Hebrew). You can't begin to blend together the letters and their sounds if you don't know this. And finally, you need to know in what direction to turn the pages in a book. English begins at the beginning, right? Well, the beginning for us is the end for other language groups. Hebrew readers start at what we think of as the back of the book. How did we manage to get all of these pieces put together so that by the end of our first grade of school we could read even little books on our own? And how do we ever find meaning among seemingly meaningless squiggles?

THE READING JOURNEY

Let's go on the same journey that children travel when they ford this critical stream. As you digest the evidence and learn what goes into reading, we hope that you will be able to relax and recognize that you are probably already providing most of what is essential to get emergent literacy off the ground. So put away your credit card, pull out your library card, put your feet up, and join us as we discover the wonders of the printed word.

When Do Babies Understand What Picture Books Are?

You've just had this gorgeous new baby, and although you may be a bit shell-shocked, you have noticed (between feedings) that some people have given you children's books as gifts. You wonder, When will Beulah be ready for books? At birth and up until about 6 months, your baby will be interested in books just as she is in any other brightly colored object in her environment. Toward the end of that period, she might even appear to listen if you read a simple book to her. But, more often than not, she will prefer to eat books, exploring them as she does everything else, with her mouth. One question you might have is whether babies see books as we do. For one thing, do they appreciate that pictures in books are not the same as the real thing?

Professor Judy DeLoache, now at the University of Virginia, and her colleagues at the University of Illinois studied the reactions of two groups of babies—one group of 9-month-olds and one group of 19-month-olds—when they were given picture books. The 9-month-olds poked and prodded and patted the pictures as if they were real objects. Many were very persistent at trying to grasp the picture as if to pull it off the page. Professor DeLoache concluded that "physically grasping at pictures helps infants to begin to mentally grasp the true nature of objects." In other words, their lack of success at pulling pictures off the page teaches them that pictures are not real objects but mere representations of real objects.

By 19 months, however, babies' manual activities were mostly replaced by pointing. The function of pointing is to single something out, to take notice of it. Pointing is not the same as trying to pull the picture off the page and reveals a more mature understanding of its two-dimensional status. But don't take this to mean that by 19 months children have understood all that they need to about pictures. It takes several more years for children to understand what pictures mean. For example, preschoolers are not yet clear that pictures don't have the properties of the real objects. When asked if a photograph of an ice cream cone would be cold if you touched it, preschoolers say yes. It also takes children years to understand the conventions we use to indicate motion in pictures, such as little lines around joints.

| Discovering Hidden Skills | Noticing Books |

Ages: 8 months to 20 months

Can you reproduce the DeLoache findings? Once your baby can sit up, give him a new hard cardboard book to explore while he is sitting in his high chair. What does the baby do to the book? Does he try to pull the picture off the page by grasping it? Does he try to feel the picture, rub it, and pat it as if it were a real object? Try this again with the same book in 3 months, and then 3 months later. It might be fun to record what the baby does in his baby book, if you keep one. Do you see a change over the 6 months? Does the baby seem to appreciate the fact that pictures in books are but two-dimensional? Does he start to point at the pictures instead of trying to pull them off the page? It's fun to chart this transformation.

A little later, into the 2nd year of life, some babies (who can sit still long enough) will enjoy hearing a book read to them. They may even recognize familiar objects and people in books and try to turn the pages. On the other hand, they may also try to rip the pages (makes a great noise), which is why cloth and cardboard books that minimize this concern are great and reduce any book battles that might ensue. Toddlers now will sit by themselves and "read" a book for a little while and may have a favorite book they insist on hearing . . . and hearing . . . and hearing. If you hand a toddler a book, she will generally know now which end is up and which way it opens. In fact, this is part of a pre-reading test that Professor Marie Clay of the University of Auckland in New Zealand devised called the Concepts about Print test. It consists of handing a child a book and seeing what they know about it, among other concepts. Do they know which is the front and which is the back? Do they know that the words go from left to right? Do they know which way the pages turn? Do they know that the story comes from the words and not the pictures? Children's scores on questions like these correlate with their reading success—above and beyond their knowledge of print. Why is this so? Probably because doing well on this test indicates that children have been read to and have a lot of familiarity with books.

| Discovering Hidden Skills | It's a Page-Turner: Becoming Familiar with Books |

Ages: 18 months to 3 years

When your child is about 18 months, you can just hand her a *new* book and watch to see what she does with it. Can she take a book she's never seen and turn it around to the front? Turn the pages the right way? If you try this about every 6 months, you can gauge how your child's familiarity with books is changing. And when her language is sufficiently developed to answer questions, you can ask her things like "Which way do we read the words?" and "Is the story in the pictures or in the words?" It's interesting to see how children answer these questions.

What Are Words, Anyway?
Come to Think of It, What Are Letters?

Now that your child is reading books with you, he is surely noticing both the pictures and the words on the page. You've probably noticed that you talk about the pictures a good deal with your child as you read. But children at around age 2 are definitely starting to notice the print, too. In fact, American children as young as 2½ have been shown to recognize brand names. What a thrill it is for us (not necessarily) to know that our young children can recognize the words "McDonald's" and "Burger King"! However, just as being able to read words from flash cards does not mean a child can read, being able to recognize common brand names does not guarantee this, either. Nor does it guarantee that children can even distinguish writing (letters and words) from designs, or pictures, or symbols. When do children know what is writing and what is not writing? Professor Linda Lavine of Cortland State University in New York took us a long way in answering this question.

For her experiment, Professor Lavine created cards with one of four different items on each: pictures; letter or words written in English (either in script or printed); writing from another language, such as Hebrew or Chinese; and doodle-like designs. She then individually tested children between 3 and 6 years who had not yet had reading instruction. Each child was asked to put the cards with writing into a play mailbox and all the others in another container. When they finished, Professor Lavine then asked each child to name what was on each card. In this way, she discovered whether 3-year-olds (and older children) could distinguish writing from other images that appear on paper. What did she find?

By the age of 3, children could distinguish true writing (in both English and Hebrew) 86 percent of the time. By age 4, they had improved to 90 percent, and by age 5 they were almost perfect at 96 percent. When she asked them to name the materials, none of the children could read the real words and many couldn't name the three real letters in the set (A, B, and E). All of the children, however, were able to name the pictures, and *none* of the children called the pictures "writing."

How do children do this? How do they know, for example, that Hebrew writing is writing? It must be the case that they have distinguished the kinds of features that make up letters in English and extrapolated their knowledge to Hebrew. This is truly amazing given that no one tells children, "Now notice that letters are made up of straight and curvy lines and that they sometimes appear in strings (words)." Children have figured this out for themselves. How? Think about our society and the pervasiveness of print. Environmental print, as it is called, is everywhere—from cereal boxes to street signs to packages in the supermarket. Children who have exposure to lots of print seem to analyze the patterns that make up writing on their own, without explicit tutelage.

We know from cross-cultural work that Professor Lavine did that the environment children are in is *crucial* for when they distinguish between writing and other sorts of designs. Professor Lavine took her cards to Mexico, both a rural village and an industrialized town in the Yucatán.

Interestingly, the Mexican children were behind the American children, particularly the children growing up in a rural village that did not abound with street signs or cereal boxes.

These findings tell us two important things about emergent literacy. First, on their own, children are figuring out lots of things about how writing works. Without prompting, children at the end of their 2nd year, having had a wide range of experiences with print, already can tell the difference between pictures and letters. Children are, by nature, pattern seekers who do not wait to be told which are letters and which are pictures or designs. On their own, they uncover the features that make up letters and generalize this knowledge to other writing systems. All that said, the second thing we learned is how critical the environment is. Pattern-seeking children must, after all, have something to bring their pattern-seeking skills to. If they are in environments rich in print, they uncover the features of writing a lot sooner than if they are not. If they are read to and are exposed to written materials, they figure out many things about books, letters, and writing before they even come to school. This is emergent literacy.

| Discovering Hidden Skills | Discovering the Written Word |

Ages: 2 years to 4 years

Take 16 index cards and on each card write a single word or a letter, or make a design (squiggle, shapes, etc.) or draw a picture. Make four cards of each type. Make the print or picture quite large, taking up virtually the whole card, and use a thick pen or pencil of the same color. Shuffle the cards when you're done. Starting at around age 2, show the cards one at a time to your child and ask if what she sees is writing. Or you could put your hands out and say, "Put the writing in this hand (moving your hand) and put all the others in this hand (indicating your other hand)." Keep track of how many your child gets right. When you're done asking the child to sort them, find out which ones (if any) your child can name. Do you see a pattern to your child's mistakes? Try this every 3 or 4 months, keeping your cards away from your child in between so that they are fresh each time. You will be watching as your child discovers the features that make up writing, a crucial emergent literacy achievement that you might not otherwise have noticed at all.

Is Learning Letter Names Important for Learning to Read?

A great controversy swirls around the question of whether children should be taught their letter names. Perhaps it is not enough for children to be able to distinguish between the letters and pictures. Perhaps they need to know what we call the letters. In other words, is it important to be able to call an "A" an "A" to learn to read? President George W. Bush thinks so, and knowing the names of the letters is a key component of his early education initiative. As he said in a speech at Pennsylvania State University:

> But (reading to your children) is more than just fun. It is a vital preschool learning experience. Consider this amazing finding: 10th grade reading scores can be predicted with surprising accuracy from a child's knowledge of the alphabet in kindergarten. Think about that. We can pretty well predict how well a child will read in the 10th grade . . . (by) whether or not the child has been given a good education early in his or her life. A child who cannot identify the letters of the alphabet in his or her first year of school runs a real risk of staying behind in school throughout her or his career.

The emphasis on emergent literacy is exactly where it should be, since we now know that there is no clear line between reading and pre-reading. However, there is concern about how President Bush's ideas will be implemented. As a column in *Education Week* states, "The president's campaign promise to require the teaching of phonics as part of his reading initiative, as well as his calls for greater accountability in education, has raised concerns among some educators that the Reading First funds would favor highly scripted programs and put a great emphasis on high-stakes testing."

Since virtually hundreds of studies clearly and unequivocally show that knowledge of letter names and letter sounds is related to success in learning to read, where's the rub? Some educators are concerned that reading will be pushed on preschool children in unhealthy ways. The worst-case scenario is that the emphasis on letter names and sounds will be poorly implemented into a "drill and kill" curriculum rather than one that emphasizes rich, authentic literacy experiences. Three- and 4-year-olds should not be doing worksheets and engaging in drill and practice.

Three- and 4-year-olds should be engaging in genuine literacy activities, like reading, writing, talking, and listening. Educators are concerned that these emergent literacy activities will be downplayed and that drills and practice on the letters will replace them. This concern is heightened in a national climate that emphasizes testing and standards. As Professor Catherine Snow, a leading literacy researcher at Harvard University, said, "Reading is clearly more than knowing letter names. After all, there are only 26 letters to memorize. Reading is so much more."

It's also helpful to consider what it really means when a child can name the letters of the alphabet. The greatest significance is that the child can get some help in reading. Why? Because some of the letter names sound like the sounds they make when they are found in words. The letter "b," for example, sounds like "buh" in any word you find it in. However, the names of other letters do not resemble the sound they make in words. Take "w." When used in the words "when" or "word," the sound it makes does not resemble its name. Or take "y" as in "you" or "k" as in "knife." So why does knowing letter names seem to correlate so highly with reading success? It's not that knowing the letter names per se matters, because even children who have reading problems can sometimes know their letter names. It's because when preschoolers know their letter names, it reveals another fact about their experience: These are children who have been read to a lot and who have had the good fortune to engage in lots of emergent literacy activities. Picking up the letter names for most of them is incidental to the many pre-reading literacy activities they have done. That's why it's not clear that teaching letter names by itself, without all the wonderful language and informal emergent literacy activities we've described, will have an impact on reading. Teaching letter names comes within the context of emergent literacy activities; it shouldn't be an end in itself.

Our advice? Keep reading and providing your children with the literacy experiences that prompt them to ask for information about letters and words. You'll probably be pleasantly surprised by all that they know.

What Sounds Do the Letters Make? Letter-Sound Correspondences

Knowing the letter names is half of the battle, but knowing the sounds that the letters make is even more important. And, as we already discussed, this can be difficult because the sounds don't all happily coincide with the name of the letter. Further, sometimes a single letter (such as "c" as in "city" versus "country") has multiple sounds; such is the case with most of the vowels.

What children have to do is to link the letters they see with the phonemes, the small sounds that make up the words, that they discover. This is challenging, for, as we mentioned above, we have only 26 letters, but 40 sounds. Further, learning the letter sounds doesn't help you blend or combine these separate sounds into a word when you're reading. After all, even if you say "buh-oo-kuh" three times real fast, you still won't really be saying the word "book." You'll be saying some three-syllable variant of the word. Linking the letters to the sounds they make is called finding the letter-sound correspondences. This step is a key ingredient for successful reading. The child who can link letters and sounds breaks the code and can translate from the print into the language he has mastered. At that point, the child can get real meaning from the text.

You Mean Those Letters *Mean* Something?

When your child asks you, "What does that say, Mommy?" he is appreciating reading and books in a whole new way. This question signals big progress. Your child now gets the idea that the squiggles on the page map to meanings! He has known all along that the pictures are fun and informative, but now he's getting a sense that the print can be, too. Print can tell stories in a way that pictures often can't.

Think about what your children are learning about reading. They are learning that the print in books corresponds to the words that adults say. And they are learning that the print carries more of the story than the pictures do. These significant insights contribute to emergent literacy.

Teachable Moments

Finding Meaning in Printed Words

There is a fun thing you can try to help your child understand that the funny squiggles on a page (words) correspond to the language they hear. You can try to do this once your child can talk in paragraphs, at around age 3. You're going to ask your child to tell you a little story, and then you will write down what he or she says, using big letters. Or, if you have a computer, you could type the story instead. This is *story dictation*, and it is the best way to show children that what comes out of their mouths can be translated directly into words. Read the story to your child when you're done and make a big fuss that he told *you* a story!

Start the story halfway down on a new page, because when you're done you'll ask your child to draw a picture to illustrate the story on the top half of the page. To prompt a story, ask your child to tell you about anything you have just done or something that your child found very exciting. Your child may not understand how to tell a story, so you will probably wind up asking leading questions that require more than yes/no answers. And write it as the child tells it. Don't pretty it up (well, maybe just a little). When your child has done some of these, I suggest framing them and hanging them somewhere—even the laundry room. They are your child's first narratives.

Is Scribbling on a Piece of Paper Just a Fun Way to Move Your Arm?

Emergent literacy involves not only reading but also writing. When do children want to write, and how should we treat their adorable (but sometimes pathetic) written products? One of the emergent literacy activities that children love is to scribble on a piece of paper. But if you were a skeptic, you might wonder whether children are doing this because they want to see the *marks* they make or whether they just like *exercising* their hand and arm in this way.

A world-famous psychologist, the late Dr. James J. Gibson of Cornell University, decided to lay that question to rest by studying children between the ages of 15 and 38 months. Imagine 16-month-old, curly-topped Allison visiting Dr. Gibson's lab with her mother, Donna. The graduate assistant gives Allison a clipboard with a blank paper and two writing implements—one that makes a mark and one that doesn't—one at a time. The assistant simply sits there with a stopwatch, noting how long Allison scribbles with each implement and anything else Allison says or does. Donna tells the graduate assistant that Allison really has no experience with crayons or writing yet and that she was surprised to be asked to participate in the study. As they chat, Allison is first handed the implement that does not write. She doesn't attempt to bring it to the paper and just looks at it. When time is up, the graduate assistant takes that tool away and gives Allison the tool that does write. Allison at first waves it about and then *by accident* makes a mark on the paper. In a flash, she notices the mark she made and begins to scribble away with great intensity. Donna laughs, surprised. The graduate assistant says that Allison has now performed the "fundamental graphic act." Other children, too, spend much more time working with the implement that makes marks. They want to see results!

"Writing" may be so much fun for children because they get to change something. They get to take pristine white sheets of paper and cover them with color and designs—in exactly the way they like. Now, this is pretty powerful stuff for children who may be used to hearing "no" all the time. They get to set the agenda and do as they wish (as long as they don't get too exuberant and start using the walls as their palette). They are also learning (albeit slowly) about how much pressure they need to use (Remember all those first-grade papers that came home with holes? That's from pressing too hard.), how to hold their fingers and hand, and how to create straight versus curved lines. These are obviously all things children will need to know for school.

| Discovering Hidden Skills | Scribble Writing |

Ages: 15 months to 24 months

Is there ever a time when your toddler doesn't care to scribble or care whether marks are made on paper when he does scribble? At what age will your child commit his first *fundamental graphic act*? All you have to do to test this idea is to provide a pencil without a point and a few sheets of scrap paper. You could try this every couple of months. How does your child react using a pencil that does not make marks on the page? Does he seem to already have the expectation that he should see marks? Does he ask you for another implement or look suspiciously at the one he has? What happens when you give him a tool that does write? This could be a moment to record in the baby book. And it sounds so impressive: His first *fundamental graphic act*! Imagine what you can tell Aunt Bertha at the family reunion.

Writing Words and Letters
Means Real Progress!

Eventually, children start trying to make letters. They get the idea, too, that letters appear in linear sequences, and sometimes they will produce little designs in sequences and call them letters. They are often overjoyed with their products, sensing that they are coming closer to the adult ideal. If your preschool child— even once she starts writing in earnest—makes reversals (b for d), or goes in the wrong order, or even incorporates pictures and words together, just relax. She will figure out how writing works eventually. And this can even be a teachable moment, when you show Rebecca the difference between b's and d's. Your child may not learn this the first 17 times, but eventually it will sink in. Children will *ask* you for your feedback and input. Give it joyfully and freely, always emphasizing how good the child's efforts are.

Why do children have trouble with letter orientation, confusing b's and d's and p's and g's, even after they start school? It's because letters are the only concept where orientation matters. Think about it. You are you whether you are seen from the left or the right or even from upside down. Same thing with objects in the world. In fact, we learn to ignore object orientation or we wouldn't be able to recognize an object if were turned on its side. And then come letters, and suddenly orientation matters; whether the bulb of the b is on the right or the left to make it a d is unexpectedly worth noting. It takes a while for children to figure this out. Since most children make these errors, do not be concerned that your child is dyslexic. When working on those letters where orientation matters (for example, g and p) children make lots of initial mistakes in reading and in naming the letters.

When, toward the end of the preschool period, children start writing in earnest, they often come up with their own marvelous spellings for words from sounding them out. You'll be surprised as they work the letter names into invented spellings, such as "RETTE" for the word "ready." This is a case of looking at the glass as either half-full or half-empty. These spellings are wrong, but consider what they reveal. They show us that children are using the alphabetic principle and trying to use letter sounds to write their words. These children are not just parrots who memorized a letter sequence. They are using their brains. This helps us to realize the tremendous progress children are making in understanding how words work. Consider what they have to do to produce these invented spellings: They have to dissect a word's sounds—exactly what we want them to do. They have to think hard, for example, in writing the word "bed," about whether it starts with a "p" sound or a "b" sound and which written letter matches up with that sound. This is great practice for both spelling and for gaining phonological awareness. Don't correct, just enjoy. If the child lets you, write what she has written in big, clear print *correctly* beneath her version. But don't stress over it; just appreciate the amazing effort.

THE ROLE OF THE PARENT IN DEVELOPING LITERACY

Remember Rachel and Nate from the vignettes that opened the chapter? Based on all the research we've reviewed, we would predict that Nate would have an easier time of learning to read than Rachel would. That doesn't mean that Rachel would have problems. It just means that Rachel might not be as familiar with how books work, the structure of stories, and the sensitivity to the components that make up words (phonemes). She might also not have the extensive vocabulary that Nate gets from his dialogic reading. All these things matter for learning to read. Without receiving flash card instruction, Nate is actually doing many more emergent literacy activities than Rachel is.

What does our prediction mean? It has nothing to do with the children's intelligence. Rather, the differences lie in the environments that the children are in. Nate's parents are making books a pleasure for him, by allowing him to use book reading as an opportunity to learn more about his world. Rachel's mother is working more toward the mechanics of reading by emphasizing the names of the letters. Both children are having emergent literacy experiences, but Nate's are not only more frequent but more useful to him in learning about how books and reading work.

It is our hope that the research reviewed in this chapter will free you to be more like Nate's parents than like Rachel's mother, less concerned with the mechanics and more concerned with providing the range and quantity of experiences that lead to emergent literacy. You can take confidence in knowing that reading does not start in first grade. Instead, all the emergent literacy activities that you engage in at home with your child or that your child engages in at day care are helping to set the stage for the reading that will come. A wonderful recent study by Professors Monique Sénéchal and Jo-Anne Lefevre at Carleton University in Ottawa, Canada, suggests that the specific experiences we give our children at home when they are in kindergarten can predict specific reading outcomes even at third grade. Shared reading at home, for example, builds language skills that are directly related to children's phonological awareness and to their third-grade reading level.

Indeed, although learning to read is a wonderful and shining achievement, even before your children enter school, you will be providing many of the necessary tools for them to use once formal reading instruction begins *in the classroom*. We have emphasized "in the classroom" because that is where reading instruction really belongs. At home, the name of the game is *balance*. We need to be our children's reading partners and mentors. We need to recognize that experiences like being read to, drawing, scribbling, and engaging in lots of dialogue are what our children require to be able to read. Your job is to involve your child in emergent literacy activities to prime the pump, as it were, for the formal instruction to follow. Your job is to make reading fun and engaging.

BRINGING THE LESSONS HOME

Make reading a part of your life—and your child's. If you share your enthusiasm about reading and your children see you absorbed in a book or a newspaper, you will be indirectly teaching the importance and enjoyment of reading. For a child, hearing a story should be a reward, something that is special and wonderful. The emotional and physical closeness that accompanies book reading with young children is a pleasure for both of you, even if *you* occasionally have trouble staying awake! And tolerate being asked to read that same book for the 30th time. Don't even think about skipping any pages. Your child will notice. Remember why he wants to hear the same book over and over again: In a child's unpredictable world, it sure is nice to have something—even if it's the text of a book—under control. It's fun to know what comes next and to be able to fill in the blanks. Along the same lines of gaining control, imagine being given a chance to go to the library and *pick out your own books*. That's exciting.

Create an environment that is rich with literacy materials. Print is everywhere, not just in traditional children's books. Try some creative options for exposing your child to print, such as alphabet magnets for the refrigerator. You can be sure your child will want you to spell out her name, and you can play a game by asking her to find letters for you. You can also take a product with a big label off the shelf in your kitchen and ask your child to copy its name on the fridge in the letters. In addition, your child will love lots of blank paper of different colors and writing materials on a low shelf where they can be easily reached. Alphabet and number blocks can be great fun too, for building towers and writing words and finding all the letters that have curved lines in them or straight lines . . . or whatever. Anything goes, because it's all increasing your child's familiarity with letters and letter sounds. A bulletin board to display your children's handiwork would be a nice addition too, so when your child starts to write—even if it doesn't look much like writing—you can display it and make a fuss.

Use stamps to help your child learn the letters. Children also love to use stamps (on the walls and on stamp pads). You could write your child's name and have the child reproduce it with alphabet stamps. This could, of course, expand into you writing down mommy's name, daddy's name, and after the relatives, all the neighbors. To do this, the child must analyze the letters in the name to pick one that matches from the stamps. Given what we have said about the difficulty children have in attending to letter orientation, this "copy me" game gives the child practice in distinguishing between the letters. Copying the letters in a name using stamps is again nothing but child's play. Notice, however, how central child's play is to emergent literacy.

Start a conversation. Remember that language is part of an environment rich in literacy. Engage your children in conversations and be sure to tell stories to them. If they don't hear stories, they won't tell them. Once reading begins, children's oral language skills are significantly related to their understanding of written materials. This is no surprise: children who are addressed in conversation and asked to reply are practicing their language comprehension skills. And children with larger rather than smaller vocabularies have had to store these words efficiently in their memory.

You can also tell joint stories. Start a story, "Once upon a time there was a dog who lived in a jungle . . ." and then let your child fill in the next part of the story. This game can be played in the car and with multiple players. With time, your child will take more and more responsibility for fleshing out the story. And the crazier the story, the better! Children also love to fill in the blanks for stories about their own experiences. "Remember the day we went to the pond and we saw the . . . ?"

Try out some word games. In addition to being educational, word games can be a lot of fun. One game is to see how many words you can say that start with the same sound. The parent starts with, for example, the "b" sound—book, baby, bottle, bike. Then it's the child's turn to add to the list. Take turns until you run out of words, and then dazzle your child with a few multisyllabic "b" words so you can feel smart! Another game is to take compound words that are composed of two shorter words and to remove one of the words and ask the child what word is left. So the parent might say, "What's 'baseball' without the 'base'?" The answer, of course, is "ball." And reading rhyming poetry, such as Shel Silverstein's work, is so much fun for children—and for grownups. Play is a key way for children to learn. You can help your child become a language artist, as opposed to just a language user. This makes it more likely that children will implicitly notice the parts that make up words—syllables and phonemes.

Engage in dialogic reading. The National Academy of Education Commission on Reading has declared that reading aloud to children is the "single most important activity" for ensuring success in learning to read. But it turns out that certain kinds of book reading are far more effective than others for promoting vocabulary development and emergent literacy. Just reading to a child is not enough. Asking the child to consider alternative outcomes, relate what's on the page to his own experiences, and talk about the sounds and the letters encountered is much more effective than just plain reading aloud. This type of reading is called dialogic reading. Not sure how to start?

The investigators who coined the term offer three main strategies. First, encourage your child to take an active role during story time. Active learning is more effective than just listening. When your child is very young, ask him to point at particular pictures or to name pictures. Once your child has some language, you can ask him to predict what will happen next or to talk about how the characters feel. You can also ask your child to talk about what would happen if the story didn't turn out the way it did (the "invent a new ending" game). All these things give your child the opportunity to think, to talk, to be an active participant in book reading.

Second, give your child feedback. Feedback can certainly take the form of praise, as in "Great job, Irving! That *is* a dinosaur!" but it can also occur when you expand on what your child has said. The child above had said, "Dat dinosaur"; note how the mother's response picked up on what the child said and repeated it by adding missing elements: That "*is* a dinosaur!" Expanding on what your child says accomplishes at least two things. It tells the child, "I hear you and honor your contribution to our dialogue," and it also gives the child a chance to hear what they said again correctly. This is called modeling, and it's a powerful way for children to learn.

Finally, continue to "up the ante" during book reading. Once your child knows the name of the object on the page, ask the child what the object does. Once your child knows the name of the whole object, point out the names of the object's parts. You're always looking for ways to go beyond (by just a little) what your child can do on his own. With your support, your child can develop his capabilities right before your eyes.

Make reading fun! If you really want to bring the reading lesson home, the most important thing we can tell you is to just have fun. Make sure book reading is a great pleasure for your child. Talk about some of the pages and take turns describing pictures. Turn taking can be great fun for preschoolers. You can also pretend to make mistakes. Children love correcting their parents, since they get corrected all the time. Follow up on the child's interests, too. If she wants to have an extended conversation about something that happened in a story or a picture, don't cut her off. Use this as an opportunity to get her to talk.

CHAPTER + 6

WELCOME TO LAKE WOBEGON:
THE QUEST TO DEFINE INTELLIGENCE

HOW NICE IT WOULD BE to live in the fictional town of Lake Wobegon, Minnesota, created by Garrison Keillor, host of the popular National Public Radio show *A Prairie Home Companion*. There, "all the women are strong, all the men are good looking, and *all* the children are above average."

Keillor puts his finger on a very American obsession—the notion that average (especially in the realm of intelligence) is to be avoided at all cost. We all want our kids to be *above* normal! In fact, this desire has become so extreme that in one recent case, a mother fabricated her son's IQ score—to disastrous effect. Like most of us, Elizabeth Chapman wanted to give her child every chance for success in life. When she saw an opportunity to falsify her son's IQ score, she took it. She transformed an average child into a genius by claiming that his IQ was 298+, the highest IQ on record! When the deceit was discovered, the story was plastered all over the national press. Her son, who became suicidal, was put in foster care.

The Chapman story is extreme. Yet it indicates the tremendous pressure parents feel to find a way to assure their child's place in a precarious world. No longer is it considered good enough for a child to be "normal." Companies are now marketing baby formula supplemented with fatty acids that are supposed to bolster IQ. One magazine advertisement even suggests that a baby will develop "the mind of a scientist" by drinking the formula! And an article in the *New York Times* tells us that some parents are paying up to $3,000 to hire advisors to help them get their children into a handful of private schools in New York City called the Baby Ivies. Further, in the fall of 2002, Jack Grubman, a powerful financial analyst in New York, manipulated stocks to get his children into the "right" preschool!

This anxiety about IQ and assuring a child's future success has trickled right into the once playful world of the preschooler, who is now required to take an IQ test to be admitted to certain preschools. In fact, President George W. Bush has even mandated that we test all 4-year-olds in Head Start programs to assure they are being adequately "taught."

What about the children who attend achievement-oriented preschools? Often the time they would normally have for creative play and self-discovery is preempted for structured lessons and worksheets. Many quickly equate learning with hard work and regimentation and express anxiety and fear that they won't "measure up" to future academic challenges—such as kindergarten!

In this chapter, we'll show you why a child's IQ has little relevance in determining his or her future success. Further, when you learn what's on an IQ test, you may well wonder if it is really adequate to measure intelligence, let alone predict a successful life. The commonly accepted definition of intelligence is that it is the ability to learn or cope with new situations and challenges or to think abstractly. *The problem is that these qualities are not readily captured on an IQ test.*

The focus on children's IQs has also led to the belief that middle-class children need tutors and academic programs in preschool to maximize IQ. As you'll see in this chapter, however, children don't learn best in academic settings. Rather, they learn best in childish ways—through play, social interaction, exploration, and enjoyment of their environment.

THE UNINTENDED EFFECT OF FOCUSING ON IQ

Today's parents and caregivers feel enormous pressure to do all they can to elevate their children's IQs. Yet our research shows that the children who know more facts are not necessarily the same children who are more intelligent than their peers.

Author Kathy Hirsh-Pasek worked with Professors Marilou Hyson of the University of Delaware and Leslie Rescorla of Bryn Mawr College to determine whether preschools with more academic curricula really produce smarter, happier, and more creative children. One hundred and twenty children participated in this study. Some of the children went to more academically oriented schools and some went to more socially oriented schools. We then asked whether the children who had been taught more letters and numbers at age 4 were the more intelligent, social, and creative children at ages 5 and 6. The answer? These children did indeed know more numbers and letters at age 5 than their peers did. However, a follow-up study by Drs. Rescorla and Betsy Richmond, a private therapist in Ardmore, Pennsylvania, found that the children in the two groups were indistinguishable from one another when they entered formal schooling. The academically oriented children were not observed (using tests of intelligence and creativity) to be more intelligent than their peers, but they did appear to be *less* creative and *less* enthusiastic about learning.

There is so much more to what makes a person successful than how they score on a single test. Psychologists have even begun to identify the ways in which people of high IQ flounder and those of modest IQ do quite well. Factors such as self-awareness, self-discipline, empathy, and understanding others are all part of being truly smart and successful.

So how does IQ relate to what we think of when we think of an intelligent person? And most importantly, is there something we can do to facilitate our children's intellectual growth? Read on for some answers.

What Is IQ, Anyway?

In 1904, the French government asked a psychologist named Alfred Binet to come up with a test to help them discern which children would be unable to learn in school so they could be sent to special schools that could accommodate them. And the rest, as they say, is history. Binet and his student Theophile Simon came up with a test that could be individually administered and that did predict how children would do in school. Here's how a typical IQ test for children is conducted:

Eight-year-old Alex sits at a table across from Ms. Simpson. When Alex feels sufficiently comfortable with her, Ms. Simpson starts asking him questions in a friendly, casual way. "A rock is hard. A pillow is . . . what,

Alex?" Ms. Simpson asks. "Soft." "Good," she always replies. "How many pints are in a quart, Alex?" "Six," he says with certainty. "Good," says Ms. Simpson, giving nothing away about the fact that his answer is incorrect. She then shows Alex four different pictures of a pitcher pouring juice into a glass. The level of juice in the glass is different in each picture. "Put the pictures in the right order so that what is happening makes sense," she instructs. Ms. Simpson continues with "Tell me what 'carpet' means."

These are some typical verbal items. Other items ask children to create block designs or repeat back a list of random numbers from memory.

What's This Quotient Thing?

When Binet created the first intelligence tests, he came up with the concept of mental age (MA) because he realized that children are capable of quite different things depending on their ages. We all know what is meant by "chronological age." But mental age refers to the number of items on the intelligence test that the child answers correctly. For example, most 7-year-olds can remember seven random digits. But they can't remember eight. So that test item *distinguishes* between children of different mental ages.

Intelligence quotient is a person's mental age divided by their chronological age, multiplied by 100. That is, $IQ = MA/CA \times 100$. If mental age is the same as chronological age, then the person's IQ is 100.

IQ scores are based on comparisons with other people. To compare the scores, we make a graph of the number of people who get each score. What we find is that the graph looks like what's called a normal curve—it resembles a camel's hump. It shows that most of the scores are piled up around the center to form the peak of the camel's hump. Those people at the center all scored around 100 on IQ. In fact, most of the scores—68 percent—range between 84 and 116. Garrison Keillor was right about not only Lake Wobegon, but the rest of us as well. Most people have truly splendid IQs! Seven out of 10 children have similar, normal IQs. Only 1.5 children in 10 have a score over 117, and 1.5 in 10 have a score under 83.

Even some of those considered mentally retarded, with scores under 70, may be married, active in the community, and employed. The IQ test alone just doesn't cut it in predicting how people will adapt to their environment. Nor does it predict who will excel.

What Does It Mean to Be Gifted?

Defying standard IQ tests, genius seems to have a life of its own. Einstein's mother didn't use flash cards, and neither have the parents of other gifted children. As you'll see with the following example, flash cards are about as useful as a wet blanket.

When she was only 2 years old, Romanian-born Alexandra Nechita was so absorbed with her coloring books that her parents worried she was becoming too isolated. They stopped buying her coloring books, hoping she would jump rope and play more with her dolls and friends. Her parents say that taking the coloring books away was like taking oxygen away from her. She simply began to draw and color her own figures on scrap computer paper her mother would bring home from work. Once she started school, she would start painting as soon as she got home. Alexandra is now 18 years old and lives in Los Angeles. In one week, she may complete several large canvases, as big as 5 feet by 9 feet. These paintings, which are in the modern tradition, sell for up to $80,000 apiece.

Yes, Alexandra is truly gifted. And yes, the gifted are as happy as anyone else, according to all the studies that have investigated this question. What's the relationship of giftedness to IQ? Generally, if your IQ is over 120 and/or you have a superior talent for something, you are considered gifted. Gifted children are often precocious—they begin to master a subject area earlier than their peers, and their learning in that area is more effortless. They also tend to learn in a qualitatively different way than their peers and need less help from adults. In fact, they often resist explicit adult instruction and make discoveries on their own and solve problems in unique ways. Most of all, they seem to show a passion to master what they are interested in and have an exceptional ability to focus. They are not children who need to be pushed by their parents. They motivate themselves.

Teachable Moments	Intelligent Play

All children, whether they're gifted or not, are motivated by something. We just need to be good observers to find out what our children are interested in and we can build from there. One of Kathy's sons, Josh, spent much of his time when he was 2 years old lining up things in pairs, facing each other. He lined up one car and one train and even shoes with socks. By offering him the opportunity to line up whatever was there, we were giving him "practice" in one to one correspondence. We never guessed that this was consistent with his later interest and acumen in mathematics. Another child might like to cook. By adding things to cake batter, for example, he is experimenting in chemistry and physics. So take the time to watch what your child is interested in and use that as a plat-form for building on his motivation as he turns play into intelligent play.

Maybe you're thinking, "Einstein and Alexandra are truly gifted. What about my children, who are unlikely to attain these heights? Wouldn't flash cards help them?" For mastering little disconnected facts, flash cards are great. But intelligence is so much more. Keep reading.

Using IQ

We now know something about how the IQ test is put together—but what use does it really serve (beyond bragging rights)? IQ tests are clearly about the kind of learning that takes place in school. So let's say your third-grader, Billy, is getting Cs and Ds. The teacher believes the work is hard for him. You always thought he was pretty smart. So you wonder what could be wrong. You have his IQ tested and it shows up as 135, which is on the high side. It occurs to you that he's in a school that is overcrowded and that he's had three different teachers this year. Maybe the problem has to do with a school that's not sufficiently challenging or rewarding. Or perhaps the unfriendly divorce you and your spouse have just been through is affecting Billy more than he's been letting on, and you realize that he may need some emotional first aid.

For analyzing how well a child should be doing in school, the IQ test is great. (Of course, that happens to be just the purpose for which it was designed.) Psychologists would say there is a strong "correlation" between IQ and school performance; your IQ score will be related to the grades you get in school. But it's not a perfect predictor. Some children are highly motivated, while others have too little stimulation and support. Other factors, such as home environment, also matter. The child with a normal IQ can certainly fail at school—or become a Nobel prize–winning scientist. Indeed, James Watson, who won the Nobel prize in 1962 for helping to discover the molecular structure of DNA, had a normal IQ (in the 68 percent range most of us belong to) and was not considered outstanding by his teachers. "But I asked a lot of questions," he explains.

One other caution about IQ: It's related to school performance—which is related to the standards of the middle class. In other words, the IQ test involves knowledge of the things that matter in middle-class culture. If you live in an isolated South Seas island village, you might score as "mentally retarded" on the IQ test. And yet you could be brilliant, a leader of your group, capable of constructing a boat that won't sink and able to use complex knowledge of stars, tides, and wave patterns to navigate great distances in the ocean. Likewise, if you are a recent immigrant or belong to a minority group, you might not have been exposed to some of the concepts readily available to the middle class. For instance, one question that used to be on the IQ test was "If a child hits you, what do you do?" The correct answer was "Walk away." But if you were brought up in the inner city, the correct answer in your culture would be " Hit him back." While the makers of the IQ test have tried to filter out these kinds of bias, it's probably impossible to completely eliminate them.

BABIES AND TODDLERS HAVE IQS, TOO

IQ testing can and has been used on infants. The motivation for this work is excellent. Take Sally, whose mother had a very difficult birth. Was Sally damaged by some period when her brain might not have received sufficient oxygen? How can we tell? If Sally acts like other children of her age when given a standardized test of infant development, we can feel assured that she is probably okay. So these baby intelligence tests serve a screening function, to see if a child appears to be developing normally. If Sally was damaged by the birth process, it would be very useful to know this so that she can get extra help even before she enters school. But how would one test such a young child?

Sally may be given the Bayley Scale of Infant Development (named for Nancy Bayley, who created the test). This test was developed for children between 1 month old and 3½ years, but it's used mostly with toddlers. It includes items like how quickly Sally turns toward a new sound, grasps an object, builds a tower with blocks, or names pictures. The score that results is a DQ, or developmental quotient. It's not surprising that Sally's later IQ scores might look different from her DQ, since the Bayley measures different things than the IQ test. Sally's DQ can't forecast whether she'll be valedictorian of her class at Harvard. Instead, the DQ is primarily concerned with identifying children who need special help.

There is another kind of test for infants and toddlers that may be more highly related to later, standard IQ scores. The test looks at how quickly infants process or remember information. Faster processing means a higher IQ. Why would this be so? Because quick thinking involves some basic cognitive processes, like attention, memory, and response to novelty, that underlie intelligent behavior at all ages.

How can we measure how babies take in and deal with information? Professor Joseph Fagan of Case Western Reserve University in Cleveland, Ohio, devised an ingenious test that measured how long an infant would look at a picture of a face before turning away. Next, he presented the child with pictures of two faces—one was the face the child already saw, and the second was a new face. He then observed to see if the child would watch the *new* face longer than the old face.

Shorter looking at the original face is an index of speed of mental processes. That is, briefer looking suggests that the child was able to re-member its features quickly. This interpretation would be bolstered if the child also preferred looking at the new face rather than the old one he'd seen. This would indicate that the child had a preference for novelty be-cause he had indeed remembered seeing the old face before.

When babies are tested this way, the scores that result are, on the av-erage, quite similar to their IQs several years later. While the use of such measures to calculate a "baby IQ score" are not uncontroversial, it is worth noting that those babies who you would think should do poorly on this kind of test do. For example, babies who will show serious delays in mental development respond poorly, as do babies whose mothers have consumed too much alcohol during pregnancy.

WHAT SHOULD PARENTS DO TO BOOST THEIR CHILDREN'S INTELLIGENCE?

Where does all of this information about IQ leave parents whose chil-dren, like most of us, are in the normal range? Should parents try to boost their children's IQs? How far can environment contribute to boosting something that is rooted in one's genes?

It seems the environment can affect IQ by as many as 15 to 20 points. Twenty points—you could put your average child right over the top into the gifted range, right? The question is—which aspects of the environment are responsible? Should you buy mobiles and flash cards? Hire tutors? Schedule lessons? Not so fast! The evidence for such environmental enhancement is weak. It comes primarily from studies of adopted twins—one raised in an impoverished environment and one raised in a middle class environment.

We think a better question is this: *What do children need in order to develop their natural intelligence to the fullest?* And this: How can we help our children to attain their fullest intellectual potential—not on the IQ test, but more broadly, in life?

One of the key features of intelligence is language ability. Language is a primary means for learning about our environment. It's how you ask questions and get answers. So it shouldn't be surprising that, among all the subtests of the modern IQ test, the section that most closely predicts the resulting end score is vocabulary. The size of one's vocabulary is a very large component of what IQ measures. And the primary thing that helps vocabulary to develop is ordinary, everyday talk, directed to children. They learn by talking with us. They also learn when we read them stories that provide information about the world beyond the room they're in.

Beyond talking with your children, there are other things you do with them at home that are key facilitators of their intellectual growth. Psychologists have developed a test called the HOME (Home Observation for the Measurement of Environment) test for children in the first 3 years of life. High HOME scores predict gains in IQ during those early years; low HOME scores predict declines as large as 15 to 20 points. HOME is a checklist for gathering information about the quality of children's home lives through an observation of and interview with the parents. It asks how much parental encouragement, involvement, and affection there is. How much do the parents talk to their children? How accepting are they? These are the environmental components that count—not the kinds of direct imparting of information to "promote IQ" being marketed in stores.

For instance, let's watch Kathleen, a single parent who works long hours at a discount store. She's anxious about how her toddler, Sean, is doing. She's constantly pressuring Sean to restrict his childish behaviors, believing that restraint will indicate superior maturity. "Enough running! Sit down!" she exclaims. "That's enough ball play. Stack those blocks," and so forth. When parents are intrusive like this, infants and toddlers actually become more distractible and show less mature forms of play, and their intelligence scores suffer. What supports the growth of children's intelligence is recognition of the value of their childish ways of enjoying the world and helping them to play ball, enjoy a story, learn a song, build a sand castle.

How Malleable Are IQ Scores?

In 1965, as part of the "war on poverty," the federal government launched the Head Start program. The theory was that education is the key to boosting people out of poverty, and that poor children entered the education system at a disadvantage. Children who live in a middle-class environment where people talk and read to them and expose them to a range of experiences are very likely to have IQs in the normal range. On the other hand, we know that poverty pulls children's IQs down and that poor children score lower than their middle-class peers. One way that we know that the environment can have a negative influence on IQ scores is from a study of African-American children reared in very disadvantaged circumstances in the South. Older siblings had lower IQs than their younger siblings. The explanation for this finding is that the longer children live with poverty and poor schools, the more it affects their IQs.

What is it about poverty that's so damaging? The households of poor children are often chaotic, and because their parents are poorly schooled, they may not provide some of the early learning experiences that prepare children to do well in school. Fortunately, Head Start programs, which involve both parents and children in the preschool experience, have been quite successful. Children in these programs scored higher on IQ tests and did better in school (at least through the first 2 or 3 years of elementary school) than did children from the same backgrounds who did not have the Head Start experience. While the gains in IQ didn't last (probably because the children remained in an impoverished environment), the Head Start children did remain ahead on real-life measures. They were less likely to be placed in special education classes or to be retained in a grade. And more of them graduated from high school.

Beyond IQ

By now, you have some idea of how limited the IQ test actually is. That's why some psychologists have begun to talk more in terms of "multiple intelligences" and include things that the IQ test doesn't even touch. For instance, Professor Howard Gardner of Harvard University believes there are really eight independent intelligences that people are born with and that they develop throughout life. They are: linguistic, logico-mathematical, musical, spatial, kinesthetic, naturalist, interpersonal, and intrapersonal. And as we discussed in chapter 1, another theorist, Daniel Goleman, co-founder of the Collaborative for Social and Emotional Learning at the Yale University Child Study Center, argues that being truly smart involves "emotional intelligence"—self-awareness, self-discipline, empathy, and so forth. Professor Robert Sternberg of Yale University says, "How simple it would be!" if all of human intelligence were reducible to just a single thing. He argues for a concept of intelligence that includes the analytic, the creative, and the practical. All of these contribute to creating "successful intelligence," or the ability to achieve success in life. Before you worry about what all these intelligences mean for your child, maybe it's time to tell you more about how children learn.

PIAGET, A TRIP TO McDONALD'S, AND THE WAY CHILDREN LEARN

To give you a sense of what it's like for your children to learn, we'll tell you a little story. Last summer, one of us was gazing out in our backyard, looking at the small lake that sits underneath some willows. It was dusk and the sky was a kind of orangey haze. Suddenly, through the haze, there appeared a large object, as big as a merry-go-round, shaped more like a Frisbee, hovering over the lake. It appeared to be made of metal. We blinked, and blinked again. Then, the thing began to move in a spiral, right up into the air, and then it disappeared.

Consider what we've described. What do you think? No, we were not taking drugs. Was it some sort of optical illusion? We don't think so. You might ask—was it a UFO? The fact is, we did not see this. But you were probably trying pretty hard to figure it out. Something was being described that didn't fit with your notion of reality. You searched for a way to explain it. And finally, you lobbed it into the catch-all category of "UFO," or unidentified flying object. Your mind was probably working hard to explain the incongruity, to understand the reality as it was presented. But it didn't match up to what you knew. You *worked* to explain it.

This is what happens with children from the start. The world is new to them, and they are busy trying to interpret it. Children are active learners, constantly seeking to understand and master their environment. You don't have to make them want to learn. Babies are constantly putting things in their mouths—not necessarily because the things taste good, but because it's babies' way of discovering what things are made of. Babies are constantly dropping their spoons on the floor, not to make you get your daily exercise, but to see: Will it always go down? At the same speed? Can I make it go faster? They are discovering the properties of gravity and velocity.

Jean Piaget, the great Swiss scholar whose ideas have so dominated developmental psychology, taught us that the *mistakes* children make are far more revealing than the answers they get right on IQ tests. After all, sometimes when children get things right, they are simply parroting what they have heard. But when they tell you how they think about the problem, you know if they really understand. Piaget defined intelligence as a kind of adaptation to the environment. To learn how young children think, Piaget watched his own three children as well as hundreds of other children. What he found was startling. *Children are the engines behind their own development.* This means that, as we argued in chapter 2, the everyday, mundane experiences children have are sufficient to fuel their drive to understand the world. They do not wait passively to be urged to engage in intellectual behaviors, nor do they conservatively avoid new experiences. To the contrary, children create much of their own stimulation by observing and actively experimenting as they play and go through their daily lives. As a result, parents can relax and relieve themselves of the mantle of responsibility for cognitive development that they have assumed.

It's hard for us to believe, but children are learning from even their simple, everyday activities. Take, for example, a trip to a fast-food restaurant for lunch. What could a child possibly learn there? Maybe not much about healthy diets, but a lot about the world they live in. Picture 4-year-old Mary walking into a fast-food establishment with her mom, Sarah. Mary knows just what to do. She rushes to the back of the line so that she can give her order and knows just what to ask her mom about the possible options. This means that Mary already has a "script" about how fast-food places work. You don't sit at the table in these places and wait to be served, and you can't eat anything from the world of possible food choices. This knowledge about how to "do" fast food also comes in handy when you visit other restaurants, like Taco Bell or Wendy's.

That's not all you know about the fast-food *script*. You know how one eats each food in your culture (for example, you know that it's okay to pick up French fries with your fingers rather than using a fork); you learn the physics of how to use that pump to get the ketchup you need for your fries; you know where to sit and how the seats swivel. And we could go on about the lessons you learn in conversation as you order or about people as you watch the parade of interesting folks around you. The point? Children are constantly learning, and there is a lot to learn that we don't even think about. The repetitive, annoying things babies and young children often do are their way of learning about the world, manipulating the parameters of the situation for fun, just to see what will happen.

What Piaget discovered, then, is that babies and young children are programmed by nature to learn in unique ways that fit their own developing brains and bodies. Show a 2-year-old some flash cards with numbers and he'll learn to parrot what you say. Let him play with M&M's, and quantity will become of great interest to him. Read him a story about Peter Rabbit, and he won't want to forget a single detail. Learning in context is the key to intelligent learning.

From Rattles to Physics: The Progression of Learning

Piaget was a genius at unlocking the process of learning in context. Although few of us have the powers of observation that he had, we, too, can learn to see our children's world in a very different and more enriching way. Consider 3-month-old Alice. If you watch her closely, you'll notice how she experiments like a little scientist with her own body. At first, by accident, she gets her thumb in her mouth. But she doesn't know how to do it again. She waves her hand around and, after many attempts, eventually succeeds in doing it again. Gradually, she learns how to do it at will.

Piaget called these processes circular reactions of the sensory-motor period of infancy. The period is called sensory-motor because it involves the five senses and the body. Circular reactions are attempts to repeat an event that the baby likes. Circular reactions serve as the building blocks for intelligence. They start out centered around the baby's own body and move out to creating events in the world. Once babies figure out how to get their own bodies to do some of the things they want, they start to notice interesting occurrences in their immediate world. Between about 4 and 10 months, babies start making "secondary circular reactions." These are repetitive actions that involve recreating events they observe *outside* of their own bodies, such as making their crib mobile shake by kicking their legs.

The next thing babies do really drives parents crazy. "Tertiary circular reactions," seen from approximately 10 to 18 months, is the fancy name for when babies do things over and over again, just a little differently each time. This is the time when parents who don't understand their children's drive to manipulate their environment can become frustrated and perhaps abusive. When a baby has thrown Cheerios off the high chair tray 14 times in a row. But this is exactly what a tertiary circular reaction is: the creation of novel variations in events. The child now operates like a little scientist, experimentally varying the throwing—throwing it hard, throwing it easy, dropping it over the left side, and then over the right, all in service to seeing what will happen. As we discussed in chapter 4, babies are born pattern seekers. They are motivated to discover some of these patterns on their own ("Oh, objects fall down—not up!") by *creating* the patterns with their repetitive actions and then evaluating them.

What Makes It Happen?: Understanding Cause and Effect

By the end of the 2nd year, babies have figured out a number of things about how the world works. They've figured these things out through play, without any coaching. They have also figured out how causes relate to effects and that events must have causes to begin with. How comforting to live in a world where things do not occur at random. You'd cry, too, if you hadn't figured out what makes things happen in your world!

Part of understanding how the world works and what causes events is learning that people are different from objects. People can be made to do things for you, too, but in different ways than we can make objects do things. Babies figure out that people need to be appealed to through communication to get them to do what you want, but objects just need to be manipulated. The roots of the distinction between the living things and objects that fill a baby's world are present very early. Even by 3 months of age, babies can tell the difference between how objects (cars, trucks) and living things (people, animals) move.

Author Roberta Golinkoff tricked babies into revealing that by the age of 16 months, they already have different expectations for what living things and objects can do. Living things can move on their own, from a resting position, but objects can't. In other words, if a person walks across the room after just standing there, you would not be surprised. If, however, a *chair* moved across the room, without a person propelling it, you might well be startled. Imagine living in a world where you were unsure of which objects could move on their own and which couldn't. So much in the world is unexpected and unpredictable until babies figure these things out for themselves.

Let's enter the baby lab and see how to fool babies into showing us what they think about animate and inanimate objects. Kristen is a shy 17-month-old. Her dad, Frank, brings her into the lab, and she quickly becomes acclimated, given the presence of toys and friendly people sitting on the floor. Unbeknowst to Kristen, there is a student sitting on the floor behind a portable screen. The student is holding on to see-through, tough plastic fishing wire, which is attached to the back legs of an ordinary chair about 4 feet in front of the wooden screen. After explaining to Frank what is about to happen, the experimenter places a new toy on the chair and calls Kristen's attention to it. As Kristen approaches the chair to retrieve the toy, the chair starts moving backward, pulled by the hidden student and the see-through wire. Kristen stops dead in her tracks. She looks at the chair, then at her Dad, and runs over to him in haste, clutching his leg for dear life. Kristen is "telling" us that in her world, chairs do not move on their own. Kristen's reaction was clear. At 16 months, many babies indicate that this should not be happening. By 24 months of age, babies are convinced and sometimes try to make it happen again by pushing it! This is yet another example of how much babies and young children learn about the world *on their own.*

Moving On Up: What Do Young Children Know about Changes in Their World?

One of the most interesting observations Piaget made concerned the shift in development from age 5 to age 7, or between what he called the pre-operational to the concrete operational stage. You might have learned about this theory in college. However, in the last 20 or 30 years, many of the details of the theory have been questioned or refuted. (Preschoolers, it turns out, are even *more* brilliant than Piaget suspected.) Nonetheless, he shared some observations that are compelling and interesting to watch. Among them is the claim that preschoolers have trouble seeing the world from two vantage points at once. Piaget called this conservation. Take 4-year-old Pierre, for example. In one experiment, Piaget placed a child like Pierre in front of two identical 8-inch-high glasses half-filled with juice. The conversation might have gone something like this.

Piaget: So, Pierre, here are two glasses of juice. Do you have more, or do I have more, or do we both have the same?

Pierre: (Studies the glasses closely) We have the same!

Piaget: But what if I pour my glass of juice into this dish (indicating a low, flat small baking dish)? Watch me.

Pierre: (Watches closely)

Piaget: Do we still have the same amount of juice? Or do I have more, or do you have more?

Pierre: (With nary a second's hesitation) Oh, I have more now! Look how high my juice is and how low yours is!

As adults, we find this response bizarre. After all, Pierre watched Piaget pour the juice. Nothing was added and nothing was taken away. How could the child say that he had more now?

If you have more than one child, do they routinely fight about who has more juice when you use glasses of different sizes? They do this because young children get hung up on the way things look. They don't understand that a change in one dimension (height of glass) is balanced out by a change in another dimension (the spread of the liquid). They can't take two factors into account and balance them out. You see this in other domains, too. Young children will sometimes get upset when their mothers get a permanent or their dads grow a beard while away on an extended vacation. It's not mommy or daddy anymore!

| Discovering Hidden Skills | Conservation |

Ages: 3 years to 6 years

You can do the conservation experiment in your own home. Gather two identical glasses, another glass that can hold the original quantity but has a very different shape, and some juice or water. First, get your child in a game-playing mood. Show her the two identical glasses with the liquid up to the same level. Say that one glass is yours and one is hers. Ask whether you have the same amount or whether she has more or you have more. You can't go on unless your child agrees that you both have the same amount. Next, you or the child can pour the liquid from your glass into the glass of a different shape. Now ask the same question as above: Who has more, or do we both have the same? What does your child do? Can you see changes in what she does when faced with this question? Is there a time when she becomes uncertain of her answer? Ask her why she says what she says and see what reasons she gives for her judgment. You may be very surprised. If you have another child you can do this with who is, say, 6 or 7 years old, you might try it with him and notice the difference in reasoning.

Can you teach conservation, the idea that while something looks different, it's still the same amount if nothing is added or taken away? The research literature says that you can, in various ways, show a child that quantity is what matters and not the way something looks. (We explained in chapter 3 about an experiment with "magic" mice that Professor Rochel Gelman did, where she taught children that number was the important dimension.) But do you want to teach conservation? We don't think so. They will eventually get this concept on their own. It's one of those learning processes that will allow you to observe the *limits* of your children's thinking. We share the conservation findings with you not so you should run out and train your children, but because it is a window on your children's paradoxical limitations. It's amazing to see a child fail at one of these tasks, and it should be a cue that training children in a rote fashion to give the right answer doesn't begin to scratch the surface of how children think about the world.

MAKING INFERENCES: ANOTHER ASPECT OF BURGEONING INTELLIGENCE

Julie came into our university laboratory with a story that she thought was amazing and surely revealed how intelligent her child was. She had been taking 29-month-old Mikayla to a gym class since she was tiny. At the end of class, each child is given a washable hand stamp (that resembles a tattoo) of Jimbo the Clown. After class one day, when Julie took Mikayla to that chain with the golden arches, they stood in line next to a man whose body was covered with tattoos. In her loud and high-pitched voice (guaranteed to carry far and wide), Mikayla said brightly, "Oh, Mommy, that man got Jimbo stamps all over him!" Mikayla had made an inference! Based on her experience, she had reached the conclusion that the tattoos all over the man's body must be Jimbo stamps. Since she had never seen the man before, or seen anyone with tattoos, she was *generalizing*, or extending her knowledge to a new instance. This is an example of inductive inference.

Young children are doing more than observing the world, even though they learn a huge amount from that process. They are also using what they learn to form *categories* and make inductive inferences about novel situations they encounter. In fact, this is one of the most important functions of having concepts. Consider the fact that you have the concept of "animal." If I tell you that a snook is a kind of animal, but tell you nothing more and show you no pictures, consider how much you know about a snook anyway:

- It breathes.

- It reproduces.

- It moves on its own.

- It eats and eliminates.

And all of this information comes "for free" once you know something about animals. Since we can make only a limited number of observations about the world, inductive inferences are the generalizations (like the list above) that concepts enable us to draw. When can babies make such inferences about categories in the world? When do babies know that animals, vehicles, and household objects, for example, are all different kinds of things with different capabilities? And how could we know, given that babies can't talk? Two professors, Jean Mandler of the University of California at San Diego, and Laraine McDonough of Brooklyn College in New York, came up with an ingenious way to tap into babies' knowledge about object categories.

They presented babies with miniatures of objects (little cars, airplanes, lions, and cows, for example) to see if babies could make inferences about what sort of actions are appropriate for these objects. If one of the researchers pretended to use a key on the car, for example, would the baby imitate her by using the key on the airplane or on the animals? If the researcher gave a drink to the lion, would the baby try to give a drink to the airplane or to the cow? The scientists discovered that babies as young as 9 months of age can make the correct inferences, using the key only on vehicles and giving a drink only to the animals. These are not things they have observed people do, either: When was the last time you saw someone open an airplane with a key or give a cow a drink? But babies are brilliant, working out much about the world under our very noses, without fancy toys or classes. Nature intended that children be able to learn lots of things about their world without special support. Developing intelligence in infancy is simply part of the terrain, as natural as eating or sleeping.

A LITTLE HELP, PLEASE?—BOOSTING YOUR BABY'S DEVELOPMENT

Like Piaget, Lev Vygotsky, the brilliant Russian developmental theorist, also believed that children are extremely active in constructing their understanding of the world. Vygotsky was interested in the role the *social environment* plays in children's cognitive growth. Parents, teachers, siblings, and even other children all help the young child learn about the world. Vygotsky introduced a term that is very popular today: the zone of proximal development, or the ZPD, for short. He recognized that there is a range, or zone, of tasks that the child cannot yet handle alone but can accomplish with the help of more skilled partners. And this, of course, is where parents and caregivers come in. Consider the following scenario.

Three-year-old Matthew is on a rug in the kitchen working on a puzzle. But he is getting very frustrated. He just can't get the wooden pieces to slide in easily. Usually he's very good at puzzles, but he refused to have a nap today and is a bit short on patience. His mother, making dinner, watches him for a bit out of the corner of her eye, and when she thinks he's tried on his own long enough, she sits down on the rug with him. Without saying a word, she turns the puzzle frame in a way that matches his puzzle piece. Voilà! He gets the piece in and she says, "Wow, Matthew, you are really good at these puzzles!" They go through this little routine seven or eight more times until the puzzle is complete. Matthew looks very pleased with himself and goes on to something else, as does his mother.

The ZPD might be translated as the "zone of near development," development just outside one's own expertise when working alone. The ZPD captures the difference between what we can do alone and what we can do with someone's help. What Matthew could do alone was one thing. But what Matthew could do with a little help was something else again. As the old Beatles song goes, "I get by with a little help from my friends." If Vygotsky had a theme song, that would be it. He argued that this is just how cognitive development works: Children develop the *leading edge* of their competence in interactions with others. We can help children to go that extra step, to progress just a little bit beyond where they are today. How do we do this? Another world-renowned psychologist gave it a name: scaffolding. Professor Jerome Bruner of New York University said that this concept of scaffolding invites parents to be participants in rather than spectators of their children's development.

Discovering Hidden Skills	Scaffolding

This time, you're going to observe a "hidden skill" that adults, rather than children, possess. Because it may be difficult to interact with your child and watch yourself in a detached, scientific way at the same time, ask another parent or adult to interact with your child as you observe. You are watching for ways in which the adult scaffolds a task for your child. Ideally, your child should be 3 years old or less. Have the adult give your child a new toy—something that requires manipulation and is a bit beyond your child's skill level. Sit back and observe the ZPD in action as the other adult goes out of her way to make the play session a success for your child. Watch how the adult manipulates the object and sets up the situation so that your child can do things with the toy. We might call these "motor hints"—things the adult does to help your child use her body to make the toy work. These include things like repositioning the toy, shaping a child's hand, pushing something closer to the child, holding the toy so that it's easier to manipulate for little hands, and so on. Also watch for "language hints"—things the adult says to tip off the child about what to try to make the toy work. Watch for encouragement and exhortations, things like "That's right! You can do it! Press a little harder." All of these adult behaviors constitute scaffolding. Adults go out of their way to make children feel and look smart by helping them to complete the tasks that children set for themselves.

It's important to note that the ZPD works best when it is *the child*, not the adult, who decides what "work" needs to get done. The parent or caregiver needs to follow the child's lead, letting the child determine which particular goal she wishes to fulfill. Parents are often amazed at how long their young child's attention span can be. The circumstances when this occurs are exactly those times when the child is pushing to get something done, not just following the adult's lead.

INTELLIGENCE AND ACHIEVEMENT— AND THE DANGER OF CONFUSING THE TWO

We have suggested that the key to intelligence is how you learn, how you adapt knowledge, and how you process what is going on around you. Yet there is tremendous pressure today to look more at *what* children know rather than at *how* they know and learn it. Eighty-year-old Aunt Babe makes this point crystal clear. Every time she saw 4-year-old Josh for their weekly card game, she asked him to recite the ABCs. She also marveled that he could name the numbers on the cards when they played War. This was a brilliant child because he could "perform." We do this all the time to our children: "Sing that song you learned in school for your grandmother." "Teddy knows how to write his name. Want to see him do it?" If a child wants to give a show and tell, there is nothing wrong with performing. We just need to understand that showing what they know does not give an indication of their intelligence. It tells instead about their *achievements*.

This confusion between intelligence, broadly conceived, and achievement is abundant and can have some serious consequences. Being able to do a limited task is not the same thing as being able to use your knowledge intelligently. For example, many are excited that in the United States, the issue of early childhood learning has finally reached the front burner. At both the state and national levels, children are finally being recognized as our greatest natural resource, and educators and policy makers are working to ensure that we have quality programs and schools for the young in which they actually learn. President Bush's early childhood initiative Good Start, Grow Smart and the related No Child Left Behind are very well-intentioned. They are designed so that the underprivileged children in our society get enough information when they are young to make them competitive learners in a global society. These initiatives will help our preschools teach what children need to learn and assure that our children are growing intellectually and socially as a result.

To increase accountability at the national level, it has been mandated that every Head Start child be tested twice a year and that progress be monitored in 13 areas, including assessments in vocabulary; print concepts (such as which way a book opens); awareness of the sounds in rhymes and words; and number knowledge. On its face, this is a good idea, but many experts fear that testing achievement in this way will force teachers to teach to the test and will divert attention from curricula that foster intelligence and problem solving. Sure, children need to know their letter names. But this, as an end in itself, would be a narrow achievement. MaryAnn, a teacher of 4-year-olds in Portland, Maine, worries, "I will have to spend much of my day teaching letters and numbers rather than reading books and giving the children time to paint."

Scholars in the areas of literacy, language, mathematics, and social skills agree. Author Kathy Hirsh-Pasek coconvened a recent meeting at Temple University in Philadelphia to discuss these issues at length. The scientists present reached remarkable consensus. They concluded that the current assessments of children's progress are culturally biased and are too focused on outcome (read that as "achievement") rather than on process. Young children need to learn how to learn and to think. If we test only whether they know their letter names rather than whether they can *use* this knowledge, we have missed the boat. If we test only how many words they know and not whether they can link them into story lines and narrative, we won't know if we have prepared them for reading. If we look only at whether they know the names of the number symbols, we will have no idea about whether they have a concept of more or less and whether they realize that adding and subtracting are related. If we test only surface markers of achievement, we will never know if we are fostering intelligence. And if we test only language and mathematics, we will not even consider the developing social skills that are so important to children's growth.

In recommendations to the government, the scholars who met in Philadelphia applauded the move to look at how children learn and at their growth over the course of a year in preschool. Such information will be critical to how we design our preschool curricula. But, they cautioned, we must look in the right places if we want to have an accurate barometer of progress. Of the myths we harbor as parents, policy makers, and professionals, one of the deepest held is that fact learning is equivalent to intelligence; that achievement and intelligence are synonymous. This is a dangerous conclusion that can have serious consequences for how we teach our children.

BRINGING THE LESSONS HOME

As we have seen, in the first few years of life children are bent on learning as much as they can about their world. Babies are brilliant! The process by which they gain intelligence is a fascinating one, and the stories we have told here just scratch the surface of the things that babies learn on their own about the world. But because our babies are brilliant does not mean that parents play no role in their cognitive development. Here are some things you can do to bring the lessons of this chapter home.

Work within your child's zone of development. Remember that children learn best when they're encouraged to move just slightly beyond what's already comfortable for them. Most likely you're already doing some of the following steps at least some of the time with your child, but describing them can help you appreciate how important your role is.

- Follow your child's interest. Don't try to make your child do a task you assign, but instead figure out what the child wants to do. Let her set up the problem she wants to work on, whether it's putting shapes into matching holes or finishing a puzzle.

- Reduce the number of steps your child has to go through to achieve the goal she has set for herself. For example, if your child wants to put shapes into a box with holes that match the shapes (a toy many of us have) but can't stabilize the box and put the shape through the hole at the same time, you stabilize the box. If your child needs to open a door and press something to make an event occur but she can't open the door, you open the door to allow the child to do the next step.

- When your child gets frustrated, encourage her to stick with the task. Don't try to *make* her stick with it; try to motivate her by saying things like "We can do it together!" or "Let me help you." Frustration is often a sign that the child can't figure out what to do next. If necessary, go back to the previous step: Break the task up into small steps.

- Demonstrate. Flagging motivation often indicates a good time to show your child how the task is done. As you demonstrate, continue to encourage your child with language such as "See? The ball went into the box! Now you do it!" Demonstrations are very helpful since we all learn from imitating others.

- Talk about the difference between what your child did and what needs to be done. By describing the child's actions, you help him understand why A doesn't work, but B will. For example, you can say something like "It doesn't work when you force it, but it might work if you put it in gently." By calling attention to the differences, you are teaching him alternative means to an end.

- Make connections for your child to things she *does* know how to do. Effective teachers for people of all ages help the learner to link what they are learning to things they already know. Say things like "This is like the toy you played with at Andrea's house. Remember? This one works almost the same way!" This helps the child bring knowledge she already has to bear on the new task she has set for herself.

Stress effort, not achievement. Your children will miss 100 percent of the shots they don't take. If we're critical and fact-driven, we're teaching our children not to take those shots. What we need to teach them more than anything is that it's okay not to be perfect, that we make mistakes, too, and that we love them for their *effort*. In contrast, an intense emphasis on early learning teaches them not to think outside the box. Yet this is just the opposite of what develops an intelligent person. We should be teaching our children to think creatively, to recognize that the walls of the box are only made of cardboard.

Have you heard the old saw about genius being 10 percent inspiration and 90 percent perspiration? Sometimes the old saws are true. One of the differences between people who achieve and people who don't is *motivation*. Professor Carol Dweck of Columbia University has made her life's work from understanding what motivates children to learn. When recently asked whether IQ was a reliable measure of children's real abilities and potential, she responded, "IQ tests can measure current skill, but nothing can measure someone's potential. . . . Research on creative geniuses shows that many of them seemed like fairly ordinary children. Yet at some point, they became obsessed with something and pursued it avidly over a long period of time. . . . Many of these contributions could not have been predicted by IQ scores."

So how can we create children who love to learn? Children start out that way—as Piaget has made so crystal clear. They are like little sponges. To keep them that way—to avoid drying up their curiosity—we need to be encouraging, not critical. We need to praise the strategies they use to solve a problem, rather than their intelligence. This implicitly says to children that with the right approach, they can do most anything. In this way, we free our children from the anxiety of disappointing us ("If I try something new and fail," they may otherwise reason, "my mom will no longer think I'm so smart.") and enable them to focus on persevering in challenging circumstances. The result is a mastery-oriented child, a child who doesn't give up when faced with a difficult task but instead embraces and enjoys the challenge. The remaining tips will help you to create and nurture a mastery-oriented child.

Don't insist that there is only one right way to do something. If your child comes up with a novel solution to a problem, that's great! An emphasis on right answers may push children to think about intelligence as an entity. On the other hand, an emphasis on creative, intellectual play will encourage children to believe that intelligence can be added to, one problem at a time.

Show your kids that you make mistakes, too, and let them correct you! Not only does this take the pressure off your children to be perfect, but it also presents learning as a lifelong pursuit.

Focus on developing your child's creativity and independent thinking—true 21st-century skills. As your child plays around with things and learns to knit facts together in new ways, he's learning skills that are valued in the 21st-century workplace. We have computers that can put information into grids for us, count faster than we ever could, and do complex math functions in a fraction of a second, but no computer can ever replicate the creativity the human brain uses to solve problems. So as parents and teachers in the 21st century, we have to have a broader view of intelligence, a view that focuses on supporting our children's talents; allows them to be creative, independent thinkers; and feeds their curiosity. If our view of intelligence focuses on test scores and ingesting tons of information, we have lost the vitality that makes for real human intelligence.

CHAPTER + 7

WHO AM I?
DEVELOPING
A SENSE OF SELF

IN 1928, the famous psychologist John Broadus Watson made an extraordinary claim. He wrote, "Give me a dozen healthy infants, well-formed, and my own specified world to bring them up in, and I'll guarantee to take any one at random and train him to become any type of specialist I might select—a doctor, lawyer, artist, merchant-chief, and yes, even a beggar-man and thief, regardless of his talents, penchants, tendencies, abilities, vocations and race of ancestors."

Watson, founder of the behaviorist school of thought in psychology, was a great believer in the power of the environment to shape character—especially when guided by *his* scientific principles. However, developmental psychologists have unearthed a few facts about the power of heredity that might now give Watson pause. Sure the environment matters; no one would deny that. But factors unique to each child, encoded in his DNA, also make a difference for who the child turns out to be and what beliefs he comes to hold about who he is.

NATURE VERSUS NURTURE: HOW DO WE DEVELOP OUR SENSE OF SELF?

Many parents are great believers in the Watson environmentalist view of their parent power. That is, until they have their second child. When the second child seems different from the first one right from the start, parents become more realistic about how much power they will have to shape their children's sense of themselves.

How *do* children come to learn who they are? Think of all the different things we know about ourselves. For example, I know that I am a woman, I know my age, and I know my race. I know what I look like and can recognize pictures of myself. I know I like broccoli and can't abide cauliflower. I know I have a temper when pushed, but that I am very quick to forgive. I know that I'm sociable rather than reserved. I know I tend to be a leader rather than a follower. I know I'm not good at math, but great at English.

By the time we are adults, we have an amazingly elaborate picture of who we are, and it's fairly balanced between positive and negative. But children don't start out this way. They construct their sense of themselves little by little. And notice the use of the verb "construct." This verb implies building something from the ground up. It implies that there is a *process* of self-formation that doesn't happen overnight. The verb "construct" also allows us to imagine that the environment can play a role in the process, and indeed it does.

In many ways, children forge their self-concept without parental assistance. This is not to say that parents don't matter. They matter enormously. But children don't wait for their parents and caregivers to tell them about themselves. As we will show in this chapter, children figure out all kinds of things about themselves on their own.

One of the dangers of the push to get children to be geniuses at an early age is that *parents act as if they were the sculptors of their children's character and self-concept.* Embracing this myth puts great pressure on parents because it leads to the corollary that they must strive to be perfect parents. Any shortcoming their children betray must surely be their fault. Johnny doesn't like spinach? It must be the way I introduced it when he was little. Sally doesn't like to do puzzles? I must have been too negative the last time we did one together. If you believe this, then the blame for any intellectual hurdle children fail to jump, or any preschool they fail to get into, must be laid squarely at the feet of the parents. A related myth for parents concerned with their children's intellectual development is a bit more specific. *Many parents believe that if they praise their children for their intelligence, they will have children who come to believe that they are intelligent and who then do well in school.* This is not a crazy idea. If we tell a child that he is handsome, he will probably come to adopt that view, too. Shouldn't being told how smart you are lead you to believe that you are indeed an intelligent person? Shouldn't being told how smart you are lead you to function more effectively at academic tasks? Unfortunately, the answer is a resounding no. As we will see, praise for intelligence works paradoxically. Praise for intelligence winds up making children conservative learners who are afraid to stretch themselves if if means risking failure. Praise for intelligence locks children inside an image of themselves that they work to maintain at all costs.

A Preschooler's Skewed Sense of Self

How do children develop a sense of themselves? And how fast does this learning come about? The self-concept that a baby has at 3 months will be very different from the child's understanding of herself at 3 years, and then at 8 years, and so forth. The University of Denver's Professor Susan Harter is an expert on how children develop a concept of self. From her interviews with children at various ages, she constructed a composite example of how 3- and 4-year-olds see themselves.

> *I'm 3 years old and I live in a big house with my mother and father and my brother, Jason, and my sister, Lisa. I have blue eyes and a kitty that is orange and a television in my room. I know all of my ABCs, listen: A-B-C-D-E-F-G-H-J-L-K-O-M-P-Q-X-Z! I can run real fast. I like pizza and I have a nice teacher at preschool. I can count up to 10, want to hear me? I love my dog Skipper. I can climb to the top of the jungle gym—I'm not scared! I'm never scared! I'm always happy. . . . I'm really strong. I can lift this chair, watch me!*

Whew! You can just picture a little child racing along telling the interviewer these things with great enthusiasm. And the child sounds so confident. He can do *anything*, he tells us, from lifting the chair to counting to 10 to reciting (his version of) the ABCs! This is typical of preschoolers; they have an exalted sense of self. (Well, perhaps not only preschoolers. . . . Some Hollywood stars and dictators may share this view!)

Why do preschoolers imagine that they are so capable when the truth is just the opposite? First, they seem to focus on just one aspect of a situation rather than several. For instance, when Kathy's son Benjy was 5, he was apparently bedazzled by several teenage macho lads who were daring each other to jump off a very high diving board at a swimming pool where the family was vacationing. Before anyone noticed, Benjy had climbed the many steps to the top and plunged into the water just as his mother turned around. It was a time in his life when he was fascinated by macho behavior and he didn't stop to compare his own small size with that of the older boys. He just focused on his one interest—doing what was macho.

Related to this single-minded focus is the fact that preschool children typically blame anything that goes wrong on factors other than themselves. For instance, one time Kathy saw her son Mikey hit another child very hard. She scolded him and his response was "I didn't do it—my hand did." If he took a swing at a baseball and missed, he'd tell his pitcher, "You threw it wrong." In fact, one study showed that even when preschoolers fail at a task several times, they think they'll get it right when next they try! In a way, this exalted view of their capabilities is a gift because they never give up. In another way, it can lead to dangerous situations because preschoolers are willing to try just about anything. Only with more development will children begin to understand the nature and extent of their own abilities. Only with more development will they take many factors into account in figuring out who they are.

Another reason preschoolers are overly confident has to do with their inability to engage in what psychologists call social comparison. We adults are terrific at this. Many of us have a little person who sits on our shoulder and judges everything we do in comparison to what others do. In fact, for some adults, the judge on the shoulder is enormous and weighs them down, stifling the risk taking needed to try new ventures. But preschoolers haven't developed this judge yet. They don't think or say things like "She's a better bowler than I am" because they don't compare themselves to others and take these discrepancies into consideration. They think they are terrific! And that's all that matters.

A More Balanced Sense of Self

By 8 years of age, children are able to see themselves as far more complex than they did when they were preschoolers. Their self-descriptions become much more balanced and abstract. They now show evidence of being able to consider the fact that they might not be perfect at everything. And they give examples of how the little judge on their shoulder has appeared, recognizing that their peers are better—and worse—at some things than they are. We see this when children immediately see through the school reading groups. They know that the blue group is better than the red group even though this is never explicitly said. They also know that the guppies are the worst swimmers in the afternoon swim group.

Older children manage to balance out their negative evaluations of themselves with positive ones. When they recognize that they are not so good at something, they decide that it isn't that important to them anyway ("Who cares if I am a guppy. I can play soccer really well!"). This serves the useful function of allowing them to continue to think well of themselves overall despite the fact that they recognize their lack of perfection. And by the time they are 8 years old, they have shifted from defining themselves through external characteristics to being aware of their psychological and social characteristics. So a typical 8-year-old might say the following about herself.

> *I'm pretty popular, at least with the girls. That's because I'm nice to people and helpful and can keep secrets. Mostly I am nice to my friends, although if I get in a bad mood I sometimes say things that can be a little mean. . . . At school, I'm feeling pretty smart in certain subjects like language arts and social studies, but I'm feeling pretty dumb in math and science, especially when I see how well a lot of the other children are doing. Even though I'm not doing well in those subjects, I still like myself as a person, because math and science just aren't that important to me. How I look and how popular I am are more important.*

What a difference between a preschooler's description and an 8-year-old's!

Ages: 2½ years to 6 years

A great book for children this age is *My Book about Me, by Me Myself with Some Help from My Friends* by Dr. Seuss. On the cover, you paste a picture of your child. And then together you describe aspects of the self that a 2- or 3-year-old would recognize as important. The book has you and your child doing all kinds of fun activities, like counting how many teeth she has and tracing her foot to see how big it is—all activities a child this age is sure to enjoy and that help her define herself as a person.

The story of the development of self is an exciting one that changes over the course of the first 5 years. In ever-widening concentric circles, the child's view of self moves from a sense of the physical self to the social and emotional self, to some understanding of the intellectual self.

THE PHYSICAL SELF: MY BODY

The first thing babies develop is a sense of their own bodies. For example, even a newborn baby can occasionally put his hand right on his face—whether by accident or design is not important. What *is* important for our purposes is the fact that the little baby can feel his hand on his cheek and his cheek on his hand. Psychologists call this double touch, and having a double touch feeling may be what tells the baby that the body he is touching is his own.

But do babies know where their bodies end and other bodies begin? To find out, Professors Philippe Rochat and Susan Hespos had the brilliant idea to see if newborn babies could tell the difference between their *own* hand touching their cheek, and someone *else's* hand touching their cheek. Cheek touching taps into something all babies are born with: the "rooting reflex." Infants show this reflex when they turn their heads to the side after you stroke their cheeks. Nature has designed babies well because they turn only to the side on which they feel the stroke. Stroke the right cheek and they turn right; stroke the left cheek and they go left. And this is a great reflex to have because turning toward a feeling of something on your cheek is very likely to lead you to the nipple—just as nature intended!

The researchers tested neonates within 24 hours of birth. They watched what happened if the *experimenter* stroked the baby's cheek or if the *baby* spontaneously touched his own cheek. If a baby can tell the difference between himself and someone else, he shouldn't show the rooting reflex when he strokes his own cheek. After all, he cannot provide himself with milk. But if he can tell the difference between his own hand touching his cheek and someone else's hand, then he should show the reflex and turn to the side of the stroke when someone else touches him. Babies showed the rooting reflex *three times* more often to the experimenter's touch than to their own touch. In a dim way, babies can distinguish between their own bodies and others' bodies when they are just 1 day old!

Distinguishing Me from You

If babies have a sense of how their own bodies work, and how they are distinct from other bodies, when do they recognize themselves? In a study done by Professor Lorraine Bahrick at Florida International University in Miami, 3-month-old babies were observed to see how long they would look at a video of themselves compared with a video of another baby of the same age and gender. Interestingly, Professor Bahrick found that babies will watch the image of the baby they've never seen longer than they will the image of themselves.

Does this mean that a 3-month-old baby recognizes himself? Not quite. It could just mean that he finds his features familiar and therefore finds the other baby more attention grabbing. We don't really know from this study if a 3-month-old baby is aware that the baby that looks familiar is himself. But what this study does tell us, even if we can't say that the baby knows he's watching himself, is that he recognizes *something* about himself. Otherwise, why spend more time looking at the new baby?

I Know What I Look Like!

While there are many milestones along the path to developing a sense of self, one research study revealed just how gradually that sense kicks in. Professor Michael Lewis of the Robert Wood Johnson Medical School and Professor Jeanne Brooks-Gunn of Teachers College of Columbia

University in New York did a very clever study to see just when children come to recognize their own physical appearances, their physical selves.

In the study, they had mothers surreptitiously dab some bright red rouge on their children's noses. They then observed whether or not the children would look longer at their images in a mirror or even try to wipe off the rouge when they saw their reflections, indicating that they recognized the image as themselves. Generally speaking, the researchers found that babies younger than 15 months did not recognize themselves in the mirror this way. By 21 months, almost all babies did.

| Discovering Hidden Skills | Sense of Physical Self |

Ages: 12 months to 24 months

Does your child have a sense of what she looks like? Try the rouge test every few months and see what happens. You'll need to be sneaky and surreptitiously place rouge on your child's nose near a large mirror and observe what happens. Does your child just look at herself for a long time? Does she try to rub it off? Does your child show it to you and smile? Or does she ignore it as if it is no big deal?

What role do parents play in babies' developing perception of self? Not much. Babies pretty much figure out these things on their own, without the aid of special classes or educational toys. Just ordinary, everyday experience combined with what baby brings into the world provides baby with the necessary opportunities to develop these primitive, yet enduring, self-understandings.

The Categorical Self: Am I a Boy or a Girl?

The physical self involves more than knowing that you have a body different from mine. It also involves seeing yourself through the lens of categories like gender, race, and ethnicity. What categories do I fit into? How do I know that I am a woman, and that I remain a woman even if I wear men's overalls or put my hair up under a hat? It is surprising to learn how early knowledge of one's own gender occurs, and yet, paradoxically, how easily it can be shaken! But the hallmarks of gender for us—the genitalia or the DNA—are not the hallmarks that young children think of. For them, it's how people look (do they have long hair? do they wear pants?) that governs whether they are perceived as a boy or a girl.

By now you've probably come to realize that learning about even gender begins in the cradle! Consider what happens when a baby is born. The first question is always "Boy or girl?" And from this moment on, that baby's life will never be the same. The baby will be treated differently based on whether we think it's a girl or a boy. How do we know this? Once again—the clever methods of laboratory research show us some startling things about ourselves.

Back in the 1970s, researchers did a number of studies we now call the "Baby X" studies. In one of the first of these studies by John and Sandy Condry of Cornell University in Ithaca, New York, a baby is shown on film reacting to a buzzer. The focus is on the participants—college students— and their responses to this baby. The students are asked to judge what emotion the child is feeling. What the students don't know is that half of them hold a response booklet that says "Dana is a 9-month-old female," while the other half hold a booklet that says "Dana is a 9-month-old male." It is really easy to dress babies and children in unisex clothing that can make it difficult to tell their sexes. In this situation, where Dana appeared to be upset, the participants who thought Dana was a boy said he experienced more anger than fear. Interestingly, the participants who thought Dana was a girl said just the opposite—more fear than anger! But it was the same baby! Sex role stereotypes are (unfortunately) alive and well.

When do babies first really know they are boys or girls? After systematically watching hundreds of children play, researchers noticed that between 12 and 18 months, children start to prefer toys considered appropriate for their gender. Girls chose to play with dolls and pink things. Boys chose the trucks and weapons. It's little wonder, in a way, given that one study showed that boys' and girls' rooms contain very different things, so the children are given a very clear message even before they are exposed to advertising or are old enough to request certain toys. Parents are the purchasers, and they outfit their children's rooms with many sex-specific items.

If children start to prefer what are considered gender-appropriate toys by the end of their 1st year, when can children *label* their own genders and those of others? It looks like they can do this between 2 and 3 years of age, and they can do it first for themselves and then for others. That should be no surprise: They hear themselves designated as either boys or girls all the time. To label other children's genders, toddlers have to guess about the criteria to use (hair length? eye color?). Given recent fashion trends, these criteria are not at all clear!

Even if children know that they are boys or girls as early as age 2, do they really understand—even after they can talk—how gender is assigned and how it doesn't (ordinarily) change? As fundamental as this knowledge is, the answer is no. Why? Because children are often limited by what they see, and they seem to use different indicators than we as adults do.

Have you ever noticed how toy stores are organized? Walk into any toy store in the land and you will be sure to see a pink, purple, and white section, usually on the left as you walk in, and everybody knows it's not for boys! That color-coding, in fact, tells you that you'll find baby dolls, Easy-Bake Oven sets, makeup kits, board games that involve learning to shop, and Barbie, Barbie, Barbie. Of course, there is no way you are going to get little Billy interested in that section. In fact, he'll be sure to head for the darker colors, rather than pastels, where his dolls will be referred to as action toys and, we might add, where there will be a wider range of choices, from science kits to sports paraphernalia to video games. And if you're the peace-loving type who doesn't want your boy to play with guns and tanks and laser-armed superheroes, in hopes that it will make him a more peace-loving adult, forget it. You won't succeed. He could make a gun out of a tulip at that age. Why? Because children's cognitive development is at a point where they are very interested in categorizing the world—especially the world of people. And since their own gender is at the center of those categories, they are busy learning the rules of what is considered socially appropriate for masculine and feminine behavior.

Our preschool children may *appear* to be knowledgeable about gender roles, but they have a long way to go. Professor Sandra Bem, a well-known developmental psychologist at Cornell University, describes how her young son, Jeremy, decided one day to wear barrettes to his nursery school. Another boy insisted repeatedly that Jeremy had to be a girl because "only girls wear barrettes." Although Jeremy argued that he was a boy because he had a penis, the other boy insisted on calling him a girl. Exasperated, Jeremy pulled down his pants to prove his sexual identity.

The other boy was not impressed: "Everybody has a penis; only girls wear barrettes," he asserted proudly.

As this example shows, young children who are in the process of developing gender schemas typically have a very narrow view of what is masculine and what is feminine. And should a boy gravitate to a Barbie or a pink makeup set, you can be sure his male friends will set him straight. Indeed, children will hold gender distinctions more firmly through middle childhood than at any other time. And because young children cannot integrate pieces of information that appear to be contradictory, they will routinely deny, for example, that mommies can be construction workers and mommies, too. It's as if they first have to learn a more rigid view of what society thinks goes in the files before they can widen their categories to be more realistic. But if they see both daddy and mommy caring for babies and baking cookies, too, it may be a bit harder for them to cling to rigid, gender-stereotyped categories. Once they've figured out the real rules for being a boy or a girl, they'll feel more comfortable in not holding such rigid gender standards, especially if parents have already provided the examples.

What Race Am I?: Another Aspect of Categorical Self

Because children hear so much talk about gender, it is perhaps not surprising that they figure out their own gender before they figure out their own race. Phyllis Katz, Ph.D., director of the Institute for Research on Social Issues in Boulder, Colorado, is a psychologist who has devoted her life's work to understanding how children come to learn about gender and race. She found that by the age of 3 years, 77 percent of the European-American children tested could name their own race, but only 32 percent of the African-American children could. This is not because African-American children are not as good at forming categories like these; they formed *gender* categories at the same time as the European-American children. It is not until the age of 4 or 5 that *all* children are pretty sure what racial (or ethnic) group they fit into. Interestingly, when they are asked what race (or gender) they'd *prefer* to be, blacks are more likely to say they'd prefer to be white than white children are to say they'd prefer to be black. Similarly, girls are more likely to prefer to be the opposite gender than are boys. Perhaps given the power differential in our society, and the fact that members of minority groups and women are devalued, this is not surprising.

Knowledge about gender and race goes through three stages. First, children become aware of the differences, the fact that there *are* separate categories. This occurs in infancy when babies can show us through their looking responses that they have a category of male and female faces and that they can divide pictures of babies apart by race. *Awareness* of differences is followed by the second stage of *identification*, which occurs between the ages of 2 and 3. At this stage, children can label their own sex and place themselves in a group of same-sex children. But recall that identification is not the same thing as *constancy*, or a realization of the permanence of gender and race classifications. Racial constancy seems to develop even later than gender constancy, and even later in minority African-American and Asian children, who may struggle with understanding their minority status. This sequence of development is tied in with children's cognitive development. There is no rushing children's understanding of these issues and no off-the-shelf training program to hurry it up.

Discovering
Hidden Skills | ## Gender and Racial Identity

Ages: 2 years to 7 years

Try this activity every 6 months or so to gauge your child's progress. Use a magazine (maybe something like *Sesame Street* magazine) that has pictures of children of various races and genders. Sit down with your child and say you're going to play a game. Ask her to point to the boys, the girls, and the white and African-American children. It would be great if you had pictures of children who were dressed or coiffed in ways that did not match their gender roles. For example, try to find a picture of a boy with long hair or a girl with short hair wearing overalls. Interestingly, young children find it easier to label *adults'* genders than children's genders. If you ask them about the genders and races of adults in pictures, use the terms that you use with the child when you talk about adults. For example, do you use the terms "man" and "lady"? If so, use those in your questions. As you did for the pictures of children, try to find pictures of adults that stretch the child's judgment. Perhaps a picture of a man wearing a kilt or a man who has a ponytail or long hair. Or a woman dressed as a firefighter or construction worker. When you're done, go back and ask your child to justify her choices. "Why did you say that this one is a girl?" Don't laugh or be judgmental, no matter what your child says; you will gain amazing insight into how your child thinks.

THE SOCIAL/EMOTIONAL SELF: I HAVE FEELINGS

The *physical* me is only one dimension of our notion of self. We also have a *social-emotional* self. In the last 20 years, scientists have discovered how essential our first relationships are even for *normal* development. The newborn baby just can't regulate his emotional states very well. He can turn away from unpleasant stimulation and mouth and suck when his feelings get too intense, but he is easily overwhelmed. This is why you can't really spoil infants—they absolutely depend on the soothing interventions of caregivers for help in adjusting their emotional reactions. They need you to lift them to your shoulder, rock them, and talk softly in order to build a sound sense of their emotional self.

Between 2 and 4 months, the part of the baby's brain known as the cerebral cortex gradually increases the baby's tolerance for stimulation. Caregivers can start to build on this capacity by playing little face-to-face games, though they still need to be careful to adjust their pace so the infant doesn't become overwhelmed. In the next chapter, we'll describe the importance of these early relationships as prototypes for subsequent relationships. But first, let's explore how these early relationships indirectly teach the baby about her world's responsiveness and how effective she is at changing her world.

While there is no question that parents don't have to respond to every noise of discomfort (let alone cries) that a baby makes, there is still a question about how quickly and often parents should respond. How much should parents try to alleviate their babies' discomfort? And will parents who are more or less responsive implicitly teach their babies to feel more or less effective in dealing with their world? There are two sides to this story (as there often are!).

Let Them Cry It Out?

No doubt you've noticed that babies cry a lot in the first year of life. Our legendary behaviorist John B. Watson advised parents that they would be "conditioning" their babies to cry (and therefore become annoying cry-babies instead of merchant-chiefs in later life) if they picked them up every time they cried. Based on his theory, parents were advised to let their babies "cry it out" so they wouldn't spoil them. On the other side of this debate, we have Freud and Erikson. They would argue that being responsive to children helps them learn that they are powerful and frees them to learn to make requests in other ways.

Fortunately, some researchers eventually decided to put these theories to the test by looking at the actual behaviors of mothers and their babies. Did mothers who let their little babies "cry it out" have babies who cried less or more than babies whose mothers picked them up? Professors Sylvia Bell and Mary Ainsworth, both of Johns Hopkins University in Baltimore, found that babies whose cries got a response more frequently cried *less* at the end of 9 months than those who were responded to less frequently. It seems that when caregivers responded to the babies' cries, they were teaching the babies that they would be cared for—perhaps building up trust in the responsiveness of the environment.

And what replaces crying in children whose needs are consistently met? Vocalizing, pointing, grunting, and making eye contact with mother or caregiver. No question that using these communication signals is an advance over just crying. Responding to babies' discomfort, then, promotes babies' ability to communicate.

The Roots of Personality: Watson Strikes Out Again

You are probably well aware that children are not as Watson thought. There is no such thing as a little lump of clay that can be conditioned by scientific techniques into becoming anything an adult wishes, regardless of his "talents, penchants, tendencies, abilities, vocations, and race of his ancestors." Each child comes into this world a very unique being—like Gracie and Annie, for instance:

Nancy Russell relaxes at the dinner table, extended with a couple of wooden leaves to seat 14. It had been one of the best Thanksgiving meals ever, even though she was now the mother of two children and the youngest, 24 months, had sat right beside her during the long and happy meal. In fact, as they all chatted over coffee and pumpkin pie, Nancy realized they had been sitting there for close to 2 hours! And Gracie had contentedly participated—"Ganpa see," holding up her spoon full of sweet potatoes so grandpa could see how delicious they looked; "More milk," holding cup to mom, requesting refills; and so forth. Two hours and Gracie was still contentedly engaged! What really struck Nancy was the memory of *Annie's* Thanksgiving meals at that age. Annie was jet-propelled. Nancy couldn't keep her in the chair for more than a few minutes. Annie ate her meal like a suburban commuter—running from the table to her toys to the kitchen—in perpetual motion! In fact, she'd been wriggly in the crib and was so active that even the changing table had been a hazard.

What Nancy was noticing in her girls is what psychologists call temperament. Temperament is a word that captures the ways that people differ, even at birth, in such things as their emotional reactions, activity level, attention span, persistence, and ability to regulate their emotions. Back in the 1950s, psychiatrists Alexander Thomas, M.D., and Stella Chess, M.D., set out to study this phenomenon and to see how consistent it might be throughout life. They studied 141 children beginning when they were infants and followed them into adulthood. They identified three basic types of temperament: The "easy child," who easily establishes regular routines, is generally cheerful, and adapts readily to new experiences (40 percent of their sample); the "difficult child," who is irregular in daily routines, is slow to accept new experiences, and tends to react negatively and intensely to new things (10 percent); and the "slow-to-warm-up child," who shows mild, low-key reactions to environmental changes, is negative in mood, and adjusts slowly to new experiences (15 percent). The rest of the children did not seem to fall into any particular category and were categorized as average babies.

Drs. Thomas and Chess found that these temperaments get modified as children interact with different types of parents. They also found that some temperaments help children overcome emotional difficulties, while others leave them more vulnerable. Difficult children, for example, will do best with very sensitive parents who know when to push and when to fold, while for easy children, parental responses won't matter quite as much since these children roll with the punches.

We still have a lot to learn about how children's initial personalities or temperaments drive what they will become. We all know that happy babies make us feel better as parents, so we interact more. Difficult babies force us away and seem to create very different interactions, even from the same parents. So to some degree, our children's temperaments shape the kind of parenting they will get.

Part of our social selves also includes an internal sense of what is right and wrong. How should we act to show respect for others? How do we learn to be fair and just people? These questions form the basis for our moral selves.

Morality Emerges!

The issue of morality has been a concern of some of the major theorists of psychology (indeed of Western thought), including Sigmund Freud, B. F. Skinner, and Jean Piaget. An important part of our concept of self is our feeling that we can do what is right and make judgments about fairness and justice. But children differ from adults. While young children protest "That's not fair" in the face of real or imagined injustices, their parents often answer (and mean it!), "Life just isn't always fair."

When young children transgress, do they do so out of weak morals, out of evil, or out of ignorance? And when our children fail to heed our lessons, and seem to feel no moral shame, does this mean they are headed to the slammer?

Imagine, for example, that 22-month-old Alice puts her finger in the electric socket. You rush over and say, "No, no!" She does it again. You pick her up and put her on the other side of the room and again say, "No!" She waits until you're not looking and then returns to the socket while you hunt for a blocking plug for it in the kitchen. Is Alice simply a willful child who will grow up to be a handful? Have you failed in some way to instill in her a sense of right from wrong?

Perhaps there is a simpler explanation that has to do with the development of Alice's self. Perhaps Alice can't respond to your punishments because she doesn't yet see herself as a distinct entity capable of being evaluated. If she can't see herself as a person capable of being judged (by herself or others), then why would she resist the temptation to misbehave yet again when your back is turned? Self-regulation is out of the question if Alice doesn't realize her behavior can be held to some standard. For this reason, perhaps, she doesn't have the capacity to experience the shame and remorse an older child would when they do something wrong. In fact, some researchers have reported that little children often show their parents that they have done something wrong with no particular emotion. "See? Break TV." Why don't these children get upset? Maybe because they don't realize that they have done something bad.

To test this theory, Professor Deborah Stipek and her colleagues at UCLA gave the mothers of 123 children between the ages of 14 and 40 months a 22-item questionnaire to fill out at home. Mothers were urged to observe their children's behavior in terms of these items before they checked "yes" or "no" to each item. One item, for example, asked whether the child could recognize himself in a mirror (an indicator of self-recognition). Another asked, "Does your child ever use general evaluative terms about herself, such as 'I'm a good girl'?" Items like this assessed whether children were capable of subjecting themselves to evaluation. And finally, mothers were asked whether children showed any kind of emotional response when they did something wrong. What did Professor Stipek and her colleagues find?

When a child Alice's age does something wrong, and then does it again after a scolding, it isn't because she is the bad seed. Alice just doesn't engage in self-evaluation yet and therefore feels no remorse when she acts out. You have to recognize that you can be evaluated, and that there are standards, before you can feel remorse! A reliable sequence occurred for all of the children. First, their mothers' responses indicated that the children could recognize themselves in a mirror or in pictures or call attention to something about their appearance pretty early. About 80 percent of the mothers of 14- to 18-month-olds said the babies could do this, and this agrees with the rouge test we described above. Then, once children can recognize themselves as entities, they become capable of self-evaluation and self-description. About 50 percent of the 19- to 24-month-olds could do that, followed by 80 percent of the 25- to 29-month-olds and almost all (91 percent) of the 30- to 40-month-olds. So it takes that long to be able to talk about yourself as an object and evaluate things about yourself. Finally, children showed an emotional response when they transgressed and attempted to control themselves from doing things that they thought were wrong. But it took a long time. Only 51 percent of the children at 25 to 29 months seemed upset or ashamed when they acted out, or tried to inhibit themselves from doing something wrong. And the percentage of children who seemed to evaluate their own behavior was not even that high at 30 to 40 months. Only 59 percent of these older children responded emotionally when they were "bad."

Moral behavior cannot occur when children do not recognize themselves as social beings whose behavior can be evaluated against some standard. How can they think about acting morally if they don't feel bad when they transgress? What makes this development happen? Once again, we turn to children's thinking and the way they are treated to help us understand. Perhaps when children learn to hold some standard in their heads and compare it with the way things really are, they can start to evaluate themselves. A child might think, "Being sticky is bad—from how it feels and from the way mom has acted in the past when my hands were sticky. I'm sticky now. That's bad." To be able to hold a standard in mind and evaluate a situation in terms of the standard shows increasing cognitive flexibility. Perhaps, too, acquiring more language helps. Now the child learns descriptive terms such as "good" and "bad," "sticky" and "clean."

Regulating the Emotional Self

Finally, the social self comes from our ability to regulate our emotions, to get what we want without overreacting or overstepping boundaries. Emotional self-regulation refers to the strategies we use to adjust our emotional states to a comfortable level of intensity so we can accomplish our goals. In the early months of life, infants have only a limited capacity to regulate their emotional states. They can turn away from unpleasant stimuli and can suck when their feelings get too intense, but they are easily overwhelmed. That's where parents come in. Parents can lift them up to their shoulder, rock them, talk to them softly—all of this helps the baby adjust her emotions.

As the cerebral cortex develops, baby's tolerance for stimulation increases. Between 2 and 4 months, caregivers start to build on this capacity by initiating face-to-face play and attention to objects. Parents arouse pleasure in the baby while sensitively adjusting the pace of their own behavior so the infant does not become overwhelmed and distressed. As a result, the baby's tolerance for stimulation increases. By 4 months, babies can help themselves by turning away from unpleasant events, and by the end of the 1st year, they can crawl away to regulate their emotions. As caregivers help children regulate their emotional states, they contribute to the child's style of emotional self-regulation. By 2 years, children can also use language to help regulate emotion. They develop a vocabulary for talking about feelings such as "happy," "love," "yucky," "mad." While listening to a story about monsters, Suzie whimpered, "Mommy, scary!" Monica put the book down and gave Suzie a comforting hug. Suzie couldn't regulate her own emotion, but by communicating her feelings to her mother, she got the comfort she needed.

Teachable Moments	## Expressing Emotion

Our children are constantly showing us how they feel through their facial expressions, how tightly they hold our hands, or by their tentative walk. We can take these precious times to talk with them about how they feel and to listen and share our own feelings. Parents and teachers often don't take the time to talk about feelings, and yet when we do, we get enormous rewards. We give our children a vocabulary that will help them navigate through the difficult moments and celebrate the great moments with others. These are the children who will be there to say "Love you."

I Want What I Want and I Want it Now!
The Importance of Learning to Control My Emotions

Tim is in the grocery store. He is having a sit-down strike on the floor, complete with tears and wails—his way of negotiating a settlement over a bag of M&M's. Sound like the terrible twos? Will he still be doing this at 32? Should young children be able to control their frustrations and disappointments, and is there something wrong when they have tantrums? The course of what psychologists call emotional regulation does not run smooth. Furthermore, because of temperamental differences, children do not all respond best to one single remedy.

But imagine if you burst into tears every time things didn't go your way. Or imagine if you just struck out and hit a person who kept you from getting what you wanted. Could you keep a job? Could you keep friends? Would possible incarceration be in your stars? And yet it takes years, and lots of intellectual growth, to be able to figure out the best way to control and harness one's emotions. Emotional regulation involves being able to cope with positive as well as negative feelings. (Interestingly, in adults, heart attacks can be precipitated by good news as well as bad!)

We all have learned how to calm ourselves down from joyful or sad experiences because our parents and caregivers helped us regulate our emotions when we were children. Consider suspense games such as "I'm gonna getcha" and "Peekaboo." Though on the surface they might seem like just a fun way to pass the time, they actually teach children how to regulate their emotions. Daniel Stern, M.D., of the Cornell University Medical Center in New York, gives us a wonderful analysis of peekaboo and how parents help regulate the baby's emotional state.

Picture 9-month-old Irving sitting in his crib and his dad, Jeff, looking in at Irving. We are spying on a game they must have played before. Jeff takes Irving's blanket and throws it over his own head. Irving laughs uproariously as dad stands stock-still for a few moments. Irving's face is lit with expectation, and he's even blinking in anticipation of his dad throwing off the blanket. Jeff says loudly, "Peekaboo!" and whips off the blanket. Irving laughs hysterically and crawls back in his crib as if to get away from Jeff. Is there a little element of fear here? After Jeff does this two more times, he waits a long time before revealing himself again. The suspense is killing Irving this time as he waits and waits for his dad to remove his cover. Just as Irving is beginning to lose interest, Jeff whips off the blanket again and yells, "Peekaboo!" Seeing Irving's startled response and now weak laughter, Jeff implicitly judges that Irving has been stimulated enough and puts the blanket back in the crib.

As Dr. Stern points out, this typical baby–parent game cycles and crescendos several times. Irving could never create such a game himself; it takes two. And the experience is full of joyful suspense and anticipation and possibly a little fear. Dad, who is sensitive to Irving's emotional state, backs off after several rounds, thinking that Irving has had enough. This is just what we do for our children: We create excitement for them and then regulate their emotions through it. It is the rare parent (although they exist and their behavior borders on abuse) who goes too far and brings his or her baby to tears in such games.

We help regulate babies' negative emotions, too, from the very beginning. When babies cry, we pick them up. But during the night, we may decide to let the baby figure out how to calm himself down because in this culture, where most babies sleep separately from their parents, they need to learn how to get back to sleep when they wake without the warmth of another body beside them.

Emotion regulation is not learned in classes or from videos but from real life. Only real life can elicit the depth and range of emotion that might lead a toddler to have a tantrum. Can you remember when you were a child and cried so long and hard that you couldn't catch your breath? It didn't feel good at all to be so out of control. And although the pediatrician may say "Ignore the tantrum," everyone must know his or her own child. As Mary, the mother of 2½-year-old Sarah, told us, "Sarah cannot 'bring herself back' when I let her go and ignore her tantrum. I have found that a better strategy for me is to distract her. She requires an hour of holding and comforting if I let her experience the tantrum." This is because Sarah is not good enough yet at emotional regulation to help herself stop crying, to get a grip. And one response size does not fit all! Children have unique temperaments. Some children are more reactive than others and seem to feel things more deeply. Others recover quickly from disappointments and go on as if nothing had happened. Further, the child's age and, more specifically, where he is in the development of emotional regulation plays a large role. That is, what might have precipitated a tantrum at 18 months might be taken as no big deal at 20 months.

Once children can figure out a way to help themselves gain control (looking for distractions; finding an alternative to what they want; calming themselves down with their favorite stuffed animal), they will gain a sense of mastery over their emotional distress. But emotional regulation like this requires parents and caregivers to talk with their children and help them understand that there are alternatives to tantrums. And even before children can profit from such "discussions," parents have to provide the external support for helping children regulate their emotions, as when the parents distract a child who is about to go into emotional overdrive. Gradually, parents hand over the reins for this control to the child, in many cases coaching the child about how to cope constructively with the negative feelings that have been engendered: "You're really mad at me, aren't you? Can you tell me something else that would make you happy?"

Once language comes on the scene, science tells us that parents talk as much with their children between the ages of 2 and 5 about positive as they do about negative emotions. But because negative emotions are more distressing and unpleasant, and therefore need to be regulated more than positive emotions, researchers found that the conversations about positive and negative emotions were very different. Where a parent might say, "Oh, the bunny is happy now!" during an ongoing play episode, the parent might say, "Why did you cry last night in your bed?" Parents are more likely to talk about negative events that took place in the past with their children. They are also more likely to ask open-ended questions about negative emotions ("Why do you think people cry?") and to call more attention to the negative emotions other people experience ("Do you understand why daddy was angry with you yesterday?").

What functions might all this talk serve? It turns out that children who have lots of these discussions with their parents have a better under-standing of their own and others' emotions later on. And knowledge is power: Understanding your own emotions and the emotions of others helps you to behave better in situations that might lead to negative emo-tions. Learning to regulate our emotions has benefits well into adulthood. Research has shown that, as Daniel Goleman, cofounder of the Collabo-rative for Social and Emotional Learning at the Yale University Child Study Center and author of *Emotional Intelligence*, points out, "Helping people better manage their upsetting feelings—anger, anxiety, depression, pessimism, and loneliness—is a form of disease prevention."

A 2002 report from the prestigious Society for Research in Child De-velopment comes to a clear conclusion based on much research: " . . . The first few years of schooling appear to be built on a firm foundation of children's emotional and social skills." And, they write, "children who have difficulty paying attention, following directions, getting along well with others, and controlling their negative emotions of anger and distress do less well in school." Scientists who study children even have some an-swers about how these skills are acquired. Both children's temperaments and parents' and caregivers' interactions with children are responsible for how well they learn to manage their negative emotions. To do this, chil-dren must learn two skills: to be able to *recognize* an emotion when they see it or feel it and to be able to *label* it (for example, "I'm angry"). This knowledge comes from parents and caregivers talking about emotions and coaching their children to respond to the emotions they encounter.

Discovering Hidden Skills	Understanding Emotions

Ages: 3 years to 6 years

If your child is 3 or older, you might try using a picture book as a way to help him understand and talk about emotions. When something particularly bad or good happens in a story, ask your child why he thinks the event occurred. This helps children think about what causes outcomes that have emotional consequences. Probe your child about how the character who is affected by the bad or good outcome feels. "Do you think the bunny is happy or sad that she can't find her baby?" "Why is the little boy smiling?" Remember that what may seem obvious to you with your knowledge of life and how stories unfold may be far less obvious to your young child. In addition to helping children understand the causes and correlates of emotions, talking with your children about the emotional events in picture books will help them to become better readers!

THE INTELLECTUAL SELF EMERGES: CAN PRAISE REALLY BE DANGEROUS?

Erika and Rachel are sitting on their tiny chairs at a table in the day care center. They are working on puzzles designed for children just their age. The puzzles are challenging. Erika tries piece after piece, carefully putting together the picture of animals in a jungle. Rachel, on the other hand, fiddles with the pieces. She looks around the room, then takes a look at Erika's half-finished puzzle, and then at her own puzzle, which has just a few pieces in place. She gives up and wanders over to the doll corner, where she begins to scold Barbie, "Mommy is mad at you. You're a stupid. No TV for you till you can do duh puzzle."

Rachel is what psychologists call a nonpersister. Professor Carol Dweck and her colleagues have identified certain parenting practices that contribute to a lack of perseverance, and they have also noted how this aspect of the emerging sense of self predicts success later on. Remember that little rhyme your mom kept zapping at you as you groaned over a minor failure at basketball or spelling? "If at first you don't succeed, try, try again." If that was your parents' theme song, you probably have a pretty good sense of your intellectual self. A mantra about trying tells you not to attribute your failures to something essential and unchangeable about yourself. That is, you probably should not blame your failure on the fact that you are stupid or lazy or both. You evaluate yourself, and rightly so, on the amount of *effort* you put forth to achieve your goals. But if your parents emphasized and praised your ability and intelligence, you might have turned out more like Rachel, not persisting at difficult tasks.

How do children develop a healthy view of their intellectual selves? Psychologists who study this question sometimes call this the development of self-esteem. According to Professors George Bear and Kathy Minke, leading experts on children's understanding of self, the self-esteem movement in education has hit rock bottom. Links researchers thought existed between self-esteem and academic achievement have been seriously questioned and have now attained the status of myths. One of the most persistent—and pernicious—is that programs that emphasize self-esteem improve children's academic performance. Research shows that it takes more than telling children they are intelligent to boost their achievement. Yet 85 percent of the parents of young children interviewed about their beliefs about achievement thought they should praise their children's intelligence to teach them that they are smart. But, you're thinking, how could it possibly be bad for children to tell them how smart they are? Even if you don't have the expectation that telling them they are smart will make them smart, how could it be bad to bolster children's self-esteem in that way?

Professor Dweck's research provides us with the answer. She cautions us to be careful about praising our children's *intelligence* for their performance on academic tasks. She writes:

> . . . *The self-esteem people were on to something extremely important. Praise, the chief weapon in their armory, is a powerful tool. Used correctly it can help students become adults who delight in intellectual challenge, understand the value of effort, and are able to deal with setbacks. . . . But if praise is not handled properly, it can become a negative force, a kind of drug that, rather than strengthening students, makes them more passive and dependent on the opinion of others.*

Think how you would feel if you were praised for doing a task that you thought was pretty Mickey Mouse. You might conclude that the person who praised you thought that you were pretty dumb and that this task was a *stretch* for you. Rachel from the anecdote above might have been praised a lot and praised for her intelligence rather than her effort. Then when she encounters a problem, she backs off, worried that she will look dumb if she can't solve it. In experiments and in real life, children praised for their intelligence for doing tasks come to think of intelligence as a kind of "feather in their caps," rather than a tool to wield to help them solve a problem.

On the other hand, Erika doesn't back off in the face of a difficult task. Her behavior can be characterized as *adaptive*. Adaptive students aren't worried about saving face and looking smart because smarts have not been emphasized to them. Instead, the Erikas of the world don't give up easily, considering their first failure a sign that their intelligence has betrayed them. For them, initial failure is just a sign that they need to try harder and use some new strategies. It's easy to see why this style is called adaptive.

Praising children for effort keeps them at the task; praising children for intelligence makes them give up! Professor Dweck and her colleagues have found that even kindergartners respond differently when they are praised for being "smart" or "good." They act just like Rachel did, backing off when they hit setbacks and being unable to respond constructively.

Even when they are only 4 years of age, some children begin to give up easily when faced with a challenge. These children, as you guessed from Rachel's play in the doll corner, tend to have parents who berate them for small mistakes. Erika, on the other hand, is more likely to have parents who adjust their expectations to Erika's abilities, praise her for her effort, and let her choose a lot of her own challenges, rather than prescribing them all for her. Her parents are probably "authoritative"—warm and responsive, providing firm but appropriate expectations for her. Rachel's parents, by contrast, may well be "authoritarian" or coercive—conveying to her the idea that she can't manage things by herself. A third type of parent, the "indulgent" or "permissive" parent, might praise the child for everything she does, creating a false sense of self-esteem that will sooner or later result in that coworker of yours whose fault it never is. Which kind of parent are you? Does your partner have the same style?

So is the message not to praise? Not at all! But learning has to be viewed as a *process*, not the validation of one's ability. Professor Dweck urges us not to tell students that they are smart because it makes them de-pendent—hooked on—the praise, with failure being a sign of weakness! The way to make children learn to persevere is to rave about their strate-gies, their perseverance, their concentration, and their follow-through. And if children succeed readily, we should apologize for giving them a task too Mickey Mouse for them, rather than giving them the idea that we look for perfection on easy tasks. Praising intelligence to create acad-emic self-esteem turns out to be one of the biggest myths around!

REVISITING THE MYTHS

John B. Watson's famous claims notwithstanding, children bring lots to the table of self-construction. Nature has made our children unique, so that we can already identify certain tendencies in their personalities in the first few months of life. Babies are not little lumps of clay. By the same token, though, Watson was right to think that caregivers do have an important role to play in shaping children's sense of self. The most important way we influence that character is by our interactions with our children. By caring for them, by talking to them, by playing with them—they are learning fundamental lessons about their physical, social/emotional, and intellectual selves. They learn about their racial and gender identities, how to manage their emotions, and about their ability to make good moral judgments.

In other words, it is a myth to think we are *all-powerful* in shaping our children's sense of self. And it is a myth, too, to think that if we tell them all the time how smart they are, they will have more confidence. Children need to be praised for their effort, not for their intelligence. As we have shown, children construct their concept of self slowly over time. And that development occurs on many planes, from the physical self to the social/emotional self, to the intellectual self. We, as the child's parent or caregiver, can support and nurture this process. The next section suggests a few strate-gies for helping this to happen.

BRINGING THE LESSONS HOME

If we recognize that we do indeed play a role in children's evolving sense of self, then we must use this power wisely.

Pay attention to how you talk *about* your children in front of them. Most parents think that small children lack an awareness of who they are and don't know when they are being talked about. It's true that 18-month-olds have a spoken vocabulary of only about 50 words, which expands to about 200 at around 24 months. But psychologists have discovered that children *understand* much more language than they are capable of producing. We, the authors, have conducted research on language comprehension, and it's surprising how much even young children know. For example, toddlers at 17 months who say virtually nothing can understand five- and six-word sentences like "Where's Big Bird kissing Cookie Monster?" Just because your toddler isn't yet speaking doesn't mean he doesn't understand lots of what you say. If toddlers hear us talking about them in pejorative terms, this may affect their self-concept.

There is an old joke about two psychiatrists who pass each other on the street. Each one says "hello" and each smiles as they pass. Then each one thinks, "I wonder what he meant by that." If adults—even those of us who are not psychiatrists—worry and wonder about what people mean when they say things to us, imagine how our young children must feel! Knowing much less language than we do and not being capable yet of processing irony, they draw much of their sense of who they are from how we talk about and to them. "Oh, good job!" "What a pretty girl you are!" All these remarks are grist for the mill of defining self. For this reason, and because children's language understanding far exceeds what they say, it is important to be careful about what you say to and about your child in her presence.

Treat your child as an individual. This advice is particularly difficult to follow after you have already had a child or two, since you already have expectations and patterns established. The trick is to let your child be, taking into account that he or she might not approach the world as you do. One of the hardest things in parenting is parenting a child whose temperament is not much like your own. If you were shy as a child and your child is outgoing, that might be delightful but strange for you. If you were outgoing and your child is shy and slow to warm up, that might make you feel even more uncomfortable. Try not to force your children to do things that they are uncomfortable with; instead, simply offer encouragement. Some children just need more time to adjust to a range of things. If you show children how much fun it can be to try what they are not so sure about, they may volunteer the next time.

Let your children know that anything is possible. If the research shows that children figure out on their own what boys and girls—and men and women—can do, then exposing children to the range of things men and women actually do will help them to broaden their thinking. Don't be surprised, though, if at first your child denies that daddies can be nurses! However, the more they see of women doing "masculine" things and men doing "feminine" things, the more they will adapt their concepts. Regardless of what your children ultimately choose to be when they grow up, it's healthy for them to know that their choices aren't limited by virtue of their genders. Point out nonstereotypical and overlapping roles to your child every now and then by saying things like "Did you see that lady driving the truck?" and "Do you know that Dr. Judy — your pediatrician—is also a mommy?"

Talk with your children about feelings. Some of the self you become is related to how you have been treated and spoken to. If I can help you interpret events in the world, and help you understand why Victor got upset when you broke his toy, you will become a better person. Feelings are on the inside. When parents talk to children about feelings, they help bring them outside, in the light of day, where they can be examined and evaluated and understood. There are no kits to be found in the stores for making a child a better, more empathic person because that kind of learning happens only through interaction with significant others. We need to be there for our children when they need us, to help them interpret their own feelings and actions and the behavior and emotions of others. The rush to transform cognitive functioning to get our children into the Ivy League and ultimately the top of their professions will be a wasted effort if we don't actively involve ourselves in their everyday nurturing. What good will it be if the child becomes a miserable "successful" human being, unhappy, unable to regulate his emotions, unable to understand why people act the way they do? Talking about emotions has long-term consequences for adjustment and success in life.

Recognize that emotional intelligence correlates to success in life. The emotional self matters, and it matters a lot. Daniel Goleman's book *Emotional Intelligence* made this very point and made it well. It doesn't matter how smart you are and how well you did on your SATs. If you can't figure out how to get along with people, read their signals, and take their feelings into consideration, you may be a failure in life—

or at least fail to reach the heights. In his book, Dr. Goleman interviewed psychologist Howard Gardner of Harvard University, who has also emphasized the importance of emotional intelligence for making one's way successfully in life. Professor Gardner talked about "intrapersonal intelligence," or our knowledge of ourselves, our feelings, and how we use these to guide our behavior. On the other hand, "interpersonal intelligence" is our knowledge of others: our ability to perceive their moods, desires, motivations. Both are essential to making a successful life. Professor Gardner put it succinctly when he said, "Many people with IQs of 160 work for people with IQs of 100, if the former have poor intrapersonal intelligence and the latter have a high one. And in the day-to-day world no intelligence is more important than the interpersonal. If you don't have it, you'll make poor choices about who to marry, what job to take, and so on."

In other words, success in life encompasses far more than a high IQ or an impressive score on the SATs. And yet, in the hothouse environment adults have created for many children, the emphasis on developing the intellectual side of the self has eclipsed the important component of developing the self's crucial, emotional side. But since our world is filled with people, and since, first and foremost, we all want our children to be happy, perhaps it is time to recognize that there are things science tells us that we can do to foster happy, well-adjusted children. And maybe the balance should shift to concern over the quality of the sense of self that our children can construct—with our help.

CHAPTER + 8

GETTING TO KNOW YOU:
HOW CHILDREN DEVELOP SOCIAL INTELLIGENCE

AMANDA IS AN UNDERWRITER for Cigna. Jeff is a stock-broker. They are both thrilled to be parents. Yet they worry that they will not be able to provide enough "quality time" for their 4-year-old daughter, Courtney. They bought all of the books and the educational toys, and they are careful to schedule as much productive time as they can during the evenings and weekends. The results have been very satisfying. Courtney has learned all the letters of the alphabet and can now read short books. She is mastering Suzuki violin and can even add and subtract small numbers. Amanda and Jeff are very proud parents, but they now have a new concern. With such a good start from home, how will Courtney fare in kindergarten? Will she be bored by the other children who are not as advanced in music and reading? Will she be turned off by school? She already had some problems in preschool, where she was bullied by some of the children. Jeff and Amanda figured the bullying was a kind of jealousy because Courtney was so far ahead of those children. They worry that the same thing might happen in kindergarten. How can they protect Courtney while ensuring her educational success in a stimulating en-vironment?

SOCIAL SKILLS 101

Jeff and Amanda have responded like many of us do—with our focus on our children's intellectual growth and little emphasis on their social development. In fact, as parents, we often assume that our children's intellectual development needs nurturing but that their social development will take care of itself. We think that social skills are not something our children need to *learn*. Since social and emotional development are not as scripted as is academic learning, they seem much less important to us. After all, social development just happens, doesn't it?

But are these assumptions true? We don't think so. If you reflect for a moment on what it takes to manage social contacts, you'll begin to realize that negotiating your way through social situations can be a minefield. It requires regulating your own emotions (for example, you've learned that having a tantrum never helps your cause). It requires the ability to understand the emotions and social cues of others (do people have to put on their pajamas before you realize it's time to leave?). It requires the ability to express yourself to others and hopefully get them to do what you want them to do (since you have learned that people do not respond well to "orders"). And it involves learning to get along with people you just do not like (avoiding your supervisor at work, for example, is well-nigh impossible). Talk about ensuring your child's success!

It's widely believed in our culture that being happy and having friends have nothing to do with how you do in school. We tend to think of the "dorky" children as smart but not social. *Star Trek*'s Mr. Spock offers a perfect example: He is very smart, but makes social gaffes. Surprisingly, however, research shows just the opposite of what is presented in the media. The more popular children are also the ones who do better in school. In her widely respected book, *Self-Regulation in Early Childhood: Nature and Nurture*, Professor Martha Bronson of Boston College describes a variety of studies that show that peer interaction skills and acceptance by your peers are associated with higher levels of functioning both in school and in later life. Believe it or not, the extent to which kindergartners make new friends and are accepted by their classmates predicts how much they will participate in the classroom activities and even how independently they will work at more academic tasks. This means that the more social children are also the more independent learners. As kindergartners forge new friendships, they also seem to integrate themselves better into the learning environment in ways that foster academic competence.

Research tells us that social skills do indeed have to be learned. Social intelligence does not come for free. It is gained on the "job"—that is, through meaningful interaction with others in life. What children become when they grow up is in large part a result of the way we interact with them at home, at child care, and at school.

Given the pervasive overemphasis we see on enhancing children's IQs, it's not surprising that children's social intelligence may be suffering. (In fact, a new field of psychology and education is currently developing to teach social skills to children—*not* to children who have demonstrated serious problems, but to normal children who could benefit from learning some basic social techniques that harried parents have failed to help them develop.) Children learn from how their parents treat them, and how their parents treat others. Then they practice on their peers. Preschool and kindergarten are largely about the pleasures—and perils—of that practice. It's also where teachers and parents provide the social scaffolding to support children's budding social talents.

THE CONCENTRIC CIRCLES OF SOCIAL LEARNING

We learn to be social by moving through an ever-widening set of relationships, comparable to a set of concentric circles. Inside the first circle, babies begin to distinguish people from other objects. In the second circle, which surrounds the first, babies become aware of and then share the emotions of others. Finally, in the next circle, babies come to appreciate that others think differently and have different perspectives from theirs. In this chapter, we'll trace social learning from infancy and demonstrate how the mundane interactions of everyday life are the lessons that shape our children into mensches or menaces.

OTHERS AS PHYSICAL BEINGS

At the most basic level, babies need to be able to separate people from other objects in their world. Luckily, evolution seems to have provided several features for living things that make them quite attractive to infants.

For example, babies like physical symmetry, and this can be seen in their preference for faces. In laboratory tests, researchers placed two pictures side by side: One was a picture of a face where the features had been scrambled, and the second was a picture of that same face with the features unscrambled. The researchers found that babies preferred to look at the unscrambled face. Tiny babies, soon after birth, easily discriminated between the scrambled and unscrambled faces and spent more time looking at the pictures that had the two eyes symmetrically placed atop the nose and one-third of the way down from the hairline.

If you were going to "build" a baby, it makes sense that you would want it to be attracted to the face and features of the creatures (parents) that would care for it. This seems to be exactly what nature has done. As a purely physical matter, humans have all of the right features to make babies attracted to them. Given how helpless human babies are relative to other newborns in the animal world, it is good that babies look toward adults and find them a little more appealing than couches and clouds.

When you build that baby, however, you might want to have babies do more than just find their elders appealing. You might want to build babies that are primed for a social connection with the other humans that inhabit their little worlds. The first kernel of such a connection with these physical others has been investigated under the research label of imitation. Professor Andrew Meltzoff at the University of Washington is the expert in baby imitation. He rocked the scientific world when he discovered that even *newborn* babies—at just 2 days old—can *imitate* facial expressions. This is truly amazing considering the mental gymnastics involved.

Discovering Hidden Skills | Imitation

Ages: Birth to 2 months

Hold your new baby on your lap. While looking closely at her, stick out your tongue about 10 times slowly and see if she answers back by sticking her tongue out at you. If it works, this may be one of the only times that you will enjoy having someone stick their tongue out at you! Or try opening your mouth wide about 10 times slowly and see if your baby can do that. It is exciting to know that your newborn is already able to mimic your actions, thereby communicating with you.

What's so remarkable about the baby's ability to make this connection with another person? Why was the finding that babies could imitate facial expressions such startling news? Let's examine this phenomenon a bit more closely. When you stick out your tongue for a baby, the baby sees your face and this odd protrusion toward the bottom of your symmetrical face. Indeed, you look rather silly as you pump your tongue in and out of your mouth. When the baby imitates this gesture, however, he has to translate what he saw into some motor program so that his tongue now goes in and out, too.

Clearly, babies are active, contributing members to the social exchanges they have with their parents and caregivers. In the crucible of these simple social exchanges devoid of true content, babies find a sense of shared experience. This reciprocity in social exchange helps to create a sense of "you and I"—the sense that there are ways of connecting with other people.

This social connection is a key avenue for learning about others. And we do much to bring babies into the social fold. Watch any parent and baby interact and you will see that adults make a number of adjustments to their conversations when talking with babies. First, we imitate what we see the babies do. If we did that with other adults, it would be considered rude. Second, we exaggerate our facial expressions—also something that would seem weird if we did this in conversation with other adults. We open our eyes and our mouths very wide. We lift our eyebrows high enough for them to almost join our hairlines, and we radiate excitement with brilliant smiles. Our exaggerations are actually part of our lesson plan—we sense that babies need these magnifiers in order to engage with us.

Others as Emotional Beings

Have you ever been in a room full of babies, say at the pediatrician's office? When one starts to cry, it can set off a virtual chorus of sirens—all babies literally screaming at the same time. This emotional contagion is the first sign that babies have empathy—they can become aware of the emotions of others and feel the others' emotions vicariously. Without empathy, we'd be inhumane sociopaths, doing whatever worked for us and not caring a whit about how it affected others. Empathy is what motivates us to be considerate of others even when it doesn't benefit us. And empathy starts in the cradle.

Sherry, director of a preschool in Connecticut, watched intently as the 22-month-olds came in from their early-morning walk in the snow. The first who tumbled in was tired and whiny and began to cry. The second who came in looked exhausted, too (snow outfits weigh a lot!), but he was very concerned about his friend's tears. He toddled over to retrieve his own blanket and then gave it to his friend. "This is one of the reasons why it is such a pleasure to run an infant care program," Sherry remarked. "Even 2-year-olds can be sensitive to the feelings of other babies! They don't talk much yet, but they sure know when somebody feels bad and they often try to fix it."

Research in the laboratory supports what Sherry has noticed in the preschool. When researchers asked the mothers of 2-year-olds to feign sadness, their babies did amazing things. Babies offered mom their blankets, tried to distract her, and hugged her to get her to feel better. How do we come to be emotionally connected to others? How do we learn to regulate our emotions so that we don't hit or slam things when we are upset? Within the field of developmental psychology, attachment and emotional regulation are two widely studied areas.

Discovering Hidden Skills | Empathy

Ages: 1 year to 2½ years

See if you can observe the development of empathy in your own home. Make believe that you hurt yourself and that you are crying. What does your child do? By 2½, most babies will respond to someone else's sadness. If your child doesn't respond with empathy, don't fear that he or she will wind up in Sing-Sing! Your child may just be able to tell that you are "faking" it.

Attachment: The First Relationships Are Foundational

Getting baby off to a good start in the social realm is easy and requires no special classes or videos. Interaction is the key—and lots of it. It's important, however, that this interaction be responsive; it needs to follow the baby's cues. So when Aunt Gertrude says that there's no need to over-stimulate the baby, and that you talk to him and play with him too much and that's why he won't go to sleep for you, she might actually be right. Research clearly shows that babies thrive on social interaction when it hinges on or is in response to *their* social bids. Babies seem to let us know when they want to interact or not. A baby who looks at you and vocalizes is saying, "Talk to me, play with me." A baby who turns away from you is saying, "I'm tired; let me be alone for a while." These adaptive social interactions form the foundations for conversations and for subsequent social relationships. It's all in the timing. When we are sensitive to our children's needs and are responsive to their preverbal requests, we model how to take turns and to be engaging.

Mother Love or Mother Grub?

Babies like to interact with us, and they quickly develop affection for their caregivers. Babies are primed by Mother Nature to develop that strong affection and tie that we feel for special people in our lives. Psychologists call this attachment. By the second half of their 1st year, infants have become attached to familiar people—not only their mothers—who have responded to their needs for physical care and stimulation.

Sigmund Freud was among the first to say that an infant's emotional tie to the mother is the foundation for all later relationships. But he thought that love grew from the fact that a mother satisfied a baby's hunger. B. F. Skinner's behaviorist theory also posited that feeding was at the core of attachment relationships—but for slightly different reasons. Skinner believed that a baby associated the reduction of the hunger drive with the mother, who fed the baby and removed that tension.

In the 1940s, however, psychologists discovered that what was absolutely central to babies' emotional well-being was not so much *feeding*, but the *consistent involvement* of caregivers. Indeed, the question of whether infants needed mother love rather than just mother "grub" was put to a direct test with monkeys in what is now a classic study in the literature. The study was conducted in the 1950s by a young professor at the University of Wisconsin, Harry Harlow.

When Monkeys Choose Their Moms

Professor Harlow came up with a test that pitted Freud's and Skinner's theories of mother "grub" against one that examined the role of caring, comfort, and nurturing. Professor Harlow and his colleagues reared monkeys with two kinds of "mothers." Picture a wire mesh cylinder leaning at a 45-degree angle on a stand. In the mother's "chest" was a place to embed a bottle so that just the nipple stuck out. The other "mother" had the same shape and size but offered no embedded bottle. This mother, though, was covered with a huggable terry cloth fabric. Both "mothers" had plastic smiley faces. To the world's surprise, the monkeys made a clear choice. When both mothers were present, the monkeys would cling to the terry cloth "surrogate" mother and leave the other mother behind. If they were hungry, they would climb on the wire mesh mother, feed as fast as they could, and jump back to Mother Terry. Close, physical comfort was part of what babies needed to feel secure.

The implications were clear: Being fed by your mother was not what attached you to her. Rather, it is consistent, close nurturing that matters in early relationships.

How Does Attachment Develop?

The findings with monkeys had an enormous impact on a psychoanalyst, Dr. John Bowlby, who would become the father of attachment theory. In his books, Dr. Bowlby set forth the groundwork for a new vision of attachment and sketched out the stages that attachment relationships go through. According to Dr. Bowlby, the beginnings of attachment occur within the first 6 months of a baby's life with a variety of built-in signals the baby uses to keep her caregiver engaged. The baby cries, gazes into your eyes, smiles, and even grasps on to your pinkie finger. The baby is exploring you in ways that will promote interaction and pave the way for her attachment to you.

In the next couple of months, the baby really begins to show who her friends are—she smiles and babbles more freely with mom and dad than with Uncle Oscar, whom she rarely sees because he lives in Madagascar.

Once the relationship is established and becomes predictable, the toddler will even let his favorite caregivers leave (sometimes) with the assurance that they will return. In Dr. Bowlby's terms, the process that ensues is one in which children are constructing an "internal working model" of the availability of attachment figures. At first in his writings, Dr. Bowlby argued that the attachment figure had to be the mother. But significant amounts of research have now been done to suggest that babies become attached not to a single person but to a network of people. When mom isn't around, baby is happy playing with dad, and when both go out, baby can be just fine with a caring, sensitive, and responsive caregiver or babysitter. In fact, infants seem to establish emotional relationships with a number of people—just like we do—and, like us, they like some people better than others.

Further research has also made clear that the nature of early attachment relationships can have a significant impact on children's emotional and academic adjustment. The University of Wisconsin's Professor Alan Sroufe and his colleagues have done a number of studies that indicate that children who have good attachment relationships as infants make better adjustments in a number of areas later on. For example, they found that 2-year-olds who had secure attachments when they were babies had more complicated and advanced make-believe play and worked harder and more persistently when given new problems. At age 4, children with secure attachments as babies showed more empathy and had higher self-esteem than children who had problematic attachment relationships. But the link between the security of early attachment and later adjustment seems to hold only if children *continue* to be in loving and supportive circumstances. In other words, having a good attachment in infancy gives you a great start but can't carry you through life. You still need to be treated sensitively and responsively as you grow up if you are to develop favorably. And circumstances change: Families divorce, people lose jobs, relatives die, and mom takes a full-time job. All these stressors impact on the parent-child relationship. Because the nature of attachment can change with such stressors, the question of stability has been hotly debated. Attachment is probably more stable if you are from a home with fewer stressors and less stable if there is more change and risk in the environment. Fortunately, it works the other way, too: Children who have less secure attachments as infants are not doomed. That is, while children's attachments are not set in stone early in life, and the lack of a secure relationship may set the course for infants to have more difficulties later on, the infant is still capable of developing secure relationships with others as these others become available or even more responsive.

Working Mothers and Day Care

Research on attachment was unfolding at exactly the same time that mothers started entering the workforce in record numbers. With both mother and father in the workforce, families had to grapple with the central question of child care: Will our babies still love us and be attached to us if they spend all day with other adults? And even if they are attached to us—their parents—will the quality of the attachment relationship suffer? Is there some magical number of hours below which child care is acceptable and above which children are in danger of disrupting their primary attachment relationships? By the beginning of the 21st century, 66 percent of the homes with children under age 6 had two parents in the workforce. Child care is not just a family issue; it's a national issue.

Throughout the 1980s and 1990s these questions were scrutinized in the scientific literature. And by the turn of the century, there were answers to some of these oft-asked questions. The first answer is consistent with current tides in attachment research. Scientists know that infants attach to more than one caregiver and that they are developing emotional relationships with multiple caregivers at once. Thus, it should come as no surprise that children who are in child care—even a lot of child care—are still attached to their parents. In fact, an ongoing landmark study that one of us (Kathy) works on, the National Institute for Child Health and Human Behavior Study of Early Child Care and Youth Development, finds that even when children are in child care for more than 30 hours per week, the family contributes more to the child's social and cognitive well-being than does the child care arrangement. Parents matter, and children are attached to parents even when children are in care.

Surely there must be some compromise, you wonder. Are these children less well-attached? Again, the answer appears to be *no*. Sixty-seven percent of children in child care are securely attached—the same number identified in children not in child care. Further, the children in child care—at least with child care of adequate quality—appear to be within the normal ranges both academically and socially. This latter point, however, is not without contention. Some experts hold that children who are in child care show some emotional problems, in that they "act out" more or are more aggressive than those in fewer hours of care. We briefly digress to review that finding.

In April of 2000, headlines blared study findings that time spent in child care yields *better school readiness but more bullies*. Closer inspection of the data, however, reveals that children who are in child care are *not* destined to become the classroom bullies and are *not* at risk for violent behavior. They are, however, at the high end of normal when it comes to teasing and hitting. The operative term here is "normal." When a child is with a group of children and wants to get the toy she has her eye on, she has to be assertive or she will become the preschool "wimp." Whether this will translate into more pushy children or children who are more likely to become CEOs is the real question. What it does highlight, however, is the point of this chapter: Children need to *learn* how to negotiate social situations, and parents, caregivers, and teachers need to learn more about how to facilitate this process.

What, then, does the attachment literature tell us about working parents? It tells us that parents have a range of options about how to care for their children. If parents choose to stay at home, then as long as they are sensitive and responsive, their babies will become securely attached. If they choose to put their children in child care, the centers they choose should be especially sensitive and responsive for newborns and clean, safe, and stimulating as the children get older. If you offer both a high-quality home environment and a high-quality child care arrangement, your child will form numerous emotional bonds with you and with the caregivers. And the bond between parent and child will always be the strongest of these bonds.

Assessing Child Care Quality

By doing a bit of homework, you can assure that you're putting your child into the best possible facility. There are many different types of child care arrangements in the United States, ranging from care by relatives in your home or theirs to in-home care by nannies, to center care. In each case, you want to make sure that the child care arrangement that you choose not only is convenient for you, but is one that provides a strong sense of well-being and security for your child. High quality is essential for building strong attachments, so that your child feels nurtured and loved even when you aren't around.

Across the different kinds of child care arrangements, there are certain things to look for. The highest-quality places have caregivers who are more highly educated (with a BA in education or a degree in child development) and have more experience on the job. They also have low child-to-staff ratios. There should be one caregiver for no more than four infants. For toddlers through 4-year-olds, there should be one caregiver for no more than 10 children. These numbers differ by state, with some allowing many more children to each caregiver. In some states, child care facilities need to be licensed; those with licenses may well be better than those without. High-quality environments are those that are clean and that establish routines rather than allow free-for-alls.

Interview the caregiver. That's important. And get a feel for how both the caregiver and the facility operate. Ask about what typically happens on a routine day. Ask how long the caregivers have been working there. High-quality child care has lower caregiver turnover than low-quality environments. If you are touring a center, a good clue that the place is responsive to children's needs is if the caregiver interrupts her conversation with you to respond to a child's query. High-quality care happens when the caregivers are considerate of your child—sensitive to her needs and responsive to her bids for attention. High-quality care is found in a place that offers an age-appropriate and stimulating curriculum, like books for all ages; blocks for children 3, 4, and 5; and dress-up corners. It is not a place in which caregivers smoke or watch TV with your child all day.

If your child care arrangement has the markings of a high-quality environment, then your child will probably form good emotional bonds with the caregivers as she extends her social and emotional network to include others.

Using Our Emotions as a Guide for Behavior

Attachment is the formation of an emotional bond. And our initial attachments may be said to be a road map for how our relationships with others will work, as well as what kinds of relationships we will choose as we get older. Especially when we are young, we use the attachment figure as an important source of how we should feel about the world. This is called social referencing. By as early as 9 months of age, we interpret the meanings of the emotional expressions of our parents and caregivers.

Social referencing is a sophisticated ability for children. Think for a moment about what it entails. It means "I know that you see this object (knowledge that the other can see). And I know that your evaluation of it may differ from mine (that you are separate from me and make independent evaluations). In fact, your evaluation of the object is very important for me to gauge so that I can act appropriately (flee? explore?)

in the face of this novel object"—as you can see, a pretty important survival skill.

Emotion Regulation: What Kind of Parent Am I?

We not only provide the emotional interpretation of events for our children, but also help them to *regulate* their own emotions as they respond to events. This is how children learn to deal with others and the world around them. A beautiful example of the different ways in which we help our children learn to regulate their emotions comes from a study done at Temple University in Philadelphia by Professors Amanda Morris and Jennifer Silk when they were graduate students. Consider the following scenario.

Allison is a curly-topped 4-year-old whose parents have invited a research team to their home. Morris and Silk introduce themselves and explain the experiment. Then Allison is told that she will get a prize at the end of their visit. In fact, Allison is pretty excited when she's given a chance to look at 10 potential "prizes" and to rank them from the best prize to the worst prize—from a truck or doll to a broken pair of sunglasses, to a pair of socks. Allison is told further that she will get the prize she liked the best.

After Allison performs the activity, she happily waits, because she knows that it's time for her prize. But—oops. Something goes dramatically wrong. The researchers say they have made a mistake and they have to give Allison the prize that she ranked as dead last—a pair of brown socks. Hey—this is not fair. There has been a *big* mistake.

Now, here's the real research question. How does the parent help the child cope with this disappointment, and what does that tell us about how children learn to regulate their emotions? Imagine that Allison is your child. Of the four types of parental responses the researchers observed, what kind of parent are you? (1) Do you shift your child's attention away from the disappointing prize toward the nice wrapping the prize came in? (2) Do you comfort your child by holding her or verbally soothing her? (3) Do you "reframe" the situation, putting the socks on your hands and making them into a puppet or suggesting you give the socks to another child who might really like them? (4) Do you encourage your child to change the situation, for instance, by talking to the researchers and telling them that she got the wrong prize?

It turns out that the strategies we use with our children can lead to distinctly different emotional responses in them. Shifting the child's attention and cognitive reframing were associated with lower levels of both sadness and anger. These children were learning to see the silver lining. This was especially true if the children perceived their parents to be warm and responsive to them. Surprisingly, the child who was encouraged to change the situation by talking to the experimenter had more anger and sadness than those in the other conditions. Why? You might think that these children were learning to stick up for themselves. Researchers worry, however, that if you can't control your anger and if you merely vent, you are not regulating your emotion in a positive way. It's okay to complain, but it is not okay to lash out. The most important thing that we learn from this research, though, is that what we, as parents and caregivers, do matters. We help our children regulate their emotions by working with them and by serving as their models.

Teachable Moments

Coping with Frustration

There are many times when our children are disappointed with what they get—whether it is at their favorite fast-food restaurant, when the kiddy meal isn't big enough, or on the ball field, when they aren't picked for the right team. Once you are aware of these moments, you can use them as an opportunity for modeling how to handle frustration. Talk the moment out with your child. Let her know how you feel and work to solve the problem together. Ask, "What do you think we should do here? Should we buy another meal? Be happy that the meal was small so we have room for our Dairy Queen dessert?" Though disappointments are a fact of life, learning how to reframe them into something positive turns them into a growth experience.

OTHERS AS INTELLECTUAL BEINGS

Our world is built around our own and others' intentions. You stepped on my foot! Was it an accident? Was it on purpose? Were you seeking revenge for something I did? Babies start to learn about others' intentions quite early in life, and this is the beginning of their understanding that other people have minds.

To Share or Not to Share?

As they grow, babies start to learn how other people feel and think. If they really care about how others think, though, why aren't they better at sharing? After all, sharing isn't so hard—or is it? Sharing involves taking the perspective of the other, which is developmentally a fairly advanced task. Yet little is more important in the life of American mothers than having polite children who share.

A recent survey by the Zero to Three group, a research group at Harvard University, indicates that fully 51 percent of parents think that 15-month-olds should be able to share their toys. Yet nothing could be further from the truth. Even 2-year-olds are just not ready yet. Why?

Think about what is involved in sharing. It's no easy business for a child who is just learning about others. Okay, it's not even easy for us adults. Imagine that you are at work and using a great new pen that you treasure. A colleague comes up to you and says, "Wow! That really writes smoothly. Can I try it?" Also imagine that you are in the midst of some task of middle-level necessity. Do you push your colleague away? Do you turn your back on him and cover the pen with your body so he can't grab it? No, but your child—even up to age 6—might respond that way, because her ability to regulate her impulses is limited. You, however, graciously say, "Sure, give it a shot," and hand it over. Why did you do that?

Let's examine all that went on in your head to allow this act of sharing to occur. You are motivated to share for several reasons. First, you want to maintain good relations with your work peers. Second, you think that this is not a good person to alienate. After all, you might need his help in the future. And third, you are worried that you will appear petty and selfish if you don't share. Toddlers are just not capable of thinking in this complicated way. It involves thinking into the future. It involves assessing how others view them, and it involves controlling their impulses. They can barely control their drooling, let alone the impulse to grab something they want! So parents and caregivers—be patient. Your lessons are important. It just takes children some time before they can actually apply those lessons and see the world from the perspective of others.

A Matter of Perspective

Taking another's perspective is essential for sharing. It's also essential for showing empathy, let alone for becoming a nice human being. But when young children can show empathy is actually a thorny question.

There is a wonderful study by Professors Betty Repacholi and Alison Gopnik of the University of California at Berkeley showing that by 18 months, babies understand something about your desires and how these can be different from their own. In the study, babies were brought into the laboratory, which was well-stocked with broccoli and crackers. Would babies be able to take the researchers' likes and dislikes into consideration, seeing the food from the *researchers'* point of view?

The babies were 14 and 18 months old. With one group of babies (at each age), a researcher acted delighted with the taste of broccoli but disgusted with the taste of crackers. With another group of babies, the researcher did just the opposite: Crackers were her chocolate and broccoli tasted just the way George Bush Senior said it did—yuckie! Later, the babies were asked to share some food with the researcher. Donna, typical of the 14-month-olds, happily munching away on a cracker herself, offered only crackers, the type of food she preferred. In contrast, 18-month-old Steven gave the researcher whichever food he had seen her swoon over, *regardless* of his own preferences. This is a big deal. These babies recognized the desire of another and shared what they thought the other person wanted. Now, that's a matter of perspective.

Discovering Hidden Skills	Understanding Another Person's Perspective

Ages: 12 months to 24 months

Try this experiment every few months to see when your baby can take your preferences into consideration. While your baby is sitting in her high chair, offer two foods and be ecstatic about one when you demonstrate eating it, then show disgust for the other. Make sure it is very clear which food you like and which you don't. (You'd better pick something that you really don't want the baby to eventually eat when you eat the awful food, lest she remember your disgust!) Then put both foods down on the high-chair tray. Wait about 5 minutes and then ask the baby to feed you. Be sure to look in the baby's eyes and not at the tray where the food is so you don't give the baby any clues about which food you want. Does the baby feed you the food you like?

While babies might be able to understand another person's desires, that is a far cry from suggesting that babies really understand that people can have different beliefs than they have. Notice that when we have friends, we do more than just recognize their intents and desires—we try to see the world from their point of view. In fact, even recognizing that there can be more than one point of view is a serious developmental achievement. Researchers call that achievement the development of a *theory of mind*, or TOM.

Recognizing That Others Have Minds, Too

The abstract notion of other minds is a difficult one, but one that children must eventually grasp if they are going to share, tell the truth, and understand that they are not always right (we all know some people—usually ex-spouses—who have not yet achieved this milestone). Scientists who work in this area have developed a task to figure out just when children can pass that TOM hurdle. The task is called the false belief task, and children start to succeed on it around age 4. Let's look at the task to see what it tells us about the child's view of the mind of the other.

Here we meet 3-year-old Janice and her mother. The experimenter is showing her a box that has pictures of M&M's all over it, including the latest new color, a kind of Barney purple. She loves M&M's and sometimes convinces her mother to buy them for her at the store, so she has seen this box before. "What do you think is in the box?" the experimenter asks. This is a no-brainer. "M&M's!" she says with a big smile. She is, of course, correct. Then the researcher asks Janice's mother what she thinks is in the box. "M&M's," she says assertively. Then the scene changes.

Janice's mother is asked to leave the room for a moment and the researcher asks that they play a little trick. Instead of M&M's, the researcher suggests, let's put pencils in the M&M box. "What's in the box, Janice?" the researcher asks. "Pencils," she screams with delight. "Okay, when your mom comes back in the room, what will she think is in the box?"

That, of course, is the trick question. Will Janice answer correctly that her mom will think M&M's are in the box? After all, her mother never saw the trick switch. Or will Janice believe that her mother thinks there are pencils in the M&M box? If Janice says "pencils," Janice doesn't recognize much of a distinction between her mind and her mom's. The answer—drum roll, please!—is that Janice falsely concludes that her mother will say "pencils."

This experiment has been tried over and over again with different toys and different people (after all, some children have been led to believe that their moms know everything!). The bottom line is that, regardless of the specifics, 3-year-olds generally cannot pass this test, while 4-year-olds can. Four-year-olds achieve a theory of mind that eludes 3-year-olds.

Discovering Hidden Skills | The False Belief Task

Ages: 2 years to 5 years

Try the false belief task we described above. It's interesting to test children before they should pass (between 2 and 4 years) and after they should pass (older than 4) to prove this phenomenon to yourself. Find a box with a clear label that has a picture of the contents on it. You'll also need another adult or older child to play along. Go through the sequence as we have described it, with the child first naming the contents as you show them the box, naming the contents that the other adult sees, having the adult leave the room, and doing the bait and switch. Then ask the child what the adult will think is in the box when the adult returns. Will your child fail, naming the new, changed contents, or will your child pass, naming the contents the adult saw before the switch? Does your child realize yet that their knowledge is not necessarily shared by another mind?

A failure to take the perspective of others into account in this false belief task means, too, that misbehaviors by young children can never have a vengeful or vindictive quality. To do things out of spite (something some grownups are very good at) requires the following thought process: "I am angry at mommy for stopping me from doing (fill in the blank). Therefore, if I do (fill in the blank) anyway, mommy will feel really annoyed and I'll get back at her for stopping me in the first place." But if you can't conceive of mommy's mind, how can you figure all this out? How can you take her perspective and figure out what she will find annoying? You can't. Therefore, a young child can't act vengefully.

Unfortunately, not all parents appreciate their children's limitations at this age. The Zero to Three survey gave parents the following scenario to react to: Suppose a 12-month-old begins to turn the TV on and off while her parents are watching. How likely is it that the child is doing this because she is angry and trying to get back at her parents? They found that fully 39 percent of the parents they interviewed thought that 12-month-olds were capable of acting maliciously and with revenge on their minds.

Why does it matter what social cognitions parents hold about their children? Because the attributions that we link to our children's behavior control how we *respond* to them. In other words, if I think you are operating from spite, I may get really angry with you. I may even hit you. On the other hand, if I think you are just interested in fiddling with the button on the TV and find your behavior difficult to inhibit (even though I have said "No" three times), I may just remove you from the situation or try to distract you. To help children learn to interact with others appropriately, parents need to be sensitive to the natural limits of their children's abilities. This is also an issue with 2- and 3-year-olds' "lies."

Handling Those Childish Little Lies

If we grant that children cannot take the perspective of another mind until sometime around the age of 4, then we might not need to punish children for "lies" they tell, either. Consider little Alexandra, who looks up at her mother rather sheepishly and then looks down at the fragments of a china vase on the floor. "The wind came an' put it on the floor," Alexandra insists.

What is a lie? It is an attempt to manipulate what you think is in the mind of another, to alter their belief to something false, perhaps to protect yourself. ("I want you to think that the vase blew off the table, not that I broke it—which I did.") But children who cannot conceive of the contents of the mind of another cannot really be said to be lying. They are probably describing the situation as they *wish* it had occurred. That's not the same as trying to conceal the truth from you. Alexandra doesn't even understand what it takes to make someone have a false belief. As our colleagues Professor Alison Gopnik of the University of California at Berkeley and Professors Andrew Meltzoff and Patricia Kuhl of the University of Washington wrote, "Two- and 3-year-olds are such terrible liars, they hardly qualify as liars at all. A 3-year-old will stand on the other side of the street and yell back at you that he didn't cross it by himself."

Sometimes, though, if you are lucky and attentive, you might catch a glimpse of your child thinking about the existence of other minds. Author Roberta's son, Jordy, at almost 3, looked up at the moon from his stroller at dusk on a beautiful summer night and said, "Is us to them a moon?" Roberta was stunned. What Jordy was asking was about the perspective of the inhabitants of the moon!

PUTTING IT ALL TOGETHER: THE PHYSICAL, EMOTIONAL, AND INTELLECTUAL OTHER

What the information in the preceding pages tells us is that science has brought us a long way toward understanding how young children think about the people in their worlds. It takes time for children to learn about the various components that make up human beings: physical aspects, emotional qualities, and intangible intellectual powers. As adults, we still strive to understand how people feel and think (consider the divorce rate!). And if we were all equally successful at it, Dale Carnegie would be out of business. While the cradle for this knowledge is in infancy, it takes time, experience, and interactions with parents, caregivers, and other children to work it all out. If, as parents and caregivers, we understand how lengthy a process of development is involved in acquiring this knowledge, we can better comprehend some of our children's less desirable behaviors—like a failure to share or the tendency to tell little white lies. This knowledge helps us assume a new perspective on how our children treat others, why they might act the way they do, and how they form their friendships, a topic to be discussed in chapter 9.

In analyzing how children think and learn about other people, we hope to have dispelled the myth that social development simply takes care of itself and that we don't have to think about it. Caring adults provide an invaluable road map for directing children through the minefields of their emotional and social lives. And this is a process all of us work at all our lives. Overemphasizing the development of what's between the ears can wind up deemphasizing the development of what needs to be in the heart in order to foster happy, confident children who can cope with the disappointments and roadblocks life invariably metes out.

Bringing the Lessons Home

How can we help children blossom socially and emotionally? Read on for some specific tips.

Look for opportunities to discuss other people's feelings. By explaining how other people would feel if a particular act occurred, you teach your child to take the perspective of others. "If you hit Irving over the head with that truck, he will probably feel very bad and cry. Do you want that to happen?"

Creating a sensitive human being takes work! It often seems a lot easier to just stop vexing and dangerous toddler behavior without explaining what consequences would follow and why, and how someone would feel as a result. Of course, tomorrow someone will probably come out with a video that claims to teach your child how to work and play well with others. But that product would be a drop in the bucket compared with the power that comes from ongoing human relationships where both mind and heart are learning together. What fills the bucket is the *interaction* children and adults experience: a product of basic social need.

Watch your language. One way to bring up the perspectives of others is to ask your child about the characters in the stories you read together. Ask questions such as "How do you think this person (the character) feels? How would you feel if you were this person? What do you think the person's friends could do to help him to feel better?"

In fact, many of the current social and emotional programs that teach children about how to be a good person use games in which children adopt different perspectives. One example is the Interpersonal Cognitive Problem Solving program for elementary school children, which was developed by Professor Myrna Shure of Drexel University in Philadelphia. After the adult shows the children pictures of scenes or verbally describes scenarios such as a fight in school or a moment of frustration, the children are asked, "How do you think this person felt in the story? How might you feel if you were that person? How would you want others to react to you?" At Pennsylvania State University, Professor Mark Greenberg created another program of this type called PATHS (Promoting Alternative Thinking Strategies) that helps children talk about their feelings. These programs have been maximally effective in reducing aggressive behavior and are training children on how to understand others' minds. They are now used widely in school programs.

Explain to your child that there are causes for people's feelings. Research by Professor Judy Dunn and her colleagues at Pennsylvania State University examined the conversations that fifty 33-month-old children had in their homes with their mothers about feelings and about what causes them. For example, a mother might say, "You broke my glass (the cause) and that makes me sad (the outcome)." Such conversations were just what Professor Dunn and her colleagues looked for in the parent-child dialogues.

She found that at 40 months, children differed widely in their appreciation of emotions and other minds. The results of this study tell us that talk about emotions and what causes emotions impacts children's developing theory of mind. Hearing an explanation for others' behavior does at least two things. It may help stunt the natural anger that arises when you are thwarted so you can respond more constructively. It may also help you look for such mitigating explanations on your own in future altercations. And these differences, in turn, will influence how well children interact with their peers and teachers.

Stop bullying in its tracks. The extreme example of children who are not thinking of the welfare of others is the bully. If your child is frequently the target of bullies, it may be a sign that she is less socially competent and, therefore, has fewer friends and is seen as vulnerable. It turns out that children who are more socially competent and who have more friends are less likely to be bullied.

Researchers have determined that both the bullies and the bullied tend to have certain typical characteristics: The majority of victims, for instance, reinforce bullies by giving in to their demands, crying, assuming defensive postures, and failing to fight back. Victims tend to have a history of overly intrusive parenting, with parents who are controlling and overprotective. These parenting behaviors prompt anxiety, low self-esteem, and dependency, which combine to radiate vulnerability. Bullies often bank on their victim's dependency and vulnerability; they know the other child won't fight back. This makes the bully feel powerful. Of course, bullies have their own social deficits. They tend to come from families where there is little warmth or affection. The families also report trouble sharing their feelings. Sometimes parents of bullies have very punitive and rigid discipline styles. Finally, bullies feel less discomfort than average children at the thought of causing pain and suffering.

So what can be done for bullies and their victims? Preschools and kindergartens where peer socialization is integrated into the curriculum are good places to start helping them. Anxious, withdrawn children will benefit greatly from developing just one good friendship. And even when they have conflicts with their peers (yes, conflict is inevitable), they'll be learning valuable lessons in how to interpret social cues accurately. But in addition to the teaching of social skills at school, it's also important to evaluate the relationship you have with your child, especially if you suspect that he's a bully. Remember: Bullies tend to come from families where there's a lack of affection or little sharing of feelings. Take the time to ask your child how he's feeling and to *really* listen to his answer. When he expresses anger or rage, work with him to help him regulate his negative emotions and find peaceful ways to resolve them. Finally, when he talks about problems he's having with his peers, brainstorm with him to come up with skillful ways he could resolve them.

Finally, children who are not bullies or victims have a powerful role to play in shaping the behavior of other children. Teach your children to speak up on behalf of children being bullied. "Don't treat her that way; it's not nice." "Hitting is not a good way to solve problems. Let's find a teacher and talk about what happened." For more examples and role-play situations, check out Sherryll Kraizer's *The Safe Child Book*.

Make space for social time. Children sometimes just need to hang out with others or to be by themselves. It might seem as if they are doing "nothing," but there's a lot to learn from unscheduled time on their own or with other children. Children need to be able to be spontaneous—to be able to just goof off! Creating playdates for our children helps them diversify their social world and develop additional social tools for dealing with a greater variety of social challenges. And social interactions give you opportunities for discussing emotional situations and others' perspectives. This cannot be obtained on the fly, in the car between activities, but only from real social interaction that you are present to observe and comment on and coach as the occasion arises.

If your child is in child care or preschool, be sure to build

strong connections with your child's caregiver or teacher. You want your child's emotions taken seriously when he is not with you, too, and you want that emotional coaching going on whenever a conflict comes up. If you talk with the caregiver on a daily basis about how your child is doing and ask questions about how he gets along with his peers and how disagreements are handled, you'll have a better sense of whether emotional coaching and mentoring is going on. Get in the habit of building strong ties to the people whom your child spends time with. Just as it makes a difference when children get consistent messages from their parents, it's important that the messages they receive from their child care providers are consistent as well.

While there are many things we can do to foster social development, here are some general suggestions for helping your children to tune in to their own feelings.

Avoid ignoring or belittling your child's feelings. Although often you'd wish such moments would just go away, times of emotional upset can be understood as key opportunities for teaching children how to avoid or resolve such situations, while also taking the feelings of others into consideration. View these times as opportunities to teach your children how to make lemonade out of lemons, while still allowing them to experience their feelings of hurt or disappointment. A versatile recipe for lemonade will be very useful for dealing with life's inevitable frustrations.

Try to see the world through your children's eyes. Once you do, you'll recognize that the things that cause our children pain are often different from the things that cause us, as adults, pain. You don't want to treat your children any differently than you would want to be treated when you express your emotions. How would you feel if you confided in a friend about something that bothered you and she made fun of you and laughed? Make a point of teaching your child that it's okay to show negative emotion, such as sadness or fear. Likewise, try to demonstrate positive ways of coping with your own anger and negative feelings. Remember: Your children are watching you for lessons on regulating their emotions.

The bottom line for this chapter is to talk to your children and invite them to talk to you. The more you try to understand how they feel and help them understand how an event happened, the more coping skills your child will develop. And, as we have documented, social skills are *essential* for doing well, both in school and in life.

CHAPTER + 9

PLAY:
THE CRUCIBLE OF
LEARNING

MARIANNE MYERS, A SUPERVISOR for a megasize office supply store, crunches on a piece of toast and scrutinizes the big calendar anchored by magnets to the refrigerator. Her husband, Dennis, a landscaper, gulps his orange juice and heads for the door. "I know! I'll take a late lunch, pick her up at 3, and take her to Gymboree. It's okay. I've got it covered," Dennis says.

"And then . . ." Marianne prompts. She wants to write it out for him because last week he brought Alyson home after Gymboree instead of to the birthday party at Ginny Rymer's house. And their time at home was completely unproductive. Alyson just played with her stuffed animals. And despite her repeated requests, Dennis didn't join in her fantasy play, thinking that she was doing just fine on her own. Instead, he tried to catch up on his work.

"And then . . ." Dennis hesitates, hoping he does have it right today. ". . . to Mrs. Majors."

"No, dear," Marianne says as gently as she can. "We had to switch her violin class to today because of the trip to the zoo tomorrow. I know it's hard to keep it all straight. Yesterday, to tell you the truth, I took her to her art class thinking it was Thursday!"

"Oh. Right. Okay, I got it." Dennis sighs and heads for his truck. Some days, caring for trees and shrubs seems like a form of relaxation compared with caring for children. He wonders how they manage this complex organization.

While her parents have been conscientiously scheduling every free moment she has with structured, "enriching" activities, 4-year-old Alyson converses with several stuffed animals in the open dining area. She sits on the floor in front of the TV, glancing occasionally at Barney, who presents a little lesson on being nice. She is engrossed in her stuffed animals, having used blocks to make a castle and about to enact a scenario. She picks up a Beanie Baby kitty. "Okay—you be duh pwincess." Then she makes her big teddy bear take giant, crashing steps toward the "pwincess." The pwincess holds her own against the teddy bear, however, and despite her diminutive size, tells the bear to "Weave my casoo!" (translation: "Leave my castle!"). The pwincess pokes at him repeatedly as the bear backs up in a hasty retreat. As Alyson makes the bear retreat, she accidentally knocks over some blocks that were serving as the castle, causing a loud noise as they crash to the ground. Alyson jumps and her mother, startled, says, "Alyson! What are you *doing*?!"

And that's the interesting question. Alyson is playing—but what, exactly, does that mean?

WHAT'S THE POINT OF PLAY?

Marianne and Dennis, like many parents today, have gotten caught up in the false belief that free play is unimportant or even a waste of time—that children aren't learning anything when they are "just" playing. But playful moments are really learning opportunities in disguise. The evidence is very clear. Play promotes development—and in a number of domains. For instance, play promotes problem solving and creativity. It also helps to build better attention spans and encourages social development. But how could play have all these—and other—benefits? Join us as we investigate the wonders of play.

Felix, age 4, and Minerva, age 5, were among the children in a (now classic) study. Before them, but quite out of reach, was a see-through latched box. And in that box lay the jewel in this experiment: a piece of colored chalk or a marble that the children had previously chosen as a neat toy. The task before the children was simple, yet seemingly impossible: to retrieve the toy without getting out of their seats or even leaning toward the box. How could the children get the chalk out of the box? There was an actual solution, which involved connecting two long sticks that together were long enough to reach the box and rake it in.

Felix and Minerva were in the group assigned to play freely with the sticks. Even before they were given the task of retrieving the chalk, even before they were asked to choose the chalk or the marble, they were given a bunch of small sticks of different sizes to play with and no particular instructions for about 10 minutes. As children are wont to do, they explored the sticks and played a little make-believe, making the sticks into soldiers. They even discovered that some of the sticks could fit inside one another to make longer sticks. Just as their interest in the sticks started to wane, Felix and Minerva chose the chalk and were given the box retrieval task.

Did Felix and Minerva just sit there waiting for the researcher to give them a solution? Did they just bang the sticks together or dig them into the carpet? Well, maybe a little. They were silent for a moment as they looked at the precious chalk so near and yet so far. Then they reminded themselves of the rules of the game. Felix: "She says we can't stand up." Minerva: "Yeah, but . . . maybe the sticks . . ." And then they were off, figuring out which sticks could clamp together and then looking for the longest ones that would clamp together. They tackled the problem with great exuberance and with serious intensity. Finally, these little detectives found the two longest sticks, clamped them together, reached the box, and raked the prize box to them. They solved the problem. Bravo!

Other pairs of children were not given the sticks to play with in advance but just given the answer to the problem right off the bat. They watched in silence as the researcher showed them how to solve it by putting two of the sticks together. Then she left them alone with the problem, and with the same sticks Felix and Minerva had used, to see how they would solve the problem. Some of the children solved the problem instantly. After all, they had seen the experimenter solve the problem. But other children sometimes failed. And when they failed, they instantly gave up. Finally, a third group of children were given no time to play with the sticks and never saw the experimenter solve the problem. Not surprisingly, nearly all of these children failed the task.

What does this experiment and others like it tell us? Self-guided exploration through play is a learning experience that "teaches" problem solving in a fun way. Sure, some of the children who were shown the solution by an adult immediately got it right. But when they failed, they *gave up*. It was as if they thought, "That lady knows how to do it and I don't. Period." Children like Felix and Minerva, however, who played with the sticks before they were given the task, worked very persistently and eagerly to solve the problem. Researchers have discovered that play is related to greater creativity and imagination and even to higher reading levels and IQ scores. Based on the research evidence, a new equation is in order: PLAY = LEARNING.

WHEN PARENTS JOIN IN THE FUN

Research has proven another interesting fact about play: The level of children's play *rises* when adults play with them. The variety of play children engage in also increases when adults join in. And "joining in" is different from controlling. Controlling makes children follow their parents' agenda and does not lead to as much cognitive development as when parents follow their children's lead.

Imagine Khara, a brown-eyed 22-month-old. She and her mother, Maxine, have been invited to Professor Barbara Fiese's lab at Syracuse University to participate in a study on play. The researchers videotape what takes place so that they can code it later for the behaviors they are interested in studying. First, they ask Maxine to fill out a questionnaire about Khara's play habits while they watch how Khara plays alone with the toys that are available. Then they ask Maxine to get on the floor with Khara and play with her as she might at home. After that, they ask Maxine to show Khara how to do various make-believe things, like pretending to brush a doll's teeth. Finally, they observe Maxine and Khara as they play with each other without any instructions.

In this experiment, Professor Fiese was following up on other studies that showed that children are more likely to treat objects not as the *real* objects they are but as *symbols* for other objects when they played with adults (here their mothers). When that block is used like a car and made to move along the floor with a "vroom, vroom, vroom," we know that the child recognizes that things can stand for other things in the world. What's the big deal? One of the key components of development is learning to *manipulate symbols and reason abstractly*. After all, what is language but symbol manipulation? The sounds of words (take "chair") in no way resemble what they stand for (a real chair). And children need to think beyond the objects that are concretely in front of them if they are to combine new ideas in creative ways. Treating objects as though they were something else is the beginning of that important ability. And being able to use objects symbolically, to stand for something other than what they really are, is related to children's language progress.

Professor Fiese evaluated the complexity of Khara's play by considering whether the things she did were just exploratory (touching, looking at), functional (moving a little car in the expected way), or symbolic (from pretending to drink from an empty cup to make-believe pouring and then drinking, to setting up a make-believe dinner scenario). When Khara played by herself, she looked the least advanced. When her mother joined in, she looked more advanced, and when Maxine showed Khara how to make believe (like pretending to brush a doll's teeth), Khara played in the most complex way. Maxine's involvement with Khara's play helped her move to another level, a level that will promote richer and more abstract thinking.

Interestingly, mothers who just asked a lot of questions of their children, who watched a lot, and who tried to direct the play rather than joining in had children who engaged in less symbolic play and more exploratory play. When children—as in Khara's case—are allowed to take the lead, the result is more advanced play. So the next time you assume that your child is doing fine playing on her own, remember that your presence makes a difference. This is not to say that solitary play is a bad idea. Not at all. But you are not *intruding* if you play with your child; in fact, without even realizing it, you are probably helping your child learn to manipulate symbols and think more abstractly.

Discovering Hidden Skills | Evaluating Play

Ages: 12 months to 3½ years

You can recreate Professor Fiese's experiment at home, but you'll need to recruit another parent or caregiver so that you can watch your child's actions closely. First, get some new toys and let the child play on her own with them while your willing helper (who should not, by the way, know what it is you are looking for) pretends to read a magazine. Observe your child for about 8 minutes, seeing what she does with the new toys. Have your helper resist the child's entreaties to join in by saying, "In a minute." Does your child explore the toys first? Does your child begin to play make-believe with the objects, acting as if they were something different than what they really are? Can you see your child treating these objects in a symbolic way? Then have your helper join in. After they play for a while, try to see if the play shifts into make-believe. Then give your helper a piece of paper with two make-believe things to try with your child, such as pretending to set up a tea party. Does the child's level of play increase yet again? It's as if you can watch your child's mental processes stretching before your eyes as she interacts with an adult who gently guides her in the use of symbols. Play with adults clearly matters for cognitive growth.

PLAY 101

Play is an elusive concept. As Janet Moyles says in her book, *The Excellence of Play*, "Grappling with the concepts of play can be analogized to trying to seize bubbles, for every time there appears to be something to hold on to, its ephemeral nature disallows it being grasped." A 12-month-old child who is banging pots together in the kitchen is playing. An 18-month-old who is practicing all the words he knows out loud before a nap in his crib is playing. A 4-year-old who is on his first soccer team is playing. And a 5-year-old who is engaging in an elaborate fantasy game with a friend is also playing. So what is the common thread? When 500 teachers were asked to define play, there were as many responses as there were teachers! It's interesting, isn't it, that the most familiar words are sometimes the hardest to define.

According to prominent researchers, such as Professor Catherine Garvey of the University of Maine and Professor Kenneth Rubin of the University of Maryland, play has five elements. First, play must be *pleasurable and enjoyable*. This doesn't mean that you have to be falling on the ground in paroxysms of laughter to be playing. But it must be fun. Second, play must have *no extrinsic goals*. You don't go into play saying something like "Hmm, I think I'll play now so that I can get some pre-reading skills."

Play is engaged in for its own sake. It doesn't have a function; it's nonutilitarian. Third, play is *spontaneous and voluntary*, freely chosen by the player. You can't assign play. In fact, in one study, when a kindergarten teacher assigned her pupils a play activity, they thought it was work. Yet at other times, they described the very same activity as play! If you make your child play soccer because it will be good for him, that doesn't qualify as play. And if he finds it stressful, this is certainly not play. Fourth, play involves some *active engagement* on the part of the player. The player has to want to do it. If the player sits passively and is not much involved in what's going on, that's not play. And finally, play contains a certain element of *make-believe*. There is a nonliteral component, an element of suspending reality, in much of the play that young children do. A child who pretends to pour liquid and then pretends to drink what he poured is at play.

Ironically, many parents today are uncomfortable with one or more of these elements of play. When measured against these criteria, some of the activities we put our children in are not very playful. When micromanaging parents and test-conscious teachers, for example, feel compelled to choose the play experience for children rather than let the children choose, they violate some of the elements that define play. Play needs to stem from a *child's* desire. We *can*, of course, provide a limited set of choices to children and then let them choose from those options. Then we are *facilitating* their play, and that's our proper role.

The most egregious violation of the elements of play in our Roadrunner society concerns the second element: Play must have no extrinsic goals. How many of us really let our children engage in play that has no practical purpose? Even the toys we select for them have the hidden agenda of making them learn. Consider the trend: An article in the *Wall Street Journal* noted that in 1995, anything that "smacked of classroom learned was viewed as the kiss of death" for a toy. Yet by 2002, a mere 7 years later, sales of educational toys have skyrocketed. As an example (and there are many), a company called LeapFrog makes toys for learning to read and do math. It had earnings of only $3 million in its 1st year (1995)—but rang up more than $500 million in sales in 2002! Now, that is a phenomenal increase. Obviously, parents and grandparents are buying gobs of educational toys. Are these toys all bad? No! The ones that children enjoy are fine. But remember that these toys *set the agenda* for the child. It's not the child figuring out what to do next; it's the device that decides.

The same is true for the classes we enroll our young children in. Are we hoping that they'll have a good time in these classes and play with other children, or do we have in the back of our minds that by exposing them to (fill in the blank) we might develop some latent talent? When our 5-year-olds are added to the Little League baseball roster, do we really just want them to have fun? Do we think that it will be great for them to learn some new skills, like catching a ball with a glove, that will add to their further pleasure? Or are we hoping that they will make the play-offs and even win? As one father of a child who began drilling his 4-year-old son for a career in athletics said, "At times, I admit, I have behaved obnoxiously and without sufficient regard for the feelings of my children." Parental brawls at children's sporting events have become legion. These examples raise interesting questions about whether we really are letting our children play when we schedule them into organized activities.

A reporter recently posed the following question to one of us: "The activities parents sign their children up for sound like fun. Why is free play of the sort you describe necessary at all?" The answer? It is through free play that children learn not only to have fun with children in organized activities, but also to create activities themselves. They learn initiative. As Susan Bredekamp, Ph.D., of the National Association for the Education of Young Children writes, "Children will feel successful when they engage in a task that they have defined for themselves." It is not considered developmentally appropriate for teachers to use "highly structured, teacher-directed lessons almost exclusively, . . . deciding what the children will do and when while expecting the children to listen passively or do pencil and paper tasks for long periods of time." Sound ghastly? To us it does. More and more parents, however, want their preschools to have this complexion. And we have visited the preschools that offer "computer science" and "mathematics instruction." Children may look busy, but the question is, what are they sacrificing in the bargain?

Academic preschools that emphasize learning over play have become popular because parents want to make sure their children get a leg up in life. Life is tough; no question about it. But it's just not true that the best kind of learning takes place only when a big, smart adult directs the child's every move. And it's also not true that children who attend academically oriented preschools enter school with better skills and better attitudes toward learning. Years of research have shown that children need to direct their own play activities. When children have a chance to play, they show an increase in creativity and problem solving.

Now we get to another central function of play: It gives children a sense of power. And for people who are being told what to do every minute of the day, having a sense of power is not only delightful, it's instructive. In free play, children get to practice being in charge—buffered from any real-life consequences. It is through free play that the child becomes the boss in a real or imagined world, independently navigating through the choices available to him. It is through play that a child can invent something new or solve a problem that arises for the dinosaurs that are often stand-ins for real people. While organized activities have their place, we must not mistake them for play. It is play, plain and simple play, that affords many of the most essential intellectual and social advantages for children. As Yale professor and noted researcher Dorothy Singer says, "Through make-believe games children can be anyone they wish and go anywhere they want. When they engage in sociodramatic play, they learn how to cope with feelings, how to bring the large, confusing world into a small, manageable size; and how to become socially adept as they share, take turns, and cooperate with each other. When children play, they are learning new words, how to problem solve, and how to be flexible. Most of all, they are just plain having fun."

WHY A LACK OF PLAY CAN BE HARMFUL

Is too little play a problem for children? Some experts argue that "play deprivation" can lead to depression and hostility in children. After all, if you never had a break, you might get depressed, too! And consider how much more your children are dealing with in trying to understand their world. While you may not feel like it on some days, *you* are in control. Conversely, your children have very little control over what happens. Your children need breaks—breaks to assimilate things they've already learned, to master new skills, to work through scary emotional experiences, and just to have fun! The best data on too little play comes from studies with animals because it isn't ethical to do experiments in which you deprive children of play. What happens when animals are deprived of play?

Some recent research suggests that depriving animals of play may have negative effects on their brains. Work with rats by Jaak Panksepp, emeritus professor at Bowling Green University in Ohio, suggests that play has an effect on the frontal lobe, the part of the brain that houses self-control. Without play, Professor Panksepp and his student Nikki Gordon found, there were delays in the brain's maturation. When rats that already had frontal lobe damage were allowed to play, some of the damage repaired itself. Damage to the frontal lobe is considered an analogue to what children have when they suffer from attention deficit disorder (ADD). If rough-and-tumble play helps rats to be less hyper, perhaps this would also be true for children. Indeed, researchers who work with children are finding similar effects. Rough-and-tumble play may help children with ADD control their impulsivity and concentrate in school.

We already know, too, from the work of Professor Anthony Pellegrini at the University of Minnesota that providing school-age children with play breaks maximizes their attention to school tasks that involve thinking. Consider the fact that schools are increasingly eliminating opportunities for play. As Professor Pellegrini says, such a move would be "misguided and may actually do harm."

WHY PLAY IS EVEN MORE IMPORTANT IN THE 21ST CENTURY

Through our years of research, we have come to the conclusion that *play is to early childhood what gas is to a car.* It is the very fuel of every intellectual activity that our children engage in. Researchers are in universal agreement that play provides a strong foundation for intellectual growth, creativity, and problem solving. And it also serves as a vehicle for emotional development, and for the development of essential social skills. In the 21st century, creative problem solvers, independent thinkers, and people with expert social acumen will inevitably surpass those who have simply learned to be efficient at getting the right answers. Encyclopedic information is already abundantly available at our fingertips. If you know how to read, and own a computer, and you know how to use a service like Google, you can get answers to nearly any question you might have. Although the new movement in education called high-stakes testing functions as if right answers were what matter, the truly creative—the individuals who make the most significant contributions—*go beyond finding answers to already formulated problems.* How do these individuals practice asking new questions and deriving new answers? Through play. Play builds *versatile* and *supple* intellectual skills; play is the place where problem solving comes alive. But then, play is not just a concept for our time. Einstein knew the value of play all along when he said, " . . . Play seems to be the essential feature in productive scientific thought—before there is any connection with logical construction in words or other kinds of signs that can be communicated to others."

The pervasive myth in our achievement-oriented society that child's play is a waste of time is linked to the hype that parents must boost their children's intelligence. So we overschedule our children and give up on the values that we know, deep down, are important. Intelligence gets a big boost from play, yet the idea that enhancing a child's intelligence must be work has become the new gospel.

Despite the fact that the amount of time children spend in free play has been steadily decreasing since the 1980s, parents universally seem to understand the value of play. In a survey conducted in 2000 by Zero to Three, a research group at Harvard University, 87 percent of parents of 3- to 5-year-olds agreed that play was important for healthy development! Parents even know which *types* of play are most beneficial for children. In the survey, they rated certain activities—banging on blocks (at 6 months), having a pretend tea party (at 2 years), making art with art supplies (at 4 years), and playing cards with dad (at 6 years)—as maximally stimulating. Activities like playing on the computer (at age 2), making art on the computer (at age 4), and memorizing flash cards (at age 4) were considered less important for optimal growth. The survey showed that parents and researchers see eye to eye. These numbers, when viewed against the backdrop of diminishing playtime, present a travesty. *We know what to do, but we just can't bring ourselves to do it.* We are afraid that if we trust our instincts, our children will be missing out on learning some critical skills. Francis, mother of 3-year-old Rebecca, puts it best: "If she is just playing, she might be wasting precious moments when she could be learning. I don't want to hold my child back. How will I feel when all of the other kids are ahead of my child? How will Rebecca feel about herself if I let her fall behind?"

Yet as we hope you are beginning to see, free play and guided play hold the key to more fulfilling lives—not only for children but for parents as well. Play is the key to nurturing happy, intelligent children.

Before we consider more of the evidence about what play means and how important it is for children's lives, we need to take a quick peek at children of different ages who are playing. Why? Because play is different at different ages. Just as we as adults no longer play in the bathtub with boats and cups, our young children are incapable of playing Scrabble or Boggle or other word games that interest us. Play has different complexions at 12 months, 2 years, and 4 years of age. Play, as a reflection of children's minds, develops and grows in complexity, too.

How Do Children Play?

Babies engage in play as early as 3 to 6 months—as soon as they are able to grasp objects. Babies this age are perfectly content to use almost any object as a toy, whether it's a crumpled piece of paper, a shoe, or even a dollar bill!

Let's watch Carol, a 9-month-old with strawberry blonde hair, as she sits on the floor playing with a 10-inch-long pink hollow plastic hammer. She studies it with great intensity for a moment, as if to memorize its features, and runs the fingers of one hand along its curves and turns it in her hand. She then studies it again and winds up bringing it to her mouth to explore it. She pulls it out, makes a face (must not taste great), and shakes it up and down, perhaps hoping for a noise (maybe it's a rattle?), when she thrashes it by accident against a cylindrical metal can that holds her other toys. Bam! Wow, that caught her interest! She thrashes it wildly again and is fascinated to hear what she has wrought. Now, more and more purposefully, she raps the can with the hammer, not as we hold a hammer, but on its side, jumping a little each time with delight as she creates a spectacle, all on her own!

Infants between 6 and 9 months are just starting to do this kind of intense object exploration. In fact, psychologist Holly Ruff at Albert Einstein College in New York City found that babies around this age start to change how they handle an object according to the object's properties. The older they get, the less they engage in indiscriminate mouthing and looking no matter what the object is. Prior to this time, Carol would have just transferred the object from hand to hand and not rotated it and studied it and looked at it from different angles. Carol is just starting to create relations between objects—although now it's by accident, as when she hit the can in a random thrashing of her arm. The late Swiss psychologist Jean Piaget, one of the founding fathers of child development, suggested that in infancy, children engage in the purest form of play. They make objects they find interesting fit into *their* world. They largely play with objects one at a time, and they use objects only in the simplest of ways—never creating uses beyond those intended by the maker.

Now look at Carol at about 23 months, a mere 14 months later. Carol is sitting on the floor of the kitchen, surrounded by the toys she has dumped out of the can we saw before. She picks up a toy telephone and fingers the buttons carefully for a while, trying to push them to hear their binging noise. After pushing a few buttons, she holds the receiver up to her ear (okay, maybe she licks it a little before she brings it to her ear) and tries the push buttons again. She becomes bored of this and sees the hammer she used in the last episode we described. She becomes bored the phone, picks up the hammer—holding it correctly now—and bangs on the buttons on the phone with some force. This looks premeditated and involved planning. It was as if she thought, "That hammer could make a lot more keys sound than my one finger has been able to!" Occasionally (her aim isn't wonderful), she is rewarded with the binging noise the buttons make. Next to her on the floor is baby, a soft doll with a plastic face, wearing blue pajamas. Periodically as she plays, Carol picks up her baby and lays it back down and covers it up with her own blankie. The blanket is what psychologists call Carol's "transitional object," and it has helped her through a lot of tough times.

Quite a lot has changed in Carol's play, compared with when she was 9 months old. Professor Fergus Hughes, an expert on child's play from the University of Wisconsin in Green Bay, points out three ways in which play in the 2nd year of life changes. The first big change is seen in the way Carol now uses the hammer on the phone. One of the hallmarks of the advancement of play is the decrease in using objects one at a time and the increase in using them two or three at a time. Now Carol creates relations between objects, which is a much more sophisticated way to use them.

Remember how Carol used the hammer when she was 9 months old? She didn't hold it by the handle and bang on the can with its head, as we might. Instead, she rapped its side against the can. By 23 months, Carol uses the hammer like a pro. The second way that play changes with age is that children start using objects in *appropriate* ways. And Carol seems to understand how a telephone works, too, even though adults don't usually lick it before they dial (we promise she won't be licking the phone by the time she goes to college). So Carol's experience with objects in the world—whether through observation of others or her own use—allows her to use objects as they were meant to be used.

When Carol picks her baby up to cuddle it as if it were real and covers it up as if it were cold, she's showing us that she is using her imagination. She no longer has to deal just in the here and now. She can *pretend* that things are alive; she can pretend that they are real. This third change in play is the one that most captures the imagination and interest of researchers. It certainly captured the attention of Professor Piaget. He realized that when children engage in pretend play, they demonstrate that they have reached a developmental milestone. They are now able to think symbolically—to have one object *stand for* another. The use of symbols is the main characteristic of human thought that makes us distinct from other animals. This is the stuff from which language, reading, problem solving, and other types of higher-order thinking are made. Humans all over the world, whether they are raised in a hut or a high-rise, think in terms of symbols.

In our final vignette, Carol is now 3½ years old. Her taste in toys has changed, and we no longer see the same ones as before. Now there are coloring books and picture books and a toy farm set with miniature animals. That little pink plastic hammer is still around, and there's also an obsolete cell phone on the floor. We peek in on Carol as she lies on her tummy, moving the animals around in the farmyard as she quietly talks to herself. As she walks the miniature cow slowly back to the barn, she says, "Okay, cow, now you go back to the barn and go to sleep because it's getting dark outside. You'll need your baby doll to fall asleep, so we have to look for it." As she looks around for the cow's baby doll, she comes up dry (what a surprise). But instead she spies that cell phone. She says, "Oh, here's your baby doll. Her name is Lulu." She "parks" the cow in her stall, laying her on her side and placing the cell phone next to the outstretched cow's feet. "Night night," she says as she covers the cow and its cell-phone baby with the old pink plastic hammer.

Pretend play like this increases dramatically in the 4th year of life as children become the master directors in their play scenarios. And as Carol gets older, her play scenarios—especially with a parent or a peer—will become even more complex, and they'll tell whole stories, just like in their picture books. Whether or not your child turns out to be a film director, the creation of these scenes, in which inanimate objects are given functions that are very different from what they were intended for by their creators, is a very special play advancement. A cell phone has become a baby doll and a hammer has become a cover. This is progress. Why? Because Carol is no longer tied to the features of the props. She can treat them *as if* they were something else. This is exactly what takes place in generating ideas, in thinking a problem through. We think *as if* other conditions apply and circumstances can be changed, and then we come up with a new idea or a novel solution. So pretend play is practice for children in freeing themselves from what is right in front of their eyes. Pretend play allows children to consider answers outside the box. Pretend play allows our children to consider alternative worlds.

Notice what has happened across the three vignettes of Carol at play. She moved from treating all objects the same way (usually mouthing them) to treating them differently and exploring their properties. Then she treated each object differently and realistically, according to what they do in the real world (as when Carol finally held the hammer the right way and used it in a conventional manner). Finally, Carol treated objects as symbols or things that stand for other things (as when Carol used the cell phone to stand for a baby doll).

Now that we have painted a broad-brush picture of the changes you are likely to see in your children's play if you look closely, we need to ask what these changes *mean*. We have already hinted at the benefits of play and what about it is so important for children's development. But we need to dig a little more deeply, to talk about the different kinds of play (all of our examples were of solitary, object play), the emotional benefits of play, and what parents and caregivers contribute to children's play. That's what we'll do next—but in a playful way (of course!).

DOES PLAY WITH OBJECTS BENEFIT INTELLECTUAL DEVELOPMENT?

The solitary object play and exploration we've just described in the vignettes above provides children with their first understandings of the way the world works. It's their chance to do their own little experiments and figure out what objects can do and what they can't. These are things that they have to figure out firsthand for themselves; there is only so much that can be learned by watching others manipulate objects.

Children are exploring the world of objects and substances. They are little scientists—testing out the properties of physical matter. Even as babies, they are doing little experiments: "What happens when I let go of my rattle? Look! It goes down to the floor. Look! It does it again! Does it do it every time? Let's see." When our 2-year-olds bang on pots, they learn about the relationship between the force they exert and the loudness of the sound. This is baby physics. When they are in their first 2 years of life, it is as if they are asking the question, "What can I do with this?" when they encounter new objects. Infants and toddlers are learning what objects can do, how objects work, and what *they* can do to make objects do their thing.

When they build with blocks and make roads for their Matchbox cars, they learn things like eight little blocks are as long as one big block. This is mathematics! Professor Ranald Jarrell, an expert at the University of Arizona on the development of young children's mathematical thinking, tells us in no uncertain terms why play is important for understanding mathematical concepts.

> *Play is vital to the development of children's mathematical thinking. Unlike some forms of knowledge, mathematical knowledge, which deals with relationships between and among things, cannot be learned by hearing adults talk about it. Experimental research on play shows a strong relationship between play, the growth of mathematical understanding, and improved mathematical performance. . . . Without play . . . children's powers of mathematical reasoning would be seriously underdeveloped.*

Is this the kind of knowledge that can be obtained from flash cards, or even from computer games that ask children to do comparisons between sets and simple counting and addition? No. What is needed are the gritty, day-to-day experiences of exploring, manipulating, sorting, dividing, and recombining that children have as they play with objects. Even toward the end of the 1st year of life, babies show evidence of making inferences about new objects based on similar objects they have encountered in play. In one study conducted by Professors Dare Baldwin of the University of Oregon and Ellen Markman and Riikka Melartin of Stanford University, 9- to 16-

month-old babies were given a horn to play with, the kind of horn that makes a noise when you squeeze the bulb. After the children played for a while, the first horn was taken away. They were then given other horns, which had different colors and sizes but the same shape. Would the babies act as if they thought these new horns should also make a noise? If they did, it would indicate that they made an "inductive inference," by assuming that things that looked alike should have similar functions.

The babies immediately squeezed the bulbs, showing that they had made an inference about the new objects based on the old one. And when some of the horns didn't produce the desired effect because they had been purposely broken, the babies worked all the harder to make them blow! These babies were making inferences about properties of objects that you cannot *see*—their ability to make a noise. Child's play? Yes. And it is crucial for learning about the world!

| Discovering Hidden Skills | Making Inferences about Objects |

Ages: 6 months to 16 months

First, find two inexpensive toys that have the same function but don't look identical. Making a noise is a good hidden function for your child to try to find. Give the baby one of the toys and watch her play with it. See if she discovers the novel function on her own. Time how long she plays with it before she figures out its function. This is important because you will be comparing her behavior with toy 1 with that of toy 2. If she doesn't figure out how to make the hidden function occur after some time, show her how to make it happen. Let her play a bit more—hopefully she can reproduce the interesting function on her own—and then trade toys with her, giving her the new one. What happens? How long does it take (compared with when she played with the first toy) for your baby to make the second toy do its thing? Does she explore the toy for the same length of time that she explored the first one? Or does she immediately try to produce its effect? If you see a difference between the way the baby interacts with the second toy and the way she interacted with the first, remember that you are seeing the effects of a *limited amount* of play on your child's cognitive development. Imagine how much babies and young children can learn about the world if allowed lots of playtime.

Studies consistently find that the availability of play materials is important for intellectual development. And that doesn't mean buying the newest so-called educational toys, either. In the first 2 years of life, children seem to love toys that require fitting things together, putting things into openings, pushing and pulling things, musical toys, and toys that require eye-hand coordination. Toddlers with a wide variety of playthings available do seem to have enhanced intellectual development later on, at ages 3 and 4. In a study of 130 children over time, Professor Robert Bradley of the University of Arkansas found that the availability of play materials was one of the most consistent predictors of intelligence even when the children entered school. And the effect of having playthings on cognitive development is independent of the quality of parent-infant interaction. That doesn't mean that parents don't matter; we will shortly show you how much they do matter. What it means is that there is a separate, measurable effect on intellectual development of having a range of toys.

For preschoolers, intellectual development is served so beautifully through object play that there are a million examples to draw from. Take blocks, for example. As we showed above, children who play with ordinary blocks are figuring out mathematical equivalences. They face problems they create for themselves (and that is key), like "How many blocks of this size will it take to make another tower just like the first?" Block play helps develop other concepts as well. When children spontaneously sort them into categories by size, shape, or color, they are working on mastering what Piaget called logical classification. Children need to understand that the red and green blocks together make up all of the blocks. While this seems incredibly obvious to *us*, it takes time for children to figure out the relationships between the parts and the whole of a set. Even putting the blocks back (as in cleanup—yes!) teaches children about the properties of the blocks and how they are the same or different.

Clay is another medium that preschoolers love to work in. Just watch Aaron.

Aaron is busily playing with a large lump of clay. He pounds it repeatedly against the table, then pulls off a large piece, breaks it into several smaller pieces, and rolls them into balls. He soon grows tired of rolling, and so he flattens the balls into pancakes, which he distributes to the three children sitting at his table. Later he collects the pancakes and stretches them into hot dogs. Then he rolls them into balls again. Next he takes some of the balls, breaks them in half, and makes smaller balls of the broken pieces.

And so on. We could have gone on longer because Aaron did. Why does this play sequence seem so boring and mundane to us and so captivating to Aaron? Aaron is working on fundamental understandings about quantity and matter. Through our own play as children, we had the opportunity to work out these same understandings, understandings that we now take for granted. We are very sophisticated about the world and what causes change in it. Our preschoolers are not.

And we haven't even mentioned the way in which this sort of intellectual play enhances intellectual curiosity and mastery. Children are in charge; children are calling all the shots, setting up their own problems, controlling their own learning.

THE TYPES OF PLAY: CONVERGENT VERSUS DIVERGENT

Intellectual play comes in many forms. Some kinds of play may actually promote children's ability to solve problems. Psychologists talk about "convergent" problems and "divergent" problems. Convergent problems are like the one we described at the beginning of the chapter—figuring out how to get a toy out of a box by putting sticks together. There is only one possible solution to a convergent problem. The ability to solve convergent problems has been linked to successful performance on standard classroom and intelligence tests where there is one right answer. Divergent problems have multiple solutions, as when you play with blocks: There are a variety of structures that can be built. Divergent problem solving seems to require a greater amount of creativity because there is no one right answer. Several studies have looked at how play materials influence preschoolers' ability to solve divergent problems, problems that require thinking outside the box. Let's watch Amala and Michael as they participate in one of these studies.

Amala is an adorable 3½-year-old who seems mature beyond her years, one of those children who are 3 going on 13. Michael is a muscular little boy with lots of enthusiasm for whatever he does. Amala, with a group of her friends, is given a bunch of convergent materials to play with—like puzzles—toys that have a single right way to play with them. While her group is playing, Michael's group is given divergent play materials—toys, like blocks, that don't require a single outcome. Both children have fun in their respective groups playing with their peers and toys. The test comes when Amala's and Michael's groups are given some divergent problems to solve. For example, both groups are asked to build a village with 45 pieces of the play materials. The researchers watch each group closely to see what the children do, counting up the number of structures they build and the number of unique names they use to label these structures. Michael's group, which had played with the divergent materials, came up with more structures and more unique names for them. They worked away at the task and didn't give up when they reached an impasse. Michael's group used trial and error a lot. Amala's group acted very differently. Having played with convergent toys that had one right answer, they got stuck and did the same things over and over again when they couldn't do a divergent problem. They also gave up more quickly than Michael's group. It was as if they had learned that problems have a single answer, while Michael's group had learned that there is "more than one way to skin a cat," as the saying goes. Creativity seemed to flourish in Michael's group.

And what are all those expensive educational toys like on the market today? Most are convergent in nature; they usually look for a single, correct answer to a problem because they are busy teaching *skills*. Yet the research we've just described suggests that Michael's group was not only more creative in their problem solving but showed more perseverance and enthusiasm. These are the behaviors and attitudes toward problem solving we want to cultivate in our children, not a penchant for looking for the one right answer. They'll get enough of that in school. We want our children to know how to find the right answer when there is one, but we also want them to be able to think outside the box. Where does creativity come from? From play—good old unmonitored, unstructured free and open play.

In fact, pundits have recently written about how it's okay for children to be bored. All parents have heard the whiny child who says, "I'm bored. I have nothing to do." Children who are used to having all their time structured for them lose the resources necessary to amuse themselves. Amusing oneself is healthy. Living in your head a little and figuring out things you can do without classes, playdates, or television is not a bad thing. Children need to develop the ability to stimulate themselves. This, too, is part of play, and some of our children seem to have forgotten how it's done!

When you think of play and its effects, consider your new equation: PLAY = LEARNING. And up to this point, we've discussed only how *object play* enhances intellectual development. We haven't even talked about the part of play that makes childhood magical: pretend play, and what it does for intellectual development. Yet that element of *make-believe*, that nonliteral component that involves suspending reality, also makes an enormous contribution to children's intellectual growth. For example, research has shown that the more advanced children's pretend play is, the better they do on divergent problem-solving tasks. Although we cannot say that pretend play *causes* children to think more creatively, this link has been found in other studies as well. Why should there be a link between playing pretend and thinking divergently? The science of pretend play helps us understand how making believe a rock is a cup might be a cognitive catalyst.

KINGS AND QUEENS: PRETEND PLAY AND LANGUAGE DEVELOPMENT

Researchers have been able to document a sequence of pretend play behaviors that all children seem to go through. Professor Lorraine McCune at Rutgers University has been studying pretend play for years because she believes, following Piaget, that the ability to use objects as symbols for other objects is an important achievement that is related to children's language ability. This is not a crazy idea. If the word "shoe" is a symbol, and using a block to represent a shoe is a symbol, then there might well be a relationship between children's ability to deal with symbols in both these realms. To study this fascinating question, Professor McCune observed 102 children between the ages of 8 months and 24 months to see how they played with objects and what was happening in their language at the same time. She did indeed find a relationship between how children treated objects and their level of language development. Let's look at David as he traverses the five levels of representational play that Professor McCune observed.

David at 9 months has jet-black hair and enormous brown eyes. He is a happy baby who rushes over to greet Professor McCune when she comes to visit him in his house with her videotape equipment. Professor McCune takes out a set of preselected toys and places them on the floor between mommy and baby. Professor McCune sits quietly videotaping as David contentedly plays. After a few moments, David brings a cup to his lips and then puts it down. He doesn't pretend to drink or swallow. Professor McCune thinks this very early example of pretend play is not pretend at all, but just David's showing that he knows what cups are for. David doesn't say any words yet either. This is Level 1 in Professor McCune's scheme.

A few months later, though, at 13 months, David takes the cup with a great flourish and puts on a performance to make Paul Newman proud. He smacks his lips, brings the cup up to his mouth, throws his head back with exaggeration, and drinks deeply. This is a big advance over what he did with the cup at 9 months, when he just seemed to recognize what the cup is used for. Now he is clearly pretending. Not coincidentally, David and the other children who are clearly pretending in this way also seem to have a few words in their vocabularies. But notice that it is David himself who is the object of his pretending; he doesn't yet pull in other characters to pretend with. This is "self-pretending," Level 2. At Level 3 ("other-pretending"), when David is 2 months older, he takes a further step and uses *others* as the object of the pretense. Now he offers his Elmo doll a drink and holds the cup up to Elmo's lips. In practice, children who do Level 2 and Level 3 pretending are at the same level in language— using words one by one.

By 19 months, David's pretend play has advanced even further. Now he shows evidence of using pretend play gestures in *combinations*. David makes believe that he offers Elmo a drink and then his stuffed dinosaur a drink. Another time David makes believe that he is pouring liquid into the cup from another empty cup and then offers Elmo a drink. These combinations are more advanced because they reflect a more complicated mental representation in David's head. Now multiple characters—aside from himself—can play the role of drinker (Elmo and dinosaur) and multiple actions are performed with the cup (pouring and drinking). By 19 months, David is also using some word combinations, like "daddy truck" and "all gone cookie." This is Level 4.

Finally, David reaches the pinnacle of this type of solitary pretend play by getting even fancier and showing signs of planning and thinking ahead. Now, at Level 5 ("hierarchical pretend"), David outdoes himself. He sees the cup and says, "Gotta feed Elmo." He then searches for something to use as a high chair for Elmo and settles on propping Elmo up between two big blocks. Then he looks for something to serve as a bib for Elmo and finds a paper napkin that he tries to stick on Elmo's chest. Since it has no way to stick, it falls, and David tries this several times before giving up. Then he finds the cup again and tells Elmo, "Drink milk," while holding the cup to Elmo's mouth. This very complex sequence tells us that David has a plan and that he is taking steps in a logical order to execute it. David and other children who show this kind of play in which acts seem to be organized hierarchically (set up Elmo, then attach bib, then feed) also have more advanced language capabilities. They tend to use somewhat longer sentences, now 2 or 3 words in length, more often.

What is so interesting about this work is that all the children Professor McCune studied seemed to go through this sequence in their play, even if they didn't do it at exactly the same age. But children didn't seem to skip levels. Not all children she studied showed this lockstep progress between pretend play levels and language, but in general she did find these links. Why should there be a link between children's language and their level of pretend play? Perhaps the *underlying skills are the same.* As we mentioned earlier, the skill in question here is being able to deal with symbols. Pretend play allows children to practice symbol manipulation. While other mammals play, no one has found evidence of make-believe play in any babies other than human babies. Make-believe play involves separating oneself from the here and now. It involves acting *as if.* It is part of what makes us human and serves as a platform for other symbolic thinking, even beyond the domain of language—in math, physics, literature, economics, and art. When children enter the world of pretend play, they are like the kings and queens of a new world—a world that they can build and control. Instead of relying on *actual* objects as they are, they now have the power to *transform* them and to serve their own purposes. This is creative thinking at its best. And pretend play is just the kind of practice that children need for symbol manipulation.

Another way in which pretend play changes with development is in the child's selection of objects to serve as substitutes for other objects.

As David gets older, he gets better and better at selecting substitute objects that look less and less like the objects they stand for. For example, at first, when David is about 18 months, if he wants to find something in his pile of toys to stand for a telephone, he will select an object that has an ambiguous function, like a rectangular block. He will not pick something that has a clear function, such as a car. It takes more appreciation of how symbols work for David to be able to *override* the conflicting cues offered by an object that has a real function. Part of this is because, like most young children, David has trouble thinking of something in two ways at the same time. By the time David is almost 3 years old, he'll be able to use a baby bottle as a comb, a car as a telephone, or a doll as a book. David has become freed from the perceptual features of the objects he plays with. This is a giant advance. At the next level of play in preschool, children eventually won't even need the props in front of them to assert that this or that is true or happening. Now they are really launched!

Discovering Hidden Skills | Pretend Play and Language Development

Ages: 8 months to 2 years

At what level of pretend play is your child's play ? Put out some objects that are miniatures of real objects and that are likely to get pretend play going. Professor McCune found that baby dolls and stuffed animals and doll-size objects like combs and baby bottles elicited pretend play, as did a dump truck, a sponge, and a toy telephone. This is fun because it is also something you can try every few months to chart your child's pretend play and language advancement. If you keep a baby book, you can record your baby's age, what she does with the objects that you give her, what level of pretend play she exhibits, and what level of language she has (single words, combinations, little sentences). Consider your child to be at the highest level of pretend play she shows. It will be fun to compare this with later episodes and see how your child has progressed. Note, too, what objects your child selects as substitutes for other objects. Do the substitutes resemble the original objects they stand for? Or do the substitutes not resemble the original objects much at all? If the latter, then your child is demonstrating a higher level of pretend play.

Pretend Play with Peers Gets Social

Play has numerous advantages for children, and only some of those feed their intellects. In play, we do learn about objects and their relations, but we also learn about people and relationships. Play is a safe haven in which our children can conquer their fears and work out emotional problems. In fact, the only kind of therapy that can really be done with children is called play therapy. Children can also learn how to be doctors, firefighters, and superheroes with no physical risks. Play is a carefree space in which they can learn about their world and their place within it. Play is a place that allows children to deal with their hectic daily lives. As Tufts University Professor David Elkind wrote, "Play is nature's way of dealing with stress for children as well as adults."

Three-year-old children who use puppets to become Goldilocks or one of the Three Little Pigs learn about taking a perspective different from their own (they get better at this by ages 5 and 6). Children create emotional comfort for themselves through play. They cling to a favorite blanket or teddy bear. Their stuffed animal may have to take medicine along with them, or may have been the one responsible for knocking over a glass of milk.

Children do not function in a vacuum devoid of social interaction. After about 2½, pretend play starts to take place with other children and, if the child is lucky, with parents and caregivers. At first, the pretend play children engage in with others is very driven by the materials that they have in front of them. If they see an apron and put it on, they become "mommy"—no other speech or scene setting is necessary. But by late age 3, and 4 and 5, children come up with elaborate pretend play scenarios that can go on for a very long time. Sometimes one child will announce the theme of the play scenario to another child and they are off and running, as in "Let's pretend to go on a vacation to a beautiful hotel!" And then there are the play scenarios that most of us (whose families couldn't afford fancy vacations at beautiful hotels!) played: cops and robbers, house, and school. Just as we knew to take on roles and create conflicts and look for resolutions, so do our children. But psychologists now appreciate that child's play serves a number of important functions.

More Benefits of Pretend Play

Other than Piaget, the theorist who has most influenced our view of play is the late, brilliant Russian psychologist Lev S. Vygotsky. Although he died tragically at the age of 38, Professor Vygotsky's legacy to us is a play theory that places play at the very heart of children's development. Professor Vygotsky argued that children are at the *highest* level of their development when they are at play. For example, 5-year-old Jessica cannot sit still for more than 3 minutes in the classroom, even with a very supportive teacher. Yet in pretend play, she can play at being a good student with her peers, sitting and concentrating for more than 10 minutes! Professor Vygotsky said, "In play, a child is above his average age, above his daily behavior: In play it is as though he were a head taller than himself."

Professor Vygotsky believed that play served three functions. First, it creates the child's "zone of proximal development." As we discussed in chapter 6, this is where the child, with the help of a peer or an adult, goes a little further than what she can accomplish alone. Another function of play is to help the child separate thought and action. This is what we've described in how children go beyond the properties of the objects before them in pretend play. Professor Vygotsky summed this up nicely when he said, "The child sees one thing, but acts differently in relation to what he sees. Thus a condition is reached in which the child begins to act independently of what he sees." Finally, Professor Vygotsky saw play as facilitating the development of *self-regulation*. In chapter 7, we talked about how fundamental self-regulation is, from being able to stop crying as a baby to not blurting out negative remarks to others when you're feeling bad. It is an essential skill for success in life and for getting along with peers. A great example of how self-regulation gets practiced in play is that of 2½-year-old Louis, who, in playing house, takes on the role of the baby. Even at 2½, Louis knows that if he is going to pretend to cry, he must stop when the "father" comforts him. This make-believe crying takes deliberateness and thought because it is not real crying that is coming from hurt or discomfort. The fact that play requires this kind of control from little children is very important for their ability to regulate their own behavior.

Another way in which children self-regulate is that they talk to themselves. Have you ever noticed that you talk to yourself when you are trying to accomplish a hard task? Professor Vygotsky noticed, too, that children talk to themselves a good deal during pretend play—even when they are playing with others. He called this private speech and found that children were working out what they wanted to do, and how their fantasy should proceed. This is one of the reasons that children must be in environments where they can verbalize while they play.

Professor Vygotsky was among the first to realize that child's play was really *culture's* play. As we internalize "scripts" for how to act in our society, we are learning how our culture does things. Professor Vygotsky gave a lovely example of two sisters at play. Remarkably, in this example, the sisters are *playing* at being sisters and are trying to figure out just what this means. In play, they make explicit the rules that are implicit in their own behavior, saying things like "Sisters don't hit each other." Children are always making up rules in pretend play and insisting on their being followed!

These new forms of make-believe are intricate in design and show us how our children are internalizing the world they live in. Sometimes, children build forts and play out a scene in which they capture the bad guys to save the world. And sometimes they are star fairies. Sometimes our children just mimic the everyday scenes that are so commonplace to us. In the Please Touch Museum of Philadelphia, children flood into the pretend supermarket, where they can take plastic cans and produce off the shelves, where they wheel their miniature carts, and where they "pay" as they leave the store with their goodies. By the time children are shopping, they are pretending to adhere to the rules of society.

Part of the fun comes from imposing your own rules on the game of play. You would be amazed at what your children know if you just listened as they play. They have developed some very interesting theories, available to you only through their play. Can girls play construction worker? Can someone be both a mommy and a lawyer? Believe it or not, children are not always so sure about the various roles that people can play. Before age 4 or 5, they are certainly not convinced that people can have multiple roles. Professor Vygotsky told us that in pretend play, the imaginary situation is *explicit* and the rules of the game are often *implicit*. Even when we watch children emulating what we do in the broader culture, they have interpreted things in their own, unique ways.

| Discovering Hidden Skills | The Play "Script" |

Ages: 3 years to 5 years

Eavesdrop. We know that isn't a nice thing to do, but if you're going to appreciate the complexity of your child's play, you need to be a little devious. As your child engages in fantasy play, just listen in, but don't make it obvious you are doing so. Does your child talk aloud? What does she say? Does she plan ahead in her talk? Does she speak for her own benefit or that of her pretend play characters? Does she recite rules of social interaction? As they play going to McDonald's, for example, listen to whether they have that script right. What happens when we go to McDonald's? What is the "airport" script? The "riding on a bus" script? Watch for that frightening moment when your child imitates you perfectly as she interacts with her fantasy actors!

Building these event structures in pretend play requires memory and the ability to take multiple actions and to arrange them in a kind of cultural story line. This sequencing is, in and of itself, an important arena where social development intersects with intellectual growth.

Play Enhances Emotional and Social Development

Another major benefit of play is that it helps children work through difficult emotional events. Children are very serious about their pretend play and often shoo away adults who would interrupt them. Why is this so important to them? Sometimes the themes are ones that they seek to gain control over, as when they reenact a conflict that took place the day before with a friend at school. Professor Greta Fein, a world-renowned expert on children's play, argued that social pretend play is motivated by children's need to get a grip on emotional experiences they want to work through. The difference between pretend play and real life, though, is very significant: In pretend play, children can maneuver the flux and flow of events as they wish. In real life, things often happen *to* children. In pretend play, children can express the things they are not yet sophisticated enough to talk about with adults. Laurie, a newly divorced mother of a 4-year-old, described how she learned what her child's fear was by watching him play. She thought he was doing okay with her divorce after her husband moved out, and even after she and her son had to move to new, smaller quarters. But in listening to his pretend play, she heard his concern: Using his stuffed animals and talking aloud, he developed a scenario about how his mommy was going to go away, too. She was grateful for the glimpse his pretend play gave her into what concerned her son. She was careful to reassure him of her constancy at every opportunity after that.

And finally, sociodramatic play feeds into literacy because it becomes practice for storytelling. The stories children like to hear and the stories they act out in pretend play with their peers have lots in common. This type of play also allows us to suspend reality and to recognize that what we see is not always what we get. Once we can think of places and stories generated from our minds rather than strictly from what we can hold or touch, we decouple thinking from perception. We begin to build inner worlds. This is exactly what we do when we read books. We open the pages to new worlds and adventures that go well beyond what we can experience ourselves. We leave ourselves open to learning through others. Thus, this ability to imagine and to create new environments within the security of our own bedrooms is preparation for language, reading, and problem solving.

The skills that allow young children to remember, to use symbols, to create rules, and to direct are the skills that they need for school readiness. These are the stuff from which richer language, story lines, memory, attention, and planning are born. In the nexus where the social meets the intellectual, happy kids become smart kids. Through play, children build the courage and confidence to tackle learning in creative ways.

What Kind of Social Play Can I Expect at Various Ages?

Just as children play with objects in different ways as they get older, so too does the way they play with one another change as they age. At the end of the 1st year, children seem to treat one another like objects. They poke one another and seem otherwise to just play alongside one another without much recognition that another person is in the room. This has been called parallel play. You might find these children playing side by side with the lint on the carpet and totally satisfied just to be exploring!

By 13 or 14 months, children begin to use cooperative play. They might seek out one another, or take toys from one another. Sharing is not one of their better qualities at this age. But they do notice that the other person is there. And they are much more sophisticated in their play with familiar children than with unfamiliar children who come over to play. In playgroups, we actually see a higher level of play than we do on playgrounds because the children are somewhat familiar with one another.

At around age 2, children take a significant leap in peer play. For the first time, they take on roles like the bus driver or the zookeeper. They might also involve their friends in their activities. In the 3rd and 4th years, they even establish routines. Julie and Marge might take plastic telephones and start to talk to each other. Or they might play "teatime" by dressing up and sitting together at a pretend table with plastic cups and saucers. These play episodes at age 2 last for only a few minutes before the children move on to the next activity. When these same children are 3 or 4, the play becomes much more elaborate and can last for hours. "I'll play mommy and you play baby." This is typically when we meet the new superheroes in our family who zoom through the living room, rescuing the dolls in distress.

As children are motivated to play more, they also need to develop the social skills that allow them to play successfully. What does this mean? Children need to be able to figure out how play works. Imagine a scene at a playground. Julie sees four of her friends playing house, and she desperately wants to join in the fun. But she came out a little late, and things are well under way when she arrives. So, she stands there on the periphery, looking and waiting for some invitation. Now, there are a couple of ways in which this scene can end. On the brighter side, some sophisticated 4-year-old might look over, see Julie, and say in a cheerful voice, "Wanna come play?" That might happen, but it is just as likely that no one will notice that Julie is even there. What can she do? Well—she has to learn. She could rudely butt in, but that is unlikely to work and the other kids could get mad. Julie could go to the teacher, who could decide to make this a teachable moment for the others about social awareness. Or, in the best scenario yet, Julie could wait for a break in the action and then subtly join in, knowing that she is unlikely to get the really good parts in the script.

As you can now see, these episodes of make-believe are ripe with opportunities for learning about the self and about others. What if Jimmy doesn't want to be the baby? What if Sarah wants to play tea party and Jesse wants to play store? Learning how to negotiate, to compromise, and to be a director who meets all needs are tremendously important social skills. These moments also give us the chance—as teachers and parents—to help our children learn emotional regulation. If you don't get what you want, do you have a temper tantrum? Pout and make others feel guilty? Or make a bargain so that "first we do what you want and then we play store"?

Play serves the role of teaching social skills and also has an emotional role for children. Play helps children cope in a complex world. This role of play has a long history within the field of psychology. And many of us have seen it firsthand. Let's watch Mikey (Kathy's son) to get a sense of how powerful play can be in building our sense of self and in soothing our fears.

Mikey was 2 years old when Simba arrived. Yes, Simba—Mike's hero from the famous Disney movie *The Lion King*—was now sitting beside him on his bed. Beyond speech (he was so excited), he took Simba carefully out of the box and gave it a huge hug. He owned Simba, and to his knowledge, he owned the real Simba—not an impostor. Simba soon came to meet Blankie—the other well-worn and very loved object that Mike carried around the house. Within just 3 months, Simba joined us on family vacations, came into the car, and even was privileged to ride with Mike on the back of his mother's bike. Mike trusted Simba. There were many days when just before bed, Mike could be found reading a book to Simba and discussing the day's events. When Mike had a fight with his older brothers, Simba protected him. When Mike was scared, Simba was the front man. Mike's parents knew that Simba was a force to be reckoned with. As Mike got older, it was *Simba* who misbehaved. Amazingly, it was *Simba* who had thrown those animals around the bedroom. And it was *Simba* who had thrown Mike's unwanted pasta in the trash can—not Mike. He'd never do that!

In play, a child can make his world over to suit him—without asking permission from adults.

Play with Friends—But Imaginary Friends?

One of the ways in which children learn to cope through play is through the friends they create that are totally in the mind of the beholder. As we see from the comic strip Calvin and Hobbes, Hobbes is truly a good friend for Calvin—and Calvin is a rather normal little boy, and a very creative one to boot. Imaginary friends are usually the province of quite normal 3- to 5-year-old children who are blessed with wonderful imaginations. In her recent book, *Imaginary Companions and the Children Who Create Them*, Professor Marjorie Taylor tells us that children with imaginary companions tend to be more intelligent and more creative than children who don't have such friends. Now, this does not mean that we should somehow implant an imaginary friend in the minds of our children. There are other ways to help our children be smarter and more creative through play. But it does mean that we need not worry if our children walk around talking to the air sometimes. As Calvin's mom once noted, it's better to join them than to question them. (In one comic strip, she actually called for Hobbes one day—her husband thought she had lost her mind, of course.)

In the preschool years, children are just learning about the world of possibilities, and there can be a fuzzy line between fantasy and reality. One of us remembers being terrified by the MGM lion when taken to movies. When it came on the giant screen, she would repeat over and over again the mantra her parents gave her, "It's not real. It's not real. It's not real," taking comfort from their amused expressions and their own calm demeanors. Many children fret about the monster in the closet, even when repeatedly reassured that only clothes "live" there. Here, too, play can help. When 2½-year-old Benj expressed real fear about the monster, we became the monster-bashing equivalents of the ghost busters. We had a meeting, chased the monster at a particular time on a particular day, and flushed the monster down the toilet. Happily, he never returned.

The benefits of social play are many. Yet perhaps the biggest one of all crosscuts the others. Children who play more are happier. When children are happier, they tend to relate better to their peers and they tend to be more popular. Social play not only makes you happy *and* intelligent, but it builds your social skills for the future. Those who played as children are also better at reducing their stress through play as adults.

Do Parents Affect Their Children's Play? You Bet!

While children can do just fine playing by themselves or with friends, parents are actually very important playmates as well. There are "teachable moments" in play where parents can challenge their children to go just a little bit beyond what the children could do alone. Many researchers suggest that guided play is the royal road to learning. How do we find these teachable moments and build on play? If we tell stories to our children and then assign them to roles in the stories so that they can act them out, our children are more engaged, are better able to follow a story line, and are developing preliteracy skills. Professor Ageliki Nicolopoulou of Lehigh University warns, however, that we must not be too controlling in the stories that we create. As with language, we need to be *partners* with children, and we need to fit their themes into the story so that they have ownership of it.

| Teachable |
| Moments |

Playacting

To help your child develop preliteracy skills, first "borrow" a child if you don't have an extra! Take turns having each child tell you a story about an event that happened at a place you visited together. The event can be as simple as that time a shopping cart hit mommy's car while you were at the grocery store, or as exciting as a recounting of the camping trip you took to the Grand Canyon. As the child tells the story, write down what he says, prompting him when necessary to provide extra details or to fill in missing steps in the sequence of events. Then encourage him and the other children to playact the story that was just told.

WHEN CAN CHILDREN FOLLOW THE RULES OF THE GAME?

As Piaget suggests, the great finale in play is when our children not only create the rules, but can also follow them. In pretend play, children make and negotiate the rules with their friends. They learn to play together in this way. But board games and sports do not afford children the opportunity to create rules at will. Anyone who has tried to play a card game with a 3-year-old knows this! They seem to make up the rules and just expect you to follow their fancy. Thus, the child—using a brilliant strategy of game control—always emerges as the winner.

Real-world games, however, are much more complex, and each rule is part of a larger system of fixed rules. In fact, after years of watching our children play in the soccer league, some of us are still trying to figure out the intricacies of the corner kick! When are children developmentally ready to cope with the idea of teams and rules? In these complex games, the key is understanding not only what you are supposed to do, but also what the person next to you is doing and might do next. You must be able to anticipate what the person on the other team might do next. So, as a child, you might learn that you should kick the ball forward, but if that is all you do, you are not really playing the game of soccer. In fact, anyone who watches 4- or 5-year-olds on the soccer field will attest to the fact that when the ball moves into the field, you find a clump of children from both teams all trying to kick it at once. What's most fun is when young children kick the ball into their own goal—so much for rules! It is not until age 7 or 8 that our children can truly understand the rules and play with strategy and planning. The same is true for board games. The simple games they start with, like Candy Land, demand only that you move forward and backward with the role of the dice. Our children can figure this one out, so they love to play, play again, and then when *we* are bored to tears—play just "one more time."

Physical Play: The Benefits of Running Around

What's the first thing that comes to mind when we think about play? Being outside, in the sun, maybe in a playground, and running around. This is what lots of us did as children growing up—before safety concerns (not to mention lawsuits) removed monkey bars and seesaws from public parks. Many of us had the freedom—even if we grew up in cities—to walk places with friends and play hopscotch and various ball games. And did you ever wonder as a child how children everywhere seemed to know the same games? We did. Why was it that even if you went to visit your grandparents, the children there knew the hand clap games you played at home? Children play many of the same games and at the same ages because play is a mirror of children's thinking and motor abilities. Play changes over time, gaining in complexity in a predictable way as children's physical and mental capabilities change. Just as a 3-year-old doesn't yet have the capability to hop on one foot and play hopscotch, the 5-year-old doesn't yet have the mental wherewithal to repeat long strings of nonsense in hand clap games without lots of practice. Nor does the 3-year-old have the capability to play outdoor games with rules.

Of course, there are many varieties of play. Witness 4-year-old Jill, who is playing with the Brio train set—interlocking the various pieces to create an interesting track. She is practicing her fine motor skills (using her fingers). Then there is her sister, 2-year-old Samantha, who is climbing on the table in the background and who is testing out her gross motor skills (chest, legs, and arms). These physical play activities abound in our children's world and are crucial to their development because they are taking pleasure in testing their budding abilities, learning how well they work, and practicing their various uses. "If I make my legs go real fast on the pedals, can I make a loud crash when I blam into the chair? Wow! That's fun. I think I'll do it again!" they might be saying to themselves. Activities like Gymboree, swimming, art classes, or local gym programs all build upon those physical play skills. But even without organized activities, physical play opportunities are found everywhere—in backyards, in baby walkers, and even in playpens; in scribbling with crayons, in shaping with Play-Doh, in fitting puzzle pieces together, children are practicing their budding motor abilities.

If we provide them with the opportunities to play in safe spaces, children can refine their skills and tone the muscles that they will need later for sports and for writing. But they will do this "work" at the appropriate level of challenge. Children have their own paces for developing these capacities. Most pediatricians now recommend against structured exercise classes for babies, for instance, because the doctors are seeing more bone fractures and muscle strains that result from pushing the babies beyond their natural limits.

In fairness, some of the reduction in outside free play, as well as the structuring of play by parents, is a result of parents' fears about their children's safety. One parent who lived next door to a park told us, "When I was 5, I played in the park near where I lived and no one minded. Now I'm afraid to let Erin go to the park with a friend—even though it's right next door!—what with all that's happening today." This is not a concern that our parents had nearly as much. There is, though, a serious question about whether the risks to children have in fact increased or whether we are just more *attuned* to risk factors because of extensive media coverage of the things that do happen, albeit rarely. The important outcome, however, is a reduction in activities that children can do independently, re-moving some of the joy and spontaneity of childhood. Playing alone out-side—even with friends—is getting rarer and rarer. What is replacing free play outside are organized sports activities that we sign our children up for, even as young as age 4. In fact, one study showed that between the ages of 6 and 8, organized sports take up approximately 20 percent of a child's playtime. Yet organized sports aren't the only option for safe out-door play. If safety is a concern for you, perhaps you could arrange a ro-tating schedule with the parents of your child's friends so that one adult always accompanies the children as they play outdoors. Another option might be to hire a trusted high school student to supervise your child's time outdoors when you can't be there.

BRINGING THE LESSONS HOME

Play is a central component in children's mental growth. Play helps chil-dren make meaning in their world, it helps them learn about themselves, and equally crucially, it helps them to learn how to get along with others. Yet it can be difficult to resist the trends of our achievement-oriented so-ciety when we're faced with the choice of allowing our children more downtime or signing them up for the latest class, sport, or activity. The following tips can help you make play a central part of your children's—and your own—life.

Become an advocate for play. If we know play to be important, we need to let our actions speak loud. Let us transform preschool rooms back into indoor playgrounds that encourage and promote learning in a playful way. Let us open up our homes to play and let us schedule activ-ities around play rather than squeeze play around our activities. Let us also acknowledge that children need us to help them get going in their play, by providing stimulating environments and by entering in and injecting important knowledge from the wider world. By doing so, we will be sending the message that play is the answer to how we build happy, healthy, and intelligent children. Einstein knew that, and—with your help—so will the parents in your neighborhood.

Provide the resources for stimulating play. Simply having objects to play with appears to be an important component of later intellectual development. Why? Toys and play materials provide the stimulus for children's exploration. When these things are interesting to children, children learn more from them. Toys and play materials are also centerpieces for interaction. When toys are interesting to them, you are more likely to see children coming together and united in a common activity. What do we all do when we are playing together, rather than alone? We talk more, create more, and engage more. These are the foundations for learning.

But there are several caveats. The first is that almost anything can be a toy. You don't have to purchase a fancy toy to reap the benefits for learning and social interaction. Consider some of the low-cost alternatives for a change: Use blankets and chairs to make forts and tents. Our children loved this kind of play, perhaps because it made them feel safe and gave them a private space that they were in charge of (for a change!). Plastic forks make great items to use to build with, and ordinary, inexpensive white paper plates and a little string are great for making things like masks. How about using your plastic containers and different amounts of raw rice, beans, and split peas to make instruments? You can experiment with whether they sound different depending on what they're filled with and how much they are filled.

The movie *Toy Story* was fascinating for children because it made their toys come alive. Stuffed animals can be characters in elaborate fantasy scenarios that you and your child concoct together. These can be at the playground, in school, in a car—all sorts of scripts can be played out. Seashells collected on trips make great toys, as do old tennis balls and old uniforms (try Goodwill stores), various inexpensive school supplies (those colored paper clips are great fun), used paper (ever make airplanes? or hats?), and, for the older set, coins. Sorting coins can be great fun. The trick is to look around your environment from your child's perspective. Whatever it is that you are always warning your children away from is what fascinates them. Can you figure out a way to adapt it to make it safe so they can play with it, or can you find something like it?

Laura Berk, in her excellent book *Awakening Children's Minds*, provides parents and caregivers with three useful questions to ask themselves before buying that next toy: "What activities will this toy inspire? What values will the activities teach? What social rules will my children learn to follow?"

Too often we buy what our children ask for and don't stop to think about whether it will be good for them to have that toy. Yet we are in control, just as we control whether the television is on or not. And we don't have to shell out money for every educational toy that comes along or that toy the children see advertised on television. We're not bad parents if our children are occasionally unhappy.

Join in the fun. Jane Brody, popular columnist for the *New York Times*, writes, "Toys are best seen as tools of play. . . . Toys should be used as an adjunct to interactions between parent and caretaker, not as a substitute for an adult's participation in the child's play."

Joining children in play is perhaps the hardest challenge we have to meet. We are up for a board game or two, but we are not as good at joining in their world. We get bored easily ourselves. If we don't *really* believe that what they are doing is important, we have a tendency to either control the scene or to opt out of their play. Yet, whenever possible, join in rather than thinking, "Oh, good, she's playing alone. I can now make that call I need to make." Part of joining in requires that you give yourself permission to be a kid again and to see the world from that point of view. Do you remember when jumping in puddles was glorious and when you used to take apart Oreo cookies to lick the icing out of the middle? Do it again. You'll find it rewarding.

Let your child take the lead. Child-directed games will pique interest and learning. When we make play into work by controlling or limiting it, our children lose interest, and we lose opportunities to bond and to imagine with them. We need to strive to find the delicate balance between providing props for play and directing play in our homes and in our classrooms. If we are going to present our children with an art project, we need to make it one where the children determine how the end product looks. We might find that they are capable—when they are the leaders—of going well beyond what we thought was possible. A good thing to remember is that it's the *process* that counts, not the *product*.

Try to be a sensitive play partner—reading your children's signals about how much involvement they want from you. Parents who are good at being play partners don't tell children what to do or constantly ask questions or hint to children about the way to play the game.

Encourage your child to use his imagination. One way to get your child's imagination flowing is to set up a pretend play sequence and then let him take it from there. For example, act out a visit to grandma's house with your child, taking his lead. Perhaps you can get him started by using chairs to represent the seats in the car and encouraging him to drive you. You can pass all sorts of interesting things as you go and even worry about the weather because it's snowing. And you can have the snowflakes look like little stars, cows, bowls—whatever you like. A trip to the swimming pool is another good one—best done in the dead of winter! Swimming on the carpet, you can spot all sorts of fish and plants and coins and other children and family members.

One game we always used to play in our (Kathy's) house was "Imagination Is." We would sit together on a bed, cover our eyes, and say, "Imagination is when you're lying in bed, you close your eyes and open them. You're somewhere else instead." The children would take us to many fanciful places as we landed at the zoo, in a jungle, on the moon, or flying in the sky. Sometimes we were giants, and sometimes we were ants looking at the world as if we were in *Honey, I Shrunk the Kids*. We would have an adventure at each stop and when we wanted to journey on, it was as easy as announcing, "Imagination is . . ." We would all cover our eyes and set out for new, child-directed sites. Pretend play is fun not only for the children, but also for the adults.

Evaluate your child's structured activities. Obviously, there's no need for you to abandon all of the structured activities your children participate in. But when you make choices for your children, select what looks like the most fun. Visit some of the classes or activities and see what the children are doing. Is the place one in which children can take a lead and show their creativity? Is it *child-centered*? Are they engaged in pretend and social play? Is there a happy feeling, and are children free to make a mess? Structure in activities is a good thing, but too much control is not. Also ask yourself what the purpose of the activity is. It should primarily be for fun and only secondarily for learning. The more we question our own motives and our own choices, the more we can close the gap between what we know is good for children and what we are actually doing with their time.

CHAPTER + 10

THE NEW FORMULA
FOR EXCEPTIONAL
PARENTING

Because raising children who will avoid the Witness Protection Program is always a blend of groping, hoping, love, and luck . . . there are no absolute rules for it or even relative ones—except perhaps: less can be more. The enlightened way to raise children is not to use pushing, but by using a lower gear, and sometimes neutral.

—Ralph Schoenstein, author of *My Kid's an Honor Student, Your Kid's a Loser: The Pushy Parent's Guide to Raising a Perfect Child*

ALBERT EINSTEIN WAS A GREAT MIND, not because his mind had assimilated vast quantities of information, but because he was a great thinker—his greatness was all about process. Albert Einstein's mother was a pianist and had arranged for him to have music lessons at the age of 6. For years he made very little progress. But at 13, he suddenly acquired a passion for Mozart's sonatas and developed a real expertise at playing the violin. "Love is a better teacher than a sense of duty," Einstein is quoted as saying about his musical achievement.

On the other hand, Einstein needed little encouragement to develop his powers of reason. As a young child, he was eager to get things correct and unusually willing to persevere at tasks. He was often engaged in play activities that involved solving puzzles and problems. He was already demonstrating a painstaking thoroughness, making elaborate structures from building blocks and, later, houses constructed from cards. When Albert reached school age, he excelled there as well. And when he was not in school, he preferred to spend his time in mentally stimulating activities like playing with a metal construction set and a model steam engine that a relative had given him. At the age of 11, Albert liked to read about science and philosophy in books that were beyond the understanding of most children. At the same time, he became enchanted with mathematics and determined to prove Pythagoras's theorem.

What lessons can we draw from these glimpses into Einstein's childhood? Simply put—Einstein himself led the way. Much of his learning as a child took place through play. His parents and family paid attention to his interests and fed them with lessons and toys and books—and, apparently, some freedom to do as he pleased. Einstein had freedom to be by himself, freedom to pursue problems that interested him.

If Einstein's mother never used flash cards with him, why is it that modern-day parents have come to believe that they must drill their preschoolers on obscure facts, teach them to read before they enter kindergarten, and have them doing arithmetic before the age of 3? Why is it that many preschool teachers and administrators are pushing an academics-oriented curriculum that leaves children with little time to play on their own? And why are government officials intent on finding a way to quantify what preschoolers are learning and turn it into a formula for measuring the children's potential for later success in life?

These efforts are well-intentioned. Parents, teachers, and elected officials are grasping at cultural myths about child-rearing and are putting the latest advice into practice. Yet the "latest advice" is not based on the best scientific research. Despite the humorous pessimism of the quotation at the beginning of this chapter, science *has* come a long way in the last 30 years in unraveling the story of how children grow and learn, and how we as parents and educators can help children be happy while reaching their intellectual potential. Unfortunately, that message has become muddled in its translation to parents and educators.

Once we understand the problem, we can take direct action and reclaim our lives and our children's. In this chapter, we'll show you how to do just that. First, though, it is important to understand the prevailing faulty assumptions that are driving parenting and policy decisions. Then, through our four guiding principles for raising happy and intelligent children, you'll discover ways in which the products of science can easily be applied in our homes as well as in our schools. Adopting this perspective, you will be able to achieve more balance in your family's life, to rethink what is meant by "success," and to view child development through a new lens. You will be able to reflect, resist, and re-center as you walk through the mall and talk to your friends about the latest classes and products that your preschoolers simply *must* have.

WHAT WENT WRONG?

If there is so much research on children, then why does the application lag so far behind the science? Why isn't research used more in our homes and classrooms? Several factors have converged to create the current rush toward baby geniuses and away from evidence-based practice: guilt, fear, and scientific sound bites.

In most families today, both the mother and the father work. And often, they work longer hours than did previous generations. If we can't be there to raise our children, we want to make sure that they are in the best hands, and in all of the top-notch classes, so that they don't miss out on a minute of the time they would have had with us. We, both fathers and mothers, feel guilty that we are not there and want to find a substitute "us" that will fill our children with all of the education they need. We fret that our children's caregivers aren't good enough, and we resolve to make the time we do have with our children count—to make it "quality" time.

We're also motivated by fear. In our increasingly unpredictable global economy, we want to equip our children with the best possible "weapons" against failure. We want to ensure that our children will be able to make it in a world where no job is secure—in fact, no career path is secure. In such a world, the only defense is the best offense.

Finally, we are swayed by the scientific sound bites we hear in the media. In the past few decades, scientists have uncovered some astounding facts about how children learn. But in the rush to take science to the presses, journalists often leave out the complexities and give us the bottom line. Therein lies the problem. News (and products!) are not attention getting if they encourage you to maintain the status quo. "Play with your kids and they'll turn out swell." Headlines like this lack drama and luster. "Scientific ways to make your baby smarter," however, captures the imagination and offers a tool to placate the defensive parent.

MISINFORMATION: A SOCIALLY TRANSMITTED DISEASE

The fear, the guilt, and the scientific sound bites have created a panic in parents and educators. This panic has become contagious and has led our culture to make four unhealthy assumptions that guide the way we raise our children. Do any of these sound familiar?

Myth 1: Faster Is Better—Whoosh!

Our Roadrunner society holds that faster is better. Whether it's food or fuel or even fat reduction, our whole society is built around speed and getting things done in the minimal time possible.

We seem determined as a culture to accelerate our children's cognitive as well as social development. Not only do we ask them to learn academic material at an earlier and earlier age, but we dress them like miniteens in fashions of Baby Gap and Abercrombie Kids. As some anthropologists tell us, we are uncomfortable with the competence differential that we find between our children and ourselves, so we engage in the complementary practices of "self-lowering" and "child raising." In self-lowering, we adjust our behavior to suit the child. For example, we try to match our speech to what we think our children can understand. When we engage in child raising, we act as if children were more capable than they really are, as when we interpret a baby's every bodily emission as though it were a contribution to his early "conversations" with us. Neither of these practices is bad for children's development, and they may even propel children forward. The problem is that these practices have spiraled out of hand as the differences between children and adults become more and more obliterated. As we schedule tiny children for enrichment classes and coed social events, we rush them beyond childhood and children's preoccupations. We make them more and more in our hectic, hurried, frenetic, and feverish image.

Myth 2: Making Every Moment Count

"Making every moment count" is a fine thing to believe in, depending on how it is interpreted. As interpreted by hassled parents, however, it is not a general Zen calling about living in the present, but an exhortation to teach and structure children's lives as much as possible. It is the belief that not a moment can be wasted if our children are to succeed in life. Without our realizing it, our current culture has unwittingly endorsed an old view championed by the psychologist Jerome Bruner, founder of the Center for Cognitive Studies at Harvard University. Bruner wrote that we can teach children any subject at any time in an intellectually honest way.

Yet the science of developmental psychology, greatly influenced by the works of Jean Piaget and Lev Vygotsky, has shown that this belief is erroneous. Children's ways of learning are qualitatively different from our own. Children are very active learners, constructing their own view of reality, which is not the same as ours. They do not passively wait for us to fill their brains with knowledge about the world. Given our general anxiety about our children, we fail to take note of the long-standing wisdom that nature is the "hidden tutor"—that biology, too, plays a role in when children are ready to learn. Certainly, a hospitable and nurturing environment helps. And of course, that gets us back to play. Young children learn through play much that is important. Play is far from a waste of time, as PLAY = LEARNING. We need to let our children live their lives, rather than view each and every moment of their lives as part of a grand plan for their future. Life is not a rehearsal; this is life!

Myth 3: Parents Are Omnipotent

Many parents have come to believe that they, and they alone, are responsible for the development of their children's intelligence, athletic skills, artistic accomplishments, emotional makeup, and sociability. But truly, children are just passing through our lives. They come into this world as unique persons who require from us both nurturing and enjoyment. Parents are not omnipotent. At best, they are wise partners accompanying their children through the labyrinth of development. Despite their best efforts, parents cannot determine their children's future by the nature of the experiences they provide for them in the present.

While we certainly would not deny the importance of childhood (as Shakespeare said, "The child becomes the man") or the importance of parents and caregivers, our culture has gone overboard. Childhood is viewed now as just the foundation for adulthood. All the silliness and playfulness and mess and absurdity are thought of more as a disease to conquer than as a delightful stage of life! And parents are seen as responsible for getting through that childishness as rapidly as possible. Why? Because parents are now seen as the designers of children's intelligence and capabilities. But our role has been perverted. A sculpture requires a sculptor to create it, yet children do much of their own creating, having come prepared with the clay (the human brain and enormous motivation to learn) that provides the framework of the sculpture and makes it all possible. Parents can relax. They don't need to be the sculptors of their children's future lives. In fact, they fool themselves if they think they are.

Myth 4: Children Are Empty Vessels

If parents are omnipotent and responsible for teaching and inculcating all the skills and traits their children will need in the future, then where does that leave the child? Certainly not in the driver's seat, but relegated to a role in the backseat, waiting to be driven everywhere. This statement is not only literally true for parents who spend most of their time carting Junior to his many activities; it is also metaphorically true for the passive child who eagerly waits for experience to write upon her blank slate. Our children seem to be happy as they fly from activity to activity and from one class to the next knowledge station, but we might be creating a cohort of children who are too passive to learn about the world. These are the precursors to that syndrome that is so familiar in elementary school—"I'm bored." The bored child is one who is just waiting for someone to announce the next activity so that he is always engaged. The bored child is one who has never learned to be creative.

If there is one thing we have learned about child development, it is that children come into the world determined to learn about and adapt to their world. They are active consumers of all the information available to them. "Consumers," of course, not in the sense of purchasers, but in the sense of eating or "taking in." Children have an insatiable appetite for knowledge. Have you ever noticed how your children want to know everything, and are not happy with simple and half-baked explanations?

Once they can say "why?" you're answering more questions than you knew existed! Although they may see the world through a different lens than we do, they are trying hard to adopt our lens, and will, little by little, succeed.

If children are like sponges when it comes to absorbing information, then what's so bad about toys and activities that strive to quickly teach them certain facts? One problem is that we train them out of self-initiative. The other problem, however, is that the "boxed" learning we provide in terms of toys and classes is not necessarily real learning. To understand what we mean, you have to distinguish between real and superficial learning. In real learning, children can take what they have learned and apply it widely. When they learn how to ride a bike, for example, it could be any bike (within size limits). When they learn how to add two small numbers together, they can apply their counting skill to any set, regardless of the kind of objects it contains. When children can apply their knowledge beyond the original situation in which they learned it, their learning is secure. The ability to apply what we have learned is called transfer. Unfortunately, much of the early learning movement is not teaching skills that can transfer, but skills that are superficial, limited only to the context in which they are learned. And when our skills are limited to the box in which we learn them, we are not learning to be creative. We are not learning to use our information in new and exciting ways.

In sum, please understand that we are not suggesting that parents should back off and wait for their children to discover everything on their own. Imagine what it would be like to be a parent who taught nothing, who never said "No, that isn't appropriate," or who never explained how something worked or why things were that way. We *are* saying that treating children like empty vessels and making every minute count is not healthy for them or us. If every situation is a potential for instruction, children will learn nothing on their own in the absence of these highly structured circumstances. These same children will be unprepared to learn on their own when they enter school and may also feel that if they don't get the "right answers," they are failures. Some of us learn more from failing than we do when we get all the answers right. We don't want to create little perfectionists! Our job, then, is to see our children as active learners, to see the world as a virtual school yard of interesting lessons, and to find a happy medium that allows us both to teach children and to retain the unprogrammed benefits of childhood. This occurs when the teaching is incidental and part of play (as opposed to drill) and the learning is embedded in an emotionally supportive context.

These four overarching assumptions leave us in an awkward place. On the one hand, we recognize that things have gone awry and that we are treating childhood as preparatory school for adulthood, that we have lost the precious moments of childhood to the fast-paced and demanding society in which we live. "If society is moving quickly forward," you might ask, "don't we want our children to be on the fast train?" On the other hand, we join the parents and teachers who long for a place where children can play in the park with no hidden agenda and where finger and pudding painting is still part of the school schedule. Is there any way to ensure that our children learn while still granting them a childhood? Is there any way to free parents so that they can relax and enjoy parenthood? Is there any way for teachers to reclaim preschool curricula where PLAY = LEARNING and where social prowess is as valued as academic skill? The simple answer is *yes*. If we apply what we know in science, we can change the core assumptions about developing children and can find the proper equation for raising happy, healthy, and intelligent children.

FOUR PRINCIPLES FOR PARENTS TO LIVE BY

Fortunately, once we recognize that the drive to hurry our children through childhood and accelerate their intellectual development is based on misinformation, we can move forward in a healthy way, based on the following four principles.

Principle 1: The Best Learning Is Learning within Reach

As you'll recall from chapter 6, the Russian psychologist Lev Vygotsky introduced the term "zone of proximal development," or ZPD. It's a great concept. He said that children need their parents, caregivers, older siblings, friends, and teachers to challenge them at the far reaches of their natural capabilities. Parents and caregivers need to stretch their children's nascent abilities, not catapult them into a realm where they are unable to grasp basic concepts. Learning within reach captures this idea. It reminds us to help children learn things just beyond their capabilities, things that will be truly meaningful for them in their lives. Why teach rocket science to 3-year-olds when they don't yet know about the clouds?

For example, preschoolers learn math best from play, *not* from doing flash card drills. They learn from messing around with sets of objects: "Amanda, will you get me two spoons, please?" "Can you find three towels in the laundry basket?" Even just counting the number of objects on the floor can be a learning experience. These ordinary, everyday interactions between children and caregivers promote learning about number better than any flash cards can. This is learning within reach: presenting children with problems that are within their ken, that make sense to them in the context of their daily lives.

When we work within our children's zone of proximal development, we present them with information just outside of what they can do, we heighten their motivation, we help them reach, we challenge them to take that extra step. And as adults, we often scaffold a child's knowledge by adding that bit of extra support (like holding the tower so that last block won't make it fall) so that the child's budding abilities can meet the demands of the task. Learning within reach supports children's cognitive growth. On the other hand, if we ask a child to work well beyond her reach, we create frustration or, worse, feelings of helplessness. If the task is something way out of her ability range, she may even conclude that she is not so bright after all. Too much pressure to display empty knowledge and show off what she knows can even cause a child to feel depressed because so much rides on getting it right.

When we violate the principle of learning within reach by teaching things that are way outside our children's experience, they may well succeed in memorizing what we tell them. But they will not have a real understanding, and more important, they may feel frustrated and let down, because they don't have any genuine feeling for what they are supposed to value as knowledge. Learning within reach guarantees that learning will be meaningful and authentic.

Principle 2: Emphasizing Process over Product Creates a Love of Learning

The "process over product" principle recognizes the essential importance of a child's (and parent's) enjoying (and emphasizing) the process of learning. We should concern ourselves as much with *how* children learn as we do with *what* they learn. We want to have children who love to learn, not who feel compelled to perform like trained seals. It's all about process (how the thinking is done, how the answer is derived) and less about the product (whether or not the right answer is achieved). Sure, the right answer matters, and it will matter more as time goes on. But it matters much less in the preschool years, when children are just finding their way. And we don't want to create children who become paralyzed when they can't get the right answer on their very first try. Understanding how your child thinks about a problem is far more interesting to you and to her than insisting on the fact that there is one right answer.

The misplaced emphasis on "product" is now going to affect at least 1 million children, who will be tested to see if their preschool experiences have prepared them adequately for school. As part of President George W. Bush's push for accountability in education, the Head Start program, for instance, is now going to test children for school readiness. In theory, this is an excellent idea. In practice, however, the testing that is being discussed is likely to emphasize product rather than process. The new, congressionally mandated assessment in Head Start covers 13 aspects of knowledge about reading and language. Among the things that a preschooler is expected to accomplish are being able to identify at least 10 letters of the alphabet, recognize a word as a unit of print, and associate sounds with written words. But why is knowing at least 10 letter names important? Surely this is not an overwhelming task. Yet rather than read to children and engage in other emergent literacy activities that really matter for learning to read, many educators are concerned that teachers might now teach to the test, making sure students know at least 10 letters. While letter knowledge correlates with reading success, it doesn't *cause* reading success. Letter knowledge is incidental to being read to, to seeing lots of print, and to seeing people read routinely to gain information. So it's not the letters' names that matter; it's an understanding of the alphabetic principle and how it relates to print. That's a focus on process, and that's what predicts a positive outcome for children's reading.

Remember what it feels like to take a test? Would "anxious" be the best adjective? Yet we are doing more and more testing. And we are increasingly teaching our children to test well, rather than to think well. What's worse, they may become fearful learners. An emphasis on process over product creates a love of learning; an emphasis on product over process can backfire and create burnout both for the teachers and their students.

Amy, a third-grade teacher, recently remarked about the new curricula in her classroom. "Guess what we are learning this week in school," she said. "On Monday, we are doing preparation for test one. On Tuesday, we are doing preparation for test two. . . . " These children are learning how to memorize the things that will be on the test so that the school looks accountable. Perhaps we need to think of process-oriented ways to assess academic and social growth.

In fact, in the winter of 2003, one of us (Kathy) convened the Temple Forum with several colleagues. We invited distinguished professors from around the country who are scholars in mathematics, language, reading, and social skills. A strong consensus rang forth as the main conclusion from this meeting: Testing for factual knowledge as the royal road to accountability is not in the best interests of the teachers or the children. It is, of course, important to make sure that each preschool is teaching what children need to know so that they are ready for school. But there is another way to do this teaching and testing. There is another way to see whether young children are learning the basic skills involved in one-to-one correspondence, holding conversations, and reading readiness. And what would this other teaching and assessment look like? It would be based in playful experiences. It would look at learning in context. It would ask whether children could count the number of plates needed to give cake to all of the children at a birthday party or whether they know how to write their names for place cards at the party. If we focus on learning in context and through play and assess learning process along with product, we will have a much better handle on whether our children are prepared for later school. For those who can find the underlying processes, this other way to teach makes learning fun and frees teachers from teaching to the test.

Principle 3: It's EQ, Not Just IQ

Many of us grew up with Fred Rogers on his highly successful show, *Mister Rogers' Neighborhood.* Why did the show have such a powerful impact on children? Probably because of its mission to help children deal with their feelings. When Fred Rogers died in the spring of 2003, obituaries lauded his enduring influence on children. Fred Rogers provided something children sorely need in this world. "The world is not always a kind place," he is quoted as saying. "That is something all children learn for themselves, whether we want them to or not, but it's something they really need our help to understand." His program was considered highly educational. Yet it stressed the emotional side of life. Clearly, there is more to being successful than just having a high IQ.

Of course, it's important for children to reach the cognitive goals set out by school curricula. Most people have a fine IQ that is adequately stimulated and challenged by the subjects educators have chosen to teach. When IQ becomes an obsession, though, a target of comparison in the keeping-up-with-the-Joneses game, we need to step back for a moment and recognize that IQ is no index for success. It reflects but one set of capabilities. Without emotional intelligence, social savvy, and pragmatic abilities, even geniuses can have a very hard time in life.

A link between emotional intelligence and success in the classroom has even been found in kindergartners. Research tells us that children who make friends easily in kindergarten and are accepted by their classmates are also the ones who work hard in a self-directed way that fosters their academic competence. EQ (emotional intelligence) and IQ go hand in hand.

One of the things that foster both IQ and EQ is social play. Social play has emotional, cognitive, and important social benefits. What children are actually doing when they play together is rehearsing the scripts that go with the various roles people play in our culture. Listen to two typical 4-year-olds.

Jill: I'll be the bus driver. You be the crossing guard.
Jake: Bus drivers can't be a lady.
Jill: Yes, they can, but they can't be married.
Jake: But Mrs. Tuttle is married.
Jill: Oh, no, she isn't. She's divorced!

These children are working out society's rules, even if they don't always get them right. Through play, children explore the various roles society sanctions, and therefore learn how the culture works, before they get to the place where they actually have to be a mommy or daddy, a bus driver, or a veterinarian. And consider—aside from the learning involved about who can play what role and under what terms—the social knowledge that your child is accruing from such mundane interactions. While these childish disagreements may seem small and petty, your child is obtaining a crucial set of skills that are essential for getting through life: how to negotiate.

Consider what successful negotiations involve. I must recognize that you think differently than I do. Then I must evaluate what you think, and decide whether you are right or wrong. If I think you are right, I may abandon my belief. But if I think you are wrong, I will need to come up with the arguments to persuade you of your error. All of these mental machinations force the child to move from believing that his way of thinking is the only way. They help the child to consider others' points of view and recognize the existence of other minds that hold different beliefs. How important for getting along with one's peers—and one's supervisors! This is emotional intelligence, and it's just as important for success as the intelligence that's measured on IQ tests.

Play also helps children work out and regulate emotions. Have you ever heard your child using your own scolding voice directed at your daughter's baby doll? "Alexandra Beth Neale! You do not hit your baby brother. You go to your room right now!" The scary part is hearing Alexandra using the exact same words, with the exact same intonation, that you used on her just minutes ago! She's displacing her anger, getting her own sense of power and self-respect back, and feeling a lot better after giving her doll a good scolding. How does this contribute to IQ and EQ? Children who play more tend to be happier. And happier children tend to relate better to their peers, and that, in turn, seems to engage them more fully in the curriculum of the classroom. Hence, they do better in school! Both EQ and IQ are fed by play.

Principle 4: Learning in Context Is Real Learning—And Play Is the Best Teacher

The English-speaking child who hears Spanish words and phrases explained on *Sesame Street* may or may not have much interest in retaining those facts. But if his new friend in day care comes from the Dominican Republic, he will want to understand those words so he can actually use them. They are the bridge that connects the friendship. They have a real-life context and a usefulness the child can understand. The problem is that most of what we teach our children (in fact, most of what we teach adults) seems to have little or no bearing on their lives. So they tune out. Our role as educators and parents is to put learning into context. That makes learning fun and unleashes the child's natural curiosity and creativity. By now, you know that the best—in fact, the *only*—way to do this is through play.

Play is that arena in which you get to try out everything with no real-life consequences because it's all just pretend. You can play at being a castle invader and having a castle wall fall on you. No pain! And you can play with Veterinarian Barbie and practice what it's like to take care of animals. Learning within the context of play brings it into the child's world, where the child is in charge. When imagination is unleashed, learning is truly meaningful.

The opposite of learning within context is learning meaningless, disembodied facts. The motivation for this type of learning becomes pleasing the parent or teacher. The children who have to memorize and perform do more learning for love than loving to learn. Children want to please you. They will try to do as you ask. And they will try to act excited about an activity if you think it is important. But a deeper, more lasting education will take place if they have a context in which to place the newly acquired information. Learning within context is real, authentic learning.

For our young children, all learning should be fun. There should never be a situation (other than discipline) where learning is forced upon a child and presented as work. Our children's play is the quintessential meaningful context for learning and the context that lays the foundation for all future learning, even when play is no longer required to sweeten the message. This principle is captured in an ancient practice that Jewish children participate in when they start to study Hebrew. The first time they encounter some Hebrew, they are given candy. Why? To sweeten their learning. We don't need to use candy; play has the same effect!

BALANCE IS THE KEY

Where does all this information leave conscientious parents who want to do the best for their children? Where does it leave preschool teachers and legislators? If they want to use evidence-based practices, it leaves them with a set of principles for achieving balance.

The next time you're at the toy store or are urged to sign your child up for assorted lessons and activities, know that you have options. Of course, not all of the games in the store are bad. Not all lessons are time wasters. We now know that the key to childhood learning is through play. So ask yourself, "Am I buying this so that I can teach my child the ways of the adult world? Or am I interested in what will intrigue and challenge my child within his reach?" The emphasis should be on the process, not the product. It's not what you do; it's how you do it. Speak the lingo and see if you can resist buying more than you can easily afford. Look around your house, the mall, and the local fast-food restaurant to see if there is any other way to experience shapes and numbers, printed words, and moral behavior. If you buy a little less for your children—but spend a little more time with them—you can feel great about that since entering into children's play is one of the best ways to help them learn. Balance is the key.

When your friends' children are signed up for activities and want you to join in, just take a moment to tally up how much free time you and the children have. Now that you recognize the need for children to do some of their own choosing, to enjoy unstructured time where they can wander, hang out, relax, and notice the squirrels, you can "just say no" to the pressures from other Roadrunners. You are safe in the knowledge that there is a very educational side to your choice—and you, through your resistance, are modeling making good choices! For how is the child whose every moment is structured by a schedule going to become an adult who is able to make good choices? Balance is the key.

How do you recognize when you're going south as a parent when you thought you were going north? When you're always rushed and tired and not enjoying parenting, things are out of balance. The hurried parent is one who is often, although not always, misdirected. Now that you understand why Einstein's parents never used flash cards, take some of the pressure off yourself by doing a little less. Yes, sometimes less is more! If you're still bent on raising a genius, watch your child very carefully to see what interests her, and then feed that interest. Again, balance is the key.

If you are the teacher or principal and you feel the pressure to add more facts and to play less, think about the ways you can talk to parents to help them see that learning is a process. How can you structure play activities so that children are learning the information you want to teach without controlling their every activity? How can we begin to give preschool education back to the teachers and principals who understand children while addressing the pressures of our sound-bite science? Balance is the key.

And when you are the legislator who must figure out how to reach acceptable levels of accountability in your preschools, ask how scientists and lawmakers might collaborate to ensure that the congressional mandates are informed not by headlines, but by the best science. Ask how teachers can learn this science and be aware of the processes that make teachable moments. Ask how we can ensure that children learn the facts but do so in a playful environment so they are ready for school and want to learn. Balance is the key.

ACHIEVING BALANCE: THE NEW THREE R's— REFLECT, RESIST, AND RE-CENTER

There's no doubt about it: Raising a child in the 21st century can be tough, especially with the swirling forces of often conflicting child-rearing advice all around us. So it's understandable if you're feeling a bit nervous about your abilities to achieve the healthy balance we've just described. Fortunately, the key to achieving this balance is fairly simple: The New Three R's, which we first presented in chapter 1.

- *Reflect.* Ask yourself, Why am I enrolling 4-year-old Jonny in this class? Does Jonny really like (art, yoga, computer science, music, fill in the blank), or do I feel pressure to make sure that Jonny has a leg up on the other children his age? Am I trying to make every moment count? Am I acting as if I'm the architect of his mind? Would we all be happier and less frenzied if we had some extra time for unstructured play?

- *Resist.* It takes courage to resist the forces that tell us that faster is better. We hear our friends as they boast about their children's newfound talents discovered (at some cost) in Melanie's music class. We live with the anxiety of knowing that while we are at the park, Janie took Ralph to art classes and Sue had Phyllis at Chess for Cherubs! Resist. PLAY = LEARNING. Your child is learning just as much as Ralph or Phyllis. And you don't even have to drive!

- *Re-center.* With your newfound focus on the science of child development and the four principles we discussed earlier, you have made the balanced and healthy choice. Think back to the "Teachable Moments" we've discussed in each chapter. These are teachable moments not just for your child, but also for you. Each time you engage in a teachable moment—each time you play with your child—you are seeing child development in action. You are connecting in a new way with your child and have become a more sensitive and responsive parent.

When you have a moment of doubt about your child's progress, about how many *facts* he knows, return to the "Discovering Hidden Skills" sections throughout the book and treat yourself to a new view of your child's competencies. Remember that process is more important than product. It's not *what* you know (the boring facts) but *how* you know that will help build creative thinking and problem solving in math, reading, and language. And your children will even be happier with some downtime so that they can connect with you and with their friends.

IMPLEMENTING THE FOUR PRINCIPLES IN OUR OWN HOMES

Families—whatever their composition—need time together. And these precious times together are opportunities for learning and emotional sharing. Perhaps the most significant change you can make is to start eating dinner together as a family. Research shows that families who eat dinner together have children who have fewer problems when adolescence comes around. It's unlikely that it's the sharing of the food per se that is related to this effect. It's much more likely that it's something it betrays about parents' attitudes. The message you send when you make family dinners a priority is *we matter, you matter, and being together and sharing matters.* This is a powerful message. And a much more important message than having dinner on the fly and making that next class.

Think of what goes on over dinner. Everyone actually sits together and converses for a full 20 minutes or so. Doesn't sound like a lot of time, does it? But it may be just enough to help your children learn what is important to you and to them. When we sit together for dinner, the assorted phones, the mail and e-mail, the bits of work left over from the office, all get tabled while the children receive attention from the adults. (That means you have to commit to letting the phone ring without answering it.) We talk about daily events, sharing our ups and downs, taking turns talking and listening. These occasions become contexts for learning. We sequence our daily events to recount them, encouraging the development of memory and narrative. We learn to read one another's facial expressions and interpret the emotional content of what is recounted. We ask for and receive advice sometimes, and we try out ideas about how to act in this or that circumstance. It's wonderful for children to see parents asking each other for feedback. Establishing that we can count on each other and call on each other for support gets conveyed indirectly but clearly that way. A shared dinner hour (even a truncated, 20-minute dinner hour!) gives the message that that each of us, and what we do, is important in our own, unique way.

One family we know has kept a dictionary and a globe at the ready, in order to enhance and verify the information that comes up in their conversations. In fact, we even play a game called "Dictionary" where each person makes up a word and its definition and the others have to guess whether it's a real word and definition. We also discuss the limits we set together on the amount of TV and computer time our children are allowed. Children who play together around the computer or TV do not talk. They do not come up with fantasy games. They do not look at one another and learn to read facial expressions. So when it comes to requests to extend those limits, we usually "just say NO," making Nancy Reagan proud!

Find times in your busy lives to be together as a family outside of the kitchen or dining room. Say "yes" to family time whenever possible. Pick a game night. Decree a reading night (even beyond the reading you do every night at bedtime). Decree a walk night (wait until you see what amazing things are going on in your neighborhood—even the cool mushrooms and slugs near the sidewalk!). While this may sound regimented, you'd need to have nights devoted to different things only when you first start. After that, it will become natural. But don't be surprised if your children want to keep the nights devoted to different activities since they love predictable structure.

Another family we know drives 3 hours to Baltimore during baseball season to watch the Orioles play. Are the parents really rabid Orioles fans? No, not really, although they do like baseball. Are the parents just gluttons for punishment, not watching their local team but traveling to another ballpark? No, they are no fonder of driving than the rest of us. So why do they do this? They are both working parents who lead very busy lives. They recognize the value of what takes place when a family is locked in a car for 3 hours. They tell us that during the time they are together in the car, they have uninterrupted time to talk (they turn off their cell phones), make up games, and have a good time together. And what better context for the older children in the family for computing batting averages!

The problem of needing more family downtime that is unstructured is so endemic that it was captured recently in a *New Yorker* cartoon. Two 7-year-olds are walking on the sidewalk together as they talk. The caption reads, "So many toys—so little unstructured time." Don't wait until your children are in school to institute family time together. Start now, when your children are small and when you can build in this expectation about your family life. We are all so busy, and we often use weekends to catch up on tasks left undone during the week. Imagine how happy your young children would be if you took a family trip to a local site or event on just one weekend a month. A trip to the zoo or a children's museum or a movie or a children's show or a free walk in the park! If you set this schedule in motion when your children are little, it will become a predictable and looked-forward-to pleasure! On another weekend, create a family project to which all contribute, such as designing and planting a garden or cooking a gourmet meal. Even young children can help mix and stir. They love to help and be part of a family structure that is mutually supportive. They love to feel needed and essential, something that children have trouble feeling because the power differential with parents is so obvious. And of course, allow your children plenty of quality time with you—not feeding them facts but following their lead in play!

IMPLEMENTING THE FOUR PRINCIPLES IN OUR PRESCHOOLS

The very principles that we have suggested for use in the home are also powerful for teachers in preschool and kindergarten. The nature of preschool and kindergarten is changing. With research demonstrating the importance of early learning, especially for impoverished families, societies around the globe are turning attention to the need for high-quality early education. In the United States, for example, there is a new movement toward preschool for all children. States are starting to require that preschool teachers have the same qualifications as elementary school teachers and that schools be accountable for what they teach to our youngest citizens. Let's take a look at two very different kinds of preschools. Let's call one "the Academy," while the other is the preschool (let's call it "Playway") across the street.

At the Academy, the daily curriculum is the centerpiece of the bulletin board. It begins in earnest at 8:00 A.M. with pre-reading skills class, time in the art corner (in which largely preassembled projects, prescribed by teachers, are carried out by children who produce good-looking results they can carry home), Spanish class, followed by snack, and then "computer science" (yes, you read that right!), in which children, whose hands are guided by an adult's hand, learn to use the mouse to select various attractive pictures on the computer and print them out. Lunch and nap are followed by math class, in which children learn to count and recognize quantities. Then a free play period or story time, snack, and finally science class, where they are shown such things as how magnets work, information about nature, and so forth. They are tested three times a year to chart their progress. Children do seem happy, although the room is sometimes awfully quiet and children sometimes wander off to the block corner as if to say, "Enough structure! I need some space!"

At Playway, across the street, things are not so neat. The bulletin board contains scruffy-looking art projects with the children's names on them. Most of the art projects are completely unidentifiable to anyone but the creator. Yet when asked, the artist (read that as your child) will give you a full story about how the blue blob is a portrait of his mother (sorry, mom) and the red streak is her car. As we look on, we see there are a variety of sections where the children can partake of different activities. There is a play corner with dress-up clothes, a block corner, a gym area with a slide and thick mats, and a doll and stuffed animal corner with miniature clothes and furniture for use with the miniature creatures. The reading corner is the pièce de résistance! It is filled with books and assorted pillows and child-size low-slung chairs and little couches. It looks like a place adults would want to hang out in—if the furniture were just a little bigger. There is an art area with easels and watercolor paints and pastels and smocks and a huge sink at child level replete with boats and plastic containers and unbreakable cups and bottles for water play. The children also go outside when the weather is nice and play on swings and in large playhouses and on circular sliding boards.

Occasionally, they take a field trip to the zoo or the Please Touch Museum. At the zoo, a child picks up a pebble and the teacher looks at it with curiosity, too. "Why do you suppose this stone is so smooth? It's not like some of the ones we have at school that are jagged." And here is a moment for introducing some ideas about the power of water to erode, for talking about elementary physics and geology. The lesson stems from something that interests the child. The teacher watches the child closely, though, to see when he's had enough information. She is careful not to overload, but rather to just build on his budding interest.

When the teachers at Playway read stories, they talk with the children about the stories and get into the fun with them. "I like green eggs and ham, said Sam!" one teacher exclaims. She then says, "Let's see if we can beat our drumsticks to the words. We are all beating them at the same time! It's almost like a song, isn't it? Are there any unusual foods that you or your family like to eat?" The children get so involved that they holler things out, and the teacher explains that one at a time is the rule, but that they'll all get a turn and everyone will listen to them when they do.

The children are free enough to make some of their own choices. They are free to make mistakes. They are even free to get into conflicts so that the adults can show them the proper ways to resolve them. There are no tests. Indeed, the curriculum is all about enjoying the process of learning and learning to behave appropriately.

Compared with other countries, we do not do a good job of supporting parents of young children with family leave, high-quality child care, and flexible work time. Recent studies show that we do not have enough high-quality child care in this country. A new study showed that welfare mothers who went back to work were doing well, but now that they are working, there is not adequate child care to take care of their children. And our children are our most important natural resource!

How can you tell if the four principles are present in the child care settings and preschools that you are considering for your children? To evaluate this, you need to go to the school and observe. And any setting that tells you that they don't allow this should be ruled out. You can't rely on your friends to evaluate sites for you because they may want different things for their children than you want for yours. When you go observe, you can quickly get a sense of the emotional tone of the site. Is there an emphasis on play? Can the children reach the toys, or are they placed up high in an inaccessible place? Are teachers talking with the children? Playing with the children? Are there enough adults around (one caregiver for no more than four infants; one caregiver for no more than 10 toddlers through 4-year-olds)? How were the teachers educated? Are children required to master a curriculum previously reserved for older children? What goes on in a typical day? For 4- and 5-year-olds, are letters memorized, or are they learned in the context of writing and reading? Are there books and puzzles? Is the setting child-centered or adult-directed? Remember, child-centered environments have structure; they just have less adult control.

When you do put your children in day care, pay attention to the following six criteria that the National Association for the Educators of Young Children provides as guidelines.

1. Are the children in the program generally comfortable, relaxed, and happy, and involved in play and other activities?
2. Are there sufficient numbers of adults with specialized training in early childhood development and education? (The younger the child, the more individualized their care should be. Infants should be in groups of no more than 6 to 8 children; 2- and 3-year-olds, 10 to 14 children; and 4-to 5-year-olds, groups of 16 to 20 children.)
3. Do adult expectations vary appropriately for children of differing ages and interests?
4. Are all areas of a child's development stressed equally, with time and attention being devoted to cognitive development, emotional and social development, and physical development?

5. Does the staff meet regularly to plan and evaluate the program?
6. Are parents welcome to observe, discuss policies, make suggestions, and participate in the work of the program?

What if you're a preschool teacher or administrator? Is it possible to keep all of these principles in mind as you transform your school? Yes! In a northern town in Italy we find the quaint town of Reggio Emilia, an internationally acclaimed municipality that for the past 25 years has committed 12 percent of the town budget to the provision of high-quality child care for children 6 years and under. A key factor that distinguishes this program is its emphasis on children's "symbolic languages"—their drawing, sculpture, dramatic play, and writing. As part of this child-centered approach, the curriculum includes real-life problem solving among peers, with numerous opportunities for creative thinking and exploration. Teachers often work on long-term projects with small groups of children while the rest of the class engages in a wide variety of self-selected activities. Reggio teachers place a high value on their ability to improvise and respond to children's predisposition to enjoy the unexpected. Successful projects are those that generate a sufficient amount of interest and uncertainty to provoke children's creative thinking and problem solving. Projects begin with teachers observing and questioning children about the topic of interest. Based on the children's responses, teachers introduce materials, questions, and opportunities that provoke children to further explore the topic.

In this community-based program, parents are expected to take part in discussions about school policy, child development, and curriculum planning. The teachers are viewed as learners whose goal is to understand children. There is no school principal, nor is there a hierarchical relationship among the teachers. The same group of children and teachers are kept together for a period of 3 years, contributing to the sense of community and the development of relationships. Each center is staffed with two teachers per classroom (12 children in infant classes, 18 in toddler classes, and 24 in pre-primary classes). One teacher is trained in the arts, and there are several auxiliary staff members. The Reggio system is acclaimed for its internationally respected preschool program. Perhaps this child-centered, process approach is what we should be doing with our children. At least we could approximate what they do. The bottom line?

It is possible to implement these principles at home and at school; we need only the will to do so.

IMPLEMENTING THE FOUR PRINCIPLES IN OUR SOCIETY

Our culture seems schizophrenic in its attitude toward babies and young children. On the one hand, we claim to be a child-centered society. On the other hand, we make it very difficult for families where parents need or choose to work, to have sufficient time off to tend to their offspring. For example, the Family and Medical Leave Act, or FMLA, grants only 12 weeks of leave—and that without pay—but just assurances that your job or a job at a comparable level will be available upon your return. And yet we have known for years from the research evidence that babies set up relationships with their parents from the start and that such relationships are essential to children's emotional, social, and intellectual success.

Fundamental societal changes must occur if we are to live our lives according to the four principles described earlier. Parenting and children must be valued beyond lip service so that parents can breathe and provide quality care for their children. Policy makers and legislators must open their eyes to the fact that families—especially those without sufficient resources—are suffering without humane policies that value and honor parenthood. And who suffers most? The children, of course. We can make a difference; we just need to have the commitment to do so. In this book, we have sounded the warning call. We are not the first to do so. But we have gone beyond the warning to offer evidence-based solutions. We propose that the more we know about children (and we know a lot), the better equipped we will be to help them thrive.

RETURNING CHILDHOOD TO CHILDREN: FROM DEFENSIVE TO LIBERATED PARENTING

Parents, teachers, and policy makers have become hostages to cultural myths about scientific discoveries without having an opportunity to see what the science actually shows. This book has exposed these growing myths about our children's development. By taking on the distortions and evaluating them against the science, we have moved the dialogue to a new place. When we understand what really does matter to children's development and how the myths mislead us, we can feel more relaxed as parents and educators and can easily ensure that our children are intellectually stimulated and socially competent.

In the last 30 years, scientists have developed new techniques for discovering how babies and young children think, and how they function in their world. Children—even infants and fetuses—know so much more than we ever realized. The findings of this burgeoning research are indeed worthy of headlines. But in our zeal to make the world a better place, and in the media's desire to share what is new in uncomplicated sound bites, these discoveries have often been misinterpreted and spun out in ways that suit the marketplace. Unfortunately, science does not fit neatly into a sound bite. Thus, it is important to understand these findings and to put them in their rightful place. It is important to close the gap between research and practice. In this book, we join many of our colleagues who are committed to moving the latest findings from the lab to life. This book is dedicated to the researchers who hope to share their findings and to the parents, practitioners, and policy makers who want what is best for all children. This book joins others that continue the conversation between science and application. When these worlds meet, we will be able to give play back to children. Only then can we restore the balance in our lives and in our schools, so that all children can realize their full potential.

It is time to Reflect, Resist, and Re-Center.

NOTES

CHAPTER 1

p. 1   *. . . buy flash cards . . .*   [Flash cards] Baby Doolittle, Baby Van Gogh, Baby Webster, etc. Baby Einstein Company: Smallfry Productions, Atlanta, GA.

p. 2   *. . . Brainy Baby video . . .*   [Videotapes] Brainy Baby Vols. 1 and 2: Right Brain/Left Brain.

p. 2   *. . . becoming a brain architect . . .*   Werth, F. (2001). *Prenatal Parenting.* New York, NY: Regan Books.

p. 3   *. . . enhances brain development . . .*   CIVITAS Initiative, Zero to Three, Brio Corporation (2000). What grown-ups understand about child development. Published by CIVITAS, Brio, and Zero to Three.

p. 3   *. . . $1-billion-a-year business . . .*   Baby Einstein to launch juvenile products, toys, preschool TV show. (2003, April) *Home Accents Today*, 18, 4, ss28.

p. 4   *. . . a 1997 study . . .*   Kantrowitz, B., and Wingert, P. (2001, January) The parent trap. *Newsweek*, 29–49.

p. 4   *. . . no time for their family . . .*   Berk, L. (2001) *Awakening Children's Minds.* New York, NY: Oxford University Press.

p. 4   *. . . last 50 years . . .*   Lang, S. (1992, Spring): Mother's time. *Human Ecology Forum*, 27–29.

p. 5   *. . . idea of "quality time" . . .*   Lang, S. (1992) op. cit.

p. 5   *. . . not in the van . . .*   Kantrowitz, B., and Wingert, P. (2001) op. cit.

p. 5   *. . . "Family Night" . . .*   Newman, M. (2002, March 27). A town calls a timeout for overextended families. *The New York Times*, B1+.

p. 5   *. . . Jean-Jacques Rousseau . . .*   Rousseau, J. (1957). *Emile.* New York, NY: Dutton.

p. 6   *. . . to prepare youth . . .*   Toffler, A. (1980). *The Third Wave.* New York, NY: Bantam.

p. 6   *. . . children could be studied . . .*   Elkind, D. (2001). *The Hurried Child.* Cambridge, MA: Perseus.

p. 6   *. . . Dr. Benjamin Spock . . .*   Spock, B. (1946). *Baby and Child Care.* New York, NY: Dutton.

p. 6   *. . . After World War II . . .*   Cohen, P. (2003, April 5). Visions and revisions of child-raising experts. *The New York Times.*

p. 6   *. . . Ken Adams . . .*   Adams, K. (1997). *Bring Out the Genius in Your Child.* London: Sterling Publications.

p. 6   *. . . Smarter Preschooler . . .*   Burton, M. R., MacDonald, S. G., and Miller, S. (1999). *365 Ways to a Smarter Preschooler.* Publications International.

p. 6   *. . . The Hurried Child . . .*   Elkind, D. (2001) op. cit.

p. 6   *. . . Awakening Children's Minds . . .*   Berk, L. (2001) op. cit.

p. 6   *. . . My Kid's an Honor Student . . .*   Schoenstein, R. (2002). *My Kid's an Honor Student, Your Kid's a Loser.* Cambridge, MA: Perseus.

p. 8   *. . . play had diminished . . .*   Chua-Eoan, H. (1999, May 31). Escaping from the darkness. *Time,* 153, 44–49.

p. 9   *. . . depressed children . . .*   McDonald, A. (2001, March). The prevalence and effects of test anxiety in school children. *Educational Psychology,* 1, 89+.

p. 9   *. . . interferes with performance . . .*   Weingarden J. D. (2001, May/June). More than a mood. *Psychology Today,* 34, 26+.

p. 9   *. . . environmental threats . . .*   Goleman, D. (1997). *Emotional Intelligence: Why It Can Matter More Than IQ.* New York, NY: Bantam.

p. 9   *. . . rejected from Carlthorp . . .*   Weingarden, J. D. (2001) op. cit.

p. 10   *. . . The Hurried Child . . .*   Elkind, D. (2001) op. cit.

p. 11   *. . . Neurons to Neighborhoods . . .*   Shonkoff, J., and Phillips, D. (Eds.) (2001). *Neurons to Neighborhoods: The Science of Early Childhood Development.* Washington, DC: National Academy Press.

p. 12   *. . . Another study found that . . .*   Hart, C. H., Burts, D. C., Durland, M., Charlesworth, R., DeWolf, M., and Fleegon, P. O. (1998). Stress behavior and activity type participation of preschoolers in more or less developmentally appropriate classrooms: SES and sex differences. *Journal of Research on Child Education,* 12, 176–196.

CHAPTER 2

p. 16   *. . . they are to be the architects . . .*   Werth, F. (2001). *Prenatal Parenting.* New York, NY: Regan Books.

p. 17   *. . . A recent study found . . .*   Campbell, D. (2000). *The Mozart Effect for Children.* New York, NY: William Morrow, flyleaf, 4; *The Mozart Effect: Music for Babies,* (1998); *The Mozart Effect: Music for Children* (1997), compiled by Don Campbell, produced by The Children's Group, Inc.

p. 17   *. . . called the Mozart effect . . .*   Pope, K. (2001, March). Marketing Mozart. *Parenting,* 15, 24+.

p. 18   *. . . could not reproduce . . .*   Steele, K. M., Bass, K. E., and Crook, M. D. (1999, July). The mystery of the Mozart effect: failure to replicate. *Psychological Science,* 10, 366–69.

p. 20   . . . *researcher Harry Chugani* . . .   (1998, March). Childhood's harsh deadlines. *Joining Forces: The Magazine*, 4–5.

p. 21   . . . *in* Newsweek *magazine* . . .   Begley, S. (1996, February 19). Your child's brain. *Newsweek*, 52.

p. 24   . . . *Carla Shatz* . . .   Shatz, C. White House Conference in Early Childhood Development and Learning: What New Research on the Brain Tells Us about Our Youngest Children. Retrieved from http://npin.org/library/2001/n00530/IIEarlychildhood.html on 5/1/02.

p. 25   . . . *more than twice as active* . . .   Shatz, C. (2002) op. cit.

p. 25   . . . *40 percent of cortical synapses* . . .   Shatz, C. *Early Childhood Development and Learning: What New Research on the Brain Tells Us about Our Youngest Children*. White House Conference, April, 1997. Report found at http://www.ed.gov/pubs/How-Children/foreword.html.

p. 25   . . . *brain's permanent circuitry* . . .   Fox, N., Leavitt, L., and Warhol, J. (1999). *The role of early experience in infant development: pediatric roundtable*. Johnson and Johnson Pediatric Institute, 12–13.

p. 26   . . . *develop on different timetables* . . .   Huttenlocher, P. R. (1979). Synaptic density in human frontal cortex—developmental changes of aging, *Brain Research*, 163: 195–205; Huttenlocher, P. R. and Dabholkar, A. S. (1997). Regional differences in synaptogenesis in human cerebral cortex, *Journal of Comparative Neurology*, 387, 167–178.

p. 26   . . . *Scientists later found* . . .   [TV Series] WNET 5-part series on the brain. 2001. "Secret Life of the Brain," Part 1: Dr. Heidelise Als, Harvard Medical School.

p. 27   . . . *Professor Donald Hebb* . . .   Hebb, D. (1947). The effects of early experience on problem solving at maturity. *American Psychologist*, 2, 737–745.

p. 27   . . . *Dr. Mark R. Rosenzweig* . . .   Renner, M. J., and Rosenzweig, M. R. (1987). *Enriched and Impoverished Environments: Effects on Brain and Behavior*. New York, NY: Springer-Verlag.

p. 27   . . . *the Disneyland rats* . . .   Greenough, W. T., and Black, J. E. (1992). Induction of brain structure by experience: substrates for cognitive development. In Gunnar, M., and Nelson, C. A., (Eds.) *Developmental Behavioral Neuroscience*. Hillsdale, NJ: Erlbaum.

p. 28   . . . *Professor Greenough* . . .   Greenough, W. T., Black, J. E., and Wallace, C. S. (1987). Experience and brain development, *Child Development*, 58, 539–559; Greenough and Black. (1992) op. cit.

p. 28   . . . *rapid synapse formation* . . .   Bruer, J. (1999). *The Myth of the First Three Years: A New Understanding of Early Brain Development and Lifelong Learning*. New York, NY: The Free Press.

p. 29   . . . *Experience-dependent* . . .   Shonkoff, J., and Phillips, D. (Eds.) (2001). *Neurons to Neighborhoods: The Science of Early Childhood Development*. Washington, DC: National Academy Press, 188.

p. 29   . . . *neurological "crowding"* . . .   Huttenlocher, P. R. (2002) op. cit., 204.

p. 29   . . . *Too much early learning* . . .   Huttenlocher, P. R. (2002) op. cit.

p. 30   . . . *Edward Zigler* . . .   Zigler, E. F., Finn-Stevenson, M., and Hall, N. W. (2002). *The First Three Years and Beyond*. New Haven, CT: Yale University Press.

p. 31   . . . *Professor Elissa Newport* . . .   Johnson, J. S., and Newport, E. L. (1989). Critical period effects in second language learning: the influence of maturational state on the acquisition of English as a second language. *Cognitive Psychology*, 21, 60–99.

p. 31 ... *Professor Newport's study* ... Hakuta, K., Bialystok, E., and Wiley, E. (2003). Critical evidence: a test of the critical period hypothesis for second language acquisition. *Psychological Science*, 14, 31–38.

p. 32 ... *Professor Ross Thompson from the University* ... Thompson, R., and Nelson, C. (2001). Developmental science and the media: early brain development. *American Psychologist*, 56, 5–15.

p. 32 ... *As Dr. Irving Sigel* ... Sigel, I. E. (1987). Does hothousing rob children of their childhood? *Early Childhood Research Quarterly*, 2, 211–225.

p. 33 ... *Indeed, it is what* ... Bruer, J. (1999). *The Myth of the First Three Years: A New Understanding of Early Brain Development and Lifelong Learning.* New York, NY: The Free Press.

p. 36 ... *a wonderful book* ... Hoberman, M.A. (1982). *A House Is a House for Me.* London, UK: Puffin.

CHAPTER 3

p. 39 ... *Karen Wynn* ... Wynn, K. (1998). Psychological foundations in number: numerical competence in human infants. *Trends in Cognitive Sciences*, 2, 296–303.

p. 39 ... *rhesus monkeys demonstrated* ... Hauser, M. D. (1996, May). Monkey see, monkey count. *Scientific American*, 274 (5), 18.

p. 40 ... *Professor Janellen Huttenlocher* ... Mix, K. S., Levine, S. C., and Huttenlocher, J. (1997). Numerical abstraction by infants: another look. *Developmental Psychology*, 33, 423–428. Mix, K. S., Huttenlocher, J., and Levine, S. C. (2001). *Quantitative Development in Infancy and Early Childhood.* New York, NY: Oxford University Press.

p. 41 ... *numerical "genius" Clever Hans* ... Pfungst, O. (1965). *Clever Hans, the Horse of Mr. Von Osten.* New York, NY: Holt, Rinehart and Winston.

p. 43 ... *Some argue that* ... Bruer, J. (1999). *The Myth of the First Three Years: A New Understanding of Early Brain Development and Lifelong Learning.* New York, NY: The Free Press, 84.

p. 46 ... *Rochel Gelman's work* ... Gelman, R. (1969). Conservation acquisition: a problem of learning to attend to relevant attributes. *Journal of Experimental Child Psychology*, 7, 67–87. See also: Gelman, R. (1998). *Annual Review;* Gelman, R., and Brenneman, K. (1994). Domain specificity and cultural variation are not inconsistent. In Hirschfeld, L.A., and Gelman, S. (Eds.) *Mapping the Mind: Domain Specificity in Cognition and Culture.* New York, NY: Cambridge University Press.

p. 53 ... *Professor Stanislas Dehaene* ... Dehaene, S. (1997). *The Number Sense: How the Mind Creates Mathematics.* New York, NY: Oxford University Press.

p. 55 ... *Professor Herbert Ginsberg* ... Ginsberg, H. P., Klein, A., and Starkey, P. (1997). The development of children's mathematical thinking. In Sigel, I. E., and Renninger, K. A. (Eds.) *Handbook of Child Psychology* (5th ed., 4). New York, NY: Wiley; Ginsberg, H. P. (1989). *Children's Arithmetic: How They Learn It and How You Teach It.* Austin, TX: Pro Ed.

p. 56 ... *Professor Geoffrey Saxe* ... Saxe, G. B., Guberman, S. R., and Gearhart, M. (1987). Social processes in early number development. *Monographs of the Society for Research in Child Development*, 52 (Serial No. 216).

p. 56 ... *Vygotsky called "scaffolding"* ... Vygotsky, L. S. (1978). *Mind in Society.* Cambridge, MA: Harvard University Press.

p. 57   . . . *independent performance improves* . . .   Freund, L .S. (1990). Maternal regulation of children's problem solving behavior and its impact on children's performance. *Child Development*, 61, 113–126.

CHAPTER 4

Golinkoff, R. M. and Hirsh-Pasek, K. (1999). *How Babies Talk: The Magic and Mystery of Language Development in the First Three Years of Life.* New York, NY: Penguin/Dutton.

p. 62   . . . *pointing and grunts* . . .   Golinkoff, R. M. (1986). I beg your pardon?: the preverbal negotiation of failed messages. *Journal of Child Language*, 13, 455–476.

p. 64   . . . *The Language Instinct* . . .   Pinker, S. (1994). *The Language Instinct: How the Mind Creates Language.* New York, NY: William Morrow and Company.

p. 65   . . . *prestigious journal* Science . . .   Holowka, S., and Petitto, L. A. (2002). Left hemisphere cerebral specialization for babies while babbling. *Science*, 297, 1515.

p. 66   . . . *lip-reading and speech* . . .   Goldin-Meadow, S., and Mylander, C. (1984). Gestural communication in deaf children: the effects and noneffects of parental input on early language development. *Monographs of the Society for Research in Child Development*, 49 (Nos. 3–4).

p. 66   . . . *Professor Derek Bickerton* . . .   Bickerton, D. (1995). *Language and Human Behavior.* Seattle, WA: University of Washington Press; Bickerton, D. (1984). The language bioprogram hypothesis. *Behavioral and Brain Science*, 7, 173–188.

p. 67   . . . *Professor William Fifer* . . .   Fifer, W., and Moon, C. (1995). The effects of fetal experience with sound. In Lecanuet, J., Fifer, W. P., Krasnegor, N., and Smotherman, W. P. (Eds.), *Fetal Development: A Psychobiological Perspective.* Hillsdale, NJ: Erlbaum.

p. 68   . . . *Sucking offers another* . . .   Mehler, J., Jusczyk, P., Lambertz, G., Halstead, N., Bertoncini, J., and Amiel-Tison, C. (1988). A precursor of language acquisition in young infants. *Cognition*, 29, 143–178.

p. 69   . . . *Finding the Units* . . .   Hirsh-Pasek, K., Kemler-Nelson, D. G., Jusczyk, P. W., Wright-Cassidy, K., Druss, B., and Kennedy, L. (1987). Clauses are perceptual units for young infants. *Cognition*, 26, 269–286.

p. 71   . . . *their own names* . . .   Mandel, D. R., Jusczyk, P. W., and Pisoni, D. B. (1995). Infants' recognition of the sound patterns of their own names. *Psychological Science*, 6, 315–318.

p. 72   . . . *Research conducted at Brown* . . .   Rathbun, K., Bortfeld, H., Morgan, J., and Golinkoff, R. M. (2002, November). What's in a name: using highly familiar items to aid segmentation. Paper presented at Boston Child Language Conference, Boston, MA.

p. 72   . . . *Headturn Preference* . . .   Jusczyk, P., and Aslin, R. (1995). Infants' detection of the sound patterns of words in fluent speech. *Cognitive Psychology*, 23, 1–29.

p. 73   . . . *By 8 months* . . .   Saffran, J., Aslin, R., and Newport, E. (1996). Statistical learning by 8-month-old infants. *Science*, 274, 1926–1928.

p. 73   . . . *follow our pointing fingers* . . .   Adamson, L. (1995). *Communication Development during Infancy.* Madison, WI: Brown and Benchmark.

p. 74   . . . *parent's eye gaze* . . .   Morales, M., Mundy, P., and Rojas, J. (1998). Following the direction of gaze and language development in 6-month-olds. *Infant Behavior and Development*, 21, 373–377.

p. 78   *... Baby Signs As Word Boosters? ...*   Acredolo, L., and Goodwyn, S. (1998). *Baby Signs.* Chicago, IL: Contemporary Books.

p. 79   *... 50-word watershed ...*   Brown, R. (1973). *A First Language.* Cambridge, MA: Harvard University Press.

p. 81   *... Fancier Sentences ...*   Bloom, L. (1970). *Language Development: Form and Function in Emerging Grammars.* Cambridge, MA: MIT Press.

p. 81   *... real stutterers ...*   Coplan, J. (1993). *Early Childhood Milestone Scale: Examiner's Manual* (2nd ed.). Austin, TX: Pro-Ed.

p. 81   *... sophisticated language users ...*   Marcus, G. F., Pinker, S., Ullman, M., Hollander, M., Rosen, T. J., and Xu, F. (1992). Overregularization in language acquisition. *Monographs of the Society for Research in Child Development*, 57 (4, Serial No. 428).

p. 82   *... the "wug" test ...*   Berko-Gleason, J. (1958). The child's learning of English morphology. *Word*, 14, 150–177.

p. 83   *... their first Halloween ...*   Ely, R., and Gleason, J. B. (1995). Socialization across contexts. In Fletcher, P., and MacWhinney, B. (Eds.), *The Handbook of Child Language.* Cambridge, MA: Blackwell.

p. 85   *... story development ...*   Stein, N. L. (1988). The development of children's storytelling skill. In Franklin, M. B., and Barten, S. (Eds.), *Child Language: A Book of Readings.* New York, NY: Oxford University Press.

p. 87   *... with your pediatrician ...*   Roberts, J., and Wallace, L. (1976). Language and otitis media. In Roberts, J. E., Wallace, I. F., and Henderson, F. W. (Eds.), *Otitis Media in Young Children.* Baltimore, MD: Brookes.

p. 88   *... as Language Partner ...*   Hart, B., and Risley, T. R. (1999). *Learning to Talk.* Baltimore, MD: Paul Brookes Publishing.

p. 88   *... like Professor Erica Hoff ...*   Hoff, E. (2002). Language development in childhood. In Lerner, R. M., Easterbrooks, M. A., and Mistoi, J. (Eds.), *Comprehensive Handbook of Psychology, Vol. 6: Developmental Psychology.* New York, NY: Wiley.

p. 89   *... University of Kansas ...*   Hart and Risley (1999) op. cit.

p. 92   *... Health and Human Development ...*   National Institute of Child Health and Human Development Early Child Care Research Network. (2000). The relation of child care to cognitive and language development. *Child Development*, 71, 960–980.

p. 92   *... children benefit tremendously ...*   DeTemple, J., and Snow, C. (in press). Learning words from books. In van Kleeck, A., Stahl, S. A., and Bauer, E.B. (Eds.), *On Reading to Children: Parents and Teachers.* Mahwah, NJ: Erlbaum.

p. 94   *... vocabulary and information ...*   Weizman, Z., and Snow, C. (2001). Lexical input as related to children's vocabulary acquisition: effects on sophisticated exposure and support for meaning. *Developmental Psychology*, 17, 265–279.

p. 94   *... use baby talk ...*   Fernald, A. (1991). Prosody in speech to children: prelinguistic and linguistic functions. In Vasta, R. (Ed.), *Annals of Child Development (Vol. 8).* London: Kingsley.

p. 95   *... Professor Ann Fernald ...*   Fernald, A. (1989). Intonation and communicative intent in mothers' speech to infants: is the melody the message? *Child Development*, 60, 1497–1510.

p. 95   *... limit TV time ...*   Huston, A., and Wright, J. (1998). Mass media and children's development. In W. Damon (Ed.), *Handbook of Child Psychology.* New York, NY: Wiley.

p. 95   ... *environment at child care* ...   Bredekamp, S. (1999). *Developmentally appropriate practice in early childhood programs*. National Association for Education of Young Children.

CHAPTER 5

p. 98   ... *Learning to Read* ...   Adams, M. (1990). *Beginning to Read: Thinking and Learning about Print*. Cambridge, MA: MIT Press.

p. 100   ... *pertaining to literacy* ...   Scarborough, H. S. (2001). Connecting early language and literacy to later reading (dis)abilities: evidence, theory, and practice. In Neuman, S. B., and Dickinson, D. K. (Eds.), *Handbook of Early Literacy Research*. New York, NY: Guilford Press.

p. 101   ... *birth through age 6* ...   Neuman, S. B., and Dickinson, D. K. (2001) Introduction. In Neuman, S. B., and Dickinson, D. K. (Eds.), *Handbook of Early Literacy Research*. New York, NY: Guilford Press. p. 3.

p. 101   ... emergent literacy ...   Clay, M. M. (1966). *Emergent reading behavior*. Unpublished doctoral dissertation, University of Auckland, New Zealand.

p. 101   ... *88 percent of children* ...   Whitehurst, G. J., and Lonigan, C. J. (2001). Emergent literacy: development from prereaders to readers. In Neuman, S. B., and Dickinson, D. K. (Eds.), *Handbook of Early Literacy Research*. NY: Guilford Press.

p. 101   ... *were less educated* ...   Venezky, R. (1998). *Reading to children in the home: practices and outcomes*. Unpublished paper, U.S. Department of Education.

p. 102   ... *the Abecedarian project* ...   Campbell, F., Miller-Johnson, S., Burchinal, M., Ramey, M., and Ramey, C. T. (2001). The development of cognitive and academic abilities: growth curves from an early childhood educational experiment. *Developmental Psychology*, 37, 231–242.

p. 102   ... *benefit of enrichment* ...   Ramey, S. L., and Ramey, C. T. (1999). What makes kids do well in school? *Work and Family Life*, 13, 2–6; Ramey, S. L., and Ramey, C. T. (in press) Intelligence and experience. In Sternberg, R. J. (Ed.) *Environmental Effects on Intellectual Functioning*. New York, NY: Cambridge University Press.

p. 103   ... *and literacy ability* ...   Chall, J. S., Jacobs, V. A., and Baldwin, L. E. (1990). *The Reading Crisis: Why Poor Children Fall Behind*. Cambridge, MA: Harvard University Press.

p. 103   ... *their children's capabilities* ...   Moerk, E. (1983). *The Mother of Eve—As a First Language Teacher*. Norwood, NJ: Ablex.

p. 103   ... *Professor Susan Engel* ...   Engel, S. (1999). *The Stories Children Tell*. New York, NY: W.H. Freeman

p. 104   ... *Good stories contain* ...   Berman, R. A., and Slobin, D. (1994). *Relating Events in Narrative: A Cross Linguistic Developmental Study*. Hillsdale, NJ: Erlbaum.

p. 104   ... *Several studies find* ...   Snow, C. E. (1983). Literacy and language: relationships during the preschool years. *Harvard Educational Review*, 53, 165–189.

p. 104   ... The Frog Story ...   Mayer, M. (1969). *Frog, Where Are You?* New York, NY: Dial Press.

p. 106   ... *Say 'top'* ...   Juel, C., Griffith, P. L., and Gough, P. B. (1986). Acquisition of literacy: a longitudinal study of children in first and second grade. *Journal of Educational Psychology*, 78, 243–255.

p. 106 ... *Dr. Isabelle Liberman* ... Liberman, I. Y., Shankweiler, D., Fischer, F. W., and Carter, B. (1974). Explicit syllable and phoneme segmentation in the young child. *Journal of Experimental Child Psychology*, 18, 201–212.

p. 108 ... *children who have this knowledge* ... Adams, M. (1990) op. cit.

p. 110 ... *Professor Judy DeLoache* ... DeLoache, J. S., Pierroutsakos, S. L., Utall, D. H., Rosengren, K., and Gottlieb, A. (1998). Grasping the nature of pictures. *Psychological Science*, 9, 205–210.

p. 111 ... *preschoolers say yes* ... Beilin, H., and Pearlman, E. G. (1991). Children's iconic realism: object versus property realism. In Reese, H. W. (Ed.), *Advances in Child Development and Behavior (Vol. 23)*. New York, NY: Academic Press.

p. 111 ... *lines around joints* ... Friedman, S. L., and Stevenson, M. B. (1975). Developmental changes in the understanding of implied motion in two-dimensional pictures. *Child Development*, 46, 773–778.

p. 112 ... *Concepts about Print test* ... Clay, M. M. (1979). *The Early Detection of Reading Difficulties* (3rd ed.). Portsmouth, NH: Heinemann.

p. 112 ... *"McDonald's" and "Burger King"*... Baghban, M. (1984). *Our daughters learn to read and write*. Newark, DE: International Reading Association.

p. 113 ... *Professor Linda Lavine* ... Lavine, L. O. (1977). Differentiation of letterlike forms in prereading children. *Developmental Psychology*, 13, 89–94.

p. 115 ... *President George W. Bush* ... [Speech] President Bush speaking at Pennsylvania State University, April 2002.

p. 115 ... *column in* Education Week ... Retrieved from *Education Week*, 20 (22) online, on 2/14/01.

p. 115 ... *Since virtually hundreds* ... Adams, M. (2001). Alphabetic anxiety and explicit, systematic phonics instruction: a cognitive science perspective. In Neuman, S. B., and Dickinson, D. K., (Eds.), *Handbook of Early Literacy Research*. New York, NY: Guilford Press.

p. 115 ... *authentic literacy experiences* ... Kantrowitz, B. and Wingert, P. (2002, April 29). The right way to read. *Newsweek*.

p. 116 ... *Reading is clearly more* ... Snow, C. (2002, August). Personal communication.

p. 118 ... *Dr. James Gibson* ... Gibson, J. J., and Yonas, P. (1968). A new theory of scribbling and drawing in children. In *The analysis of reading skill*. Final report, project 5-1213. Cornell University and Office of Education, 355–370.

p. 120 ... *into invented spellings* ... Read, C. (1975). *Children's categorization of speech sounds in English*. (NCTE Research Report 17). Urbana, IL: National Council of Teachers of English.

p. 121 ... *beneath her version* ... Shivers, *Invented spelling*. Retrieved from http://hall. gresham.k12.or.us/Shspell.html on 1/17/03.

p. 122 ... *Professors Monique Sénéchal* ... Sénéchal, M., and Lefevre, J. (2002) Parental involvement in the development of children's reading skill: a five-year longitudinal study. *Child Development*, 73, 2,445–460.

p. 123 ... *Create an environment* ... Dougherty, D. (2001). *How to Talk to Your Baby: A Guide to Maximizing Your Child's Language and Learning Skills*. New York, NY: Perigee.

p. 123 ... *Once reading begins* ... Pikulski, J., and Tobin, A. W. (1989). Factors associated with long-term reading achievement of early readers. In McCormick, S., Zutell, J.,

Scharer, P., and O'Keefe, P. (Eds.), *Cognitive and social perspectives for literacy research and instruction.* Chicago, IL: National Reading Conference.

p. 124   . . . *Shel Silverstein's work* . . .   Silverstein, S. (1981). *A Light in the Attic.* New York: Harper and Row.

CHAPTER 6

p. 126   . . . *Elizabeth Chapman* . . .   Goode, E. (2002, March 12). The uneasy fit of the precocious and the average. *The New York Times,* 1.

p. 126   . . . *baby formula* . . .   Retsinas, G. (2003, June 1) The marketing of a superbaby formula. *The New York Times.*

p. 127   . . . *Jack Grubman* . . .   Gross, J. (2002, November 15). No talking out of preschool. *The New York Times,* 1 Metro Sec.

p. 127   . . . *definition of intelligence* . . .   *Webster's Ninth New Collegiate Dictionary.* (1991). Springfield, MA: Merriam-Webster, 629.

p. 128   . . . *The academically oriented children* . . .   Rescorla, L., Hyson, M., Hirsh-Pasek, K., and Cone, J. (1990). Academic expectations in parents of preschool chidren. *Early Education and Development,* 1, 165–184.

p. 128   . . . *rock is hard* . . .   Berk, L. E. (2003). *Child Development.* Boston, MA: Longman, 454.

p. 130   . . . *Alexandra Nechita* . . .   About Alexandra Nechita. Biographical sketch supplied by Lewis and Bond Fine Art. Retrieved from www.lewisbond.com/nechita/about on 1/22/03.

p. 132   . . . *James Watson* . . .   [TV Program] 1984. Investigation of IQ in "The IQ Myth" with Dan Rather.

p. 133   . . . *Professor Joseph Fagan* . . .   Fagan, J., and Detterman, D. K. (1992). The Fagan Test of Infant Intelligence: a technical summary. *Journal of Applied Developmental Psychology,* 13, 173–193.

p. 133   . . . *not uncontroversial* . . .   Fagan, J. (1989). Commentary. *Human Development,* 32, 172–176.

p. 133   . . . *serious delays in mental development* . . .   Fagan, J. and Detterman, D. K. (1992) op. cit.

p. 133   . . . *alcohol during pregnancy* . . .   Jacobson, S. W., Jacobson, J. L., Dowler, J. K., Fein, G. G., and Schwartz, P. M. (1983). *Sensitivity of Fagan's Recognition Memory Test to subtle intrauterine risk.* Paper presented at the American Psychological Association Meetings, Los Angeles.

p. 134   . . . *(Home Observation for the Measurement of Environment) test* . . .   Bradley, R. H. (1981). The HOME Inventory: a review of findings from the Little Rock Longitudinal Study. *Infant Mental Health Journal,* 2, 198–205.

p. 135   . . . *When parents are intrusive* . . .   Berk, L. E. (2003) op. cit.

p. 135   . . . *African-American children* . . .   Jensen, R. (1972). *Genetics and Education.* New York: Harper and Row.

p. 135   . . . *Head Start experience* . . .   Head Start Bureau. 2000. Head Start Fact Sheet. Retrieved from www2.acf.dhhs.gov/programs/hsb/research/00–hsfs.htm on 1/13/03.

p. 136   . . . *graduated from high school* . . .   Royce, J. M., Darlington, R. B., and Murray, H. W. (1983). Pooled analyses: findings across studies. In Consortium for Longitudinal Studies (Ed.), *As the Twig Is Bent: Lasting Effects of Preschool Programs* (pp. 411–459). Hillsdale, NJ: Erlbaum.

p. 136   . . . *Professor Howard Gardner* . . .   Gardner, H. (1993). *Multiple Intelligences.* New York, NY: Basic Books.

p. 136   . . . *Daniel Goleman* . . .   Goleman, D. (1995). *Emotional Intelligence.* New York, NY: Basic Books.

p. 136   . . . *Professor Robert Sternberg* . . .   Sternberg, R. J. (2002). Beyond *g:* the theory of successful intelligence. In Sternberg, R. J., and Grigorenko, E. L. (Eds.), *The General Facor of Intelligence.* Mahwah, NJ: Erlbaum; Sternberg, R. J. (1997). Educating intelligence: infusing the Triarchic Theory into school instruction. In Sternberg, R. J., and Grigorenko, E. L. (Eds.), *Intelligence, Heredity, and Environment.* New York, NY: Cambridge University Press.

p. 137   . . . *Piaget defined intelligence* . . .   Piaget, J. (1929). *The Child's Conception of the World.* London: Routledge and Kegan Paul.

p. 139   . . . *Piaget called these processes* . . .   Piaget, J. (1952). *The Origins of Intelligence in Children.* NY: International Universities Press.

p. 140   . . . *Even by 3 months* . . .   Arterberry, M. E., and Bornstein, M. H. (2001). Three-month-old infants' categorization of animals and vehicles based on static and dynamic attributes. *Journal of Experimental Child Psychology,* 80, 333–346.

p. 140   . . . *Let's enter the baby lab* . . .   Golinkoff, R. M., Harding, C. G., Carlson-Luden, V., and Sexton, M. E. (1984). The infant's perception of causal events: the distinction between animate and inanimate objects. In Lipsitt, L. P. (Ed.), *Advances in Infancy Research* (Vol. 3). Norwood, NJ: Ablex.

p. 142   . . . *Can you teach conservation* . . .   Gelman, R. (1969). Conservation acquisition: a problem of learning to attend to relevant attributes. *Journal of Experimental Child Psychology,* 7, 67–87.

p. 144   . . . *Laraine McDonough* . . .   Mandler, J. M., and McDonough, L. (1998). Studies in inductive inference in infancy. *Cognitive Psychology,* 37, 60–96.

p. 144   . . . *miniatures of objects* . . .   Mandler, J. M. and McDonough, L. (1996). Drinking and driving don't mix: inductive generalization in infancy. *Cognition,* 59, 307–335.

p. 144   . . . *Like Piaget, Lev Vygotsky* . . .   Vygotsky, L. S. (1978). *Mind in Society.* Cambridge, MA: Harvard University Press.

p. 145   . . . *Professor Jerome Bruner* . . .   Bruner, J. (1983). *Child's Talk: Learning to Use Language.* New York, NY: Norton.

p. 150   . . . *Many of these contributions* . . .   Hopkins, G. (2000, February 7). How can teachers develop students' motivation—and success? Interview with Carol Dweck. *Education World;* Dweck, C. (1989). Motivation. In Lesgold, A., and Glaser, R. (Eds.), *Foundations for a Psychology of Education.* Hillsdale, NJ: Erlbaum.

CHAPTER 7

p. 152   . . . *John Broadus Watson* . . .   Watson, J. B. (1928). *Psychological care of infant and child.* As cited in Beekman, D. (1977). *The Mechanical Baby.* New York, NY: New American Library, 145–146.

p. 154   . . . *I'm 3 years old* . . .   Harter, S. (1999). *The Cognitive and Social Construction of the Developing Self.* New York, NY: Guilford Press.

p. 155   . . . *You threw it wrong* . . .   Ruble, D. N., Grosovsky, E. H., Frey, K. S., and Cohen, R. (1992). Developmental changes in competence assessment. In Boggiano, A. K., and

Pittman, T. S. (Eds.), *Achievement and Motivation: A Social Developmental Perspective*. New York, NY: Cambridge University Press.

p. 156   . . . *I'm pretty popular* . . .   Seligman, M., Reivich, K, Jaycox, L., and Gillham, J. (1995). *The Optimistic Child*. New York, NY: Houghton Mifflin.

p. 157   . . . *Professors Philippe Rochat and Susan Hespos* . . .   Rochat, P., and Hespos, S. J. (1997). Differential rooting response by neonates: evidence for an early sense of self. *Early Development and Parenting*, 6, 105–112; Rochat, P. (2001). *The Infant's World*. Cambridge, MA: Harvard University Press, 40.

p. 158   . . . *Professor Lorraine Bahrick* . . .   Bahrick, L. E., Moss, L., and Fadil, C. (1996). Development of visual self-recognition in infancy. *Ecological Psychology*, 8, 189–208.

p. 158   . . . *Professor Michael Lewis* . . .   Lewis, M., and Brooks-Gunn, J. (1979). *Social Cognition and the Acquisition of Self*. New York, NY: Plenum Press.

p. 160   . . . *John and Sandy Condry* . . .   Condry, J., and Condry, S. (1976). Sex differences: a study of the eye of the beholder. *Child Development*, 47, 812–819.

p. 160   . . . *children start to prefer toys* . . .   Caldera, Y. M., Huston, A. C., and O'Brien, M. (1989). Social interaction and play patterns of parents and toddlers with feminine, masculine, and neutral toys. *Child Development*, 60, 70–76.

p. 160   . . . *rooms contain very different* . . .   Rheingold, H. L., and Cook, K. C. (1975). The contents of boys' and girls' rooms as a function of parents' behavior. *Child Development*, 46, 445–463.

p. 160   . . . *when can children* label . . .   Ruble, D. N., Alvarez, J., Bachman, M., Cameron, J., Fuligni, A., Coll, C. G., and Rhee, E. (in press). The development of a sense of a "we": the emergence and implications of children's collective identity. In Bennett, M., and Sani, F. (Eds.), *The Development of the Social Self*. East Sussex, England: Psychology Press; Katz, P. A., and Kofkin, J. A. (1997). Race, gender, and young children. In Luthar, S. S., Burack, J. A., Cicchetti, D., and Weisz, J. (Eds.), *Developmental Psychopathology: Perspectives on Adjustment, Risk, and Disorder*. New York, NY: Academic Press; Martin, C. L., Eisenbud, L., and Rose, H. (1995). Children's gender-based reasoning about toys. *Child Development*, 66, 1453–1471.

p. 161   . . . *Professor Sandra Bem* . . .   Cole, M. and Cole, S. R. (1996). *The Development of Children* (3rd ed.). New York, NY: W. H. Freeman, 62; Slaby, R. G., and Frey, K. S. (1975). Development of gender constancy and selective attention to same-sex models. *Child Development*, 46, 849–856.

p. 162   . . . *will hold gender distinctions* . . .   Ruble, D. N., and Martin, C. L. (1998). Gender development. In Damon, D. W. (Overall ed.), *Handbook of Child Psychology* (5th ed., Vol. 3). New York, NY: Wiley.

p. 162   . . . *Phyllis Katz, Ph.D.* . . .   Katz, P. A., and Kofkin, J. A. (1997) op. cit.

p. 163   . . . *given the power differential* . . .   Ruble, D. N., and Martin, C. L. (1998) op. cit.

p. 163   . . . *Knowledge about gender* . . .   Ruble, D. N. et al. (in press)

p. 163   . . . *babies apart by race* . . .   Katz, P. A., and Kofkin, J. A. (1997) op. cit.

p. 163   . . . *their minority status* . . .   Condry, J., and Condry, S. (1976) op. cit.

p. 163   . . . *children's genders* . . .   Rhee, E., Cameron, J. A., and Ruble, D. N. (2002). Development of racial and gender constancy in European American and racial minority children. Unpublished manuscript, University of Delaware; Leinbach, M. D., and Fagot, B. I. (1986). Acquisition of gender labeling: a test for toddlers. *Sex Roles*, 15, 655–666.

p. 164   *... doesn't become overwhelmed ...*   Eisenberg, N., Cumberland, A., and Spinrad, T. L. (1998). Parental socialization of emotion. *Psychological Inquiry*, 9, 241–273.

p. 165   *... wouldn't spoil them ...*   Weill, B.C. (1930). Are you training your child to be happy? Lessons Material in Child Management. *Infant Care Bulletin*, Washington, D.C.: U. S. Government Printing Office, 1; Watson, J. B. (1928). *Psychological Care of Infant and Child*.

p. 165   *... Sylvia Bell and Mary Ainsworth ...*   Bell, S., and Ainsworth, M. (1972). Infant crying and maternal responsiveness. *Child Development*, 43, 1171–1190.

p. 166   *... regulate their emotions ...*   Rothbart, M. K., and Bates, J. E. (1998). Temperament. In Eisenberg, N. (Ed.) *Handbook of Child Psychology*, (Vol. 3). Social, emotional, and personality development (5th ed., pp. 105–176). New York, NY: Wiley.

p. 166   *... Alexander Thomas, M.D., and Stella Chess, M.D. ...*   Thomas, A., and Chess, S. (1977). *Temperament and Development*. New York, NY: Brunner/Mazel.

p. 168   *... some researchers have reported ...*   Dunn, J. (1987). The beginnings of moral understanding: development in the second year. In Kagan, J., and Lamb, S. (Eds.), *The Emergence of Morality in Young Children*. Chicago, IL: University of Chicago Press.

p. 168   *... Professor Deborah Stipek ...*   Stipek, D., Rosenblatt, L., and DiRocco, L. (1994). Making parents your allies. *Young Children*, 49, 4–9.

p. 169   *... accomplish our goals ...*   Thompson, R. A. (1994). Emotion regulation: A theme in search of definition. In Fox, N. A. (Ed.) The development of emotion regulation. *Monographs of the Society for Research in Child Development*, 59 (2–3, Serial No. 240).

p. 171   *... Daniel Stern, M.D. ...*   Stern, D. (1985). *The Interpersonal World of the Infant*. New York, NY: Basic Books, 101–106; Lagattuta, K. H., and Wellman, H. (2002). Differences in early parent-child conversations about negative versus positive emotions: implications for the development of psychological understanding. *Developmental Psychology*, 38, 564–580.

p. 174   *... Mommy is mad at you ...*   Burhans, K. K., and Dweck, C. C. (1995). Helplessness in early childhood: the role of contingent worth. *Child Development*, 66, 1719–1738; Heyman, G. D., Dweck, C. C., and Cain, K. M. (1992). Young children's vulnerability to self-blame and helplessness: relationship to beliefs about goodness. *Child Development*, 63, 401–415.

p. 175   *... Professors George Bear ...*   Bear, G. G., Minke, K. M., Griffin, S. M., and Deemer, S. A. (1997). Self-concept. In Bear, G. G., Minke, K. M., and Thomas, A. (Eds.), *Children's Needs II: Development, Problems, and Alternatives*. Bethesda, MD: National Association of School Psychologists.

p. 175   *... 85 percent of the parents ...*   Dweck, C. S., and Mueller, C. M. (1996). *Implicit Theories of Intelligence: Relation of Parental Beliefs to Children's Expectations*. Presented at the Third National Research Convention of Head Start, Washington, D.C.

p. 175   *... The self-esteem people ...*   Dweck, C. S. (1999, Spring). Caution—praise can be dangerous. *American Educator*, 4–9.

p. 176   *... solve a problem ...*   Dweck, C. S. (1999) op. cit.

p. 176   *... respond constructively ...*   Kamins, M., and Dweck, C. S. (1999). Person versus process praise and criticism: implications for contingent self-worth and coping. *Developmental Psychology*, 35, 835.

p. 176   *... They act just like Rachel did ...*   Berk, L. E. (2002). *Infants and Children* (4th ed.). New York, NY: Allyn and Bacon, 266–267, 370–386.

p. 176   . . . *Erika, on the other hand* . . .   Berk, L. E. (2000) op. cit 370.

p. 177   . . . *make children learn to persevere* . . .   Dweck, C. S. (1999) op. cit.

CHAPTER 8

p. 182   . . . *The more popular children* . . .   Bronson, M. (2000). *Self-Regulation in Early Childhood*. New York, NY: The Guilford Press, 74–75.

p. 182   . . . *Professor Martha Bronson* . . .   Pellegrini, A. S. (1992). Kindergarten children's social cognitive status as a predictor of first-grade success. *Early Childhood Research Quarterly*, 7, 565–577; Lazar, I., and Darlington, R. (1982). Lasting effects of early education: a report from the Consortium for Longitudinal Studies. *Monograph of the Society for Research in Child Development*, 47 (2–3, Serial No. 195); Bronson, M. B., Pierson, D. E., and Tivnan, T. (1984). The effects of early education on children's competence in elementary school. *Evaluation Review*, 8, 615–629.

p. 182   . . . *As kindergarteners forge* . . .   Ladd, G., Price, J., and Hart, C. (1988). Predicting preschoolers' peer status from their playground behaviors. *Child Development*, 59, 986–992; Pellegrini, A. S. (1992). Kindergarten children's social cognitive status as a predictor of first-grade success. *Early Childhood Research Quarterly*, 7, 565–577; Bronson, M. B., Pierson, D. E., and Tivnan, T. (1984). The effects of early education on children's competence in elementary school. *Evaluation Review*, 8, 615–629.

p. 184   . . . *Tiny babies, soon* . . .   Gibson, E. J. (1969). *Principles of Perceptual Learning and Development*. New York, NY: Appleton-Century-Crofts.

p. 184   . . . *He rocked the scientific* . . .   Meltzoff, A. N., and Moore, M. K. (1977). Imitation of facial and manual gestures by human neonates. *Science*, 198, 75–78.

p. 184   . . . *It is exciting to know* . . .   Golinkoff, R. M., and Hirsh-Pasek, K. (2000). *How Babies Talk: The Magic and Mystery of Language in the First Three Years of Life*. New York, NY: Dutton, 30-31.

p. 186   . . . *Research in the laboratory* . . .   Zahn-Waxler, C., Radke-Yarrow, M., and King, R. M. (1979). Childrearing and children's prosocial initiations toward victims of distress. *Child Development*, 50, 319–330.

p. 188   . . . *Professor Harlow and his colleagues* . . .   Harlow, H. F. (1958). The nature of love. *American Psychologist*, 13, 673–685.

p. 188   . . . *Dr. John Bowlby* . . .   Bowlby, J. (1969). *Attachment and Loss. Vol. 1: Attachment*. New York: Basic Books; Bowlby, J. (1973). *Attachment and Loss. Vol. 2: Separation*. New York, NY: Basic Books.

p. 189   . . . *Professor Alan Sroufe* . . .   Elicker, J., Englund, M., and Sroufe, L. A. (1992). Predicting peer competence and peer relationships in childhood from early parent-child relationships. In Parke, R. D., and Ladd, G. W. (Eds.), *Family-Peer Relationships: Modes of Linkage*. Hillsdale, NJ: Erlbaum.

p. 189   . . . *supportive circumstances* . . .   Lamb, M. E., Thompson, R. A., Gardner, W., Charnov, E. L., and Connell, J. P. (1985). *Infant-Mother Attachment: The Origins and Developmental Significance of Individual Differences in Strange Situation Behavior*. Hillsdale, NJ: Erlbaum.

p. 189   . . . *Attachment is probably* . . .   Vaughn, B. E., Egeland, B., Sroufe, L. A., and Waters, E. (1979). Individual differences in infant-mother attachment at 12 and 18 months: stability and change in families under stress. *Child Development*, 50, 971–975.

p. 190   *. . . two parents in the workforce . . .*   Eyer, D. (1996). *Motherguilt: How Our Culture Blames Mothers for What's Wrong with Society.* New York, NY: Random House, 8.

p. 190   *. . .* Study of Early Child Care and Youth Development . . .   NICHD Early Child Care Research Network. (1997). The effects of infant child care on infant-mother attachment security: results of the NICHD Study of Early Child Care. *Child Development.*

p. 190   *. . . In April of 2000, headlines blared study . . .*   NICHD Early Child Care Research Network (in press). Does amount of time spent in child care predict socioemotional adjustment during the transition to kindergarten? *Child Development.*

p. 193   *. . . Professors Amanda Morris and Jennifer Silk . . .*   Morris, A. S., and Silk, J. Parental influences on children's regulation of anger and sadness. Paper presented at the biennial meeting of the Society for Research in Child Development, Minneapolis, MN, April, 2001.

p. 195   *. . . Zero to Three group . . .*   CIVITAS Initiative, Zero to Three, Brio Corporation. (2000). What grown-ups understand about child development. Pubished by CIVITAS, Brio, and Zero to Three.

p. 196   *. . . Professors Betty Repacholi . . .*   Repacholi, B. M., and Gopnik, A. (1997). Early reasoning about desires: evidence from 14- and 18-month-olds. *Developmental Psychology,* 33, 12–21.

p. 196   *. . . regardless of his own preferences . . .*   Dunn, J., Brown, J., and Beardsall, L. (1991). Family talk about feeling states and children's later understanding of others' emotions. *Developmental Psychology,* 27, 448–455.

p. 197   *. . . false belief task . . .*   Gopnik, A., Meltzoff, A. N., and Kuhl, P. K. (1999). *The Scientist in the Crib.* New York, NY: Morrow.

p. 199   *. . . 39 percent of the parents . . .*   *Zero to Three* (2000) op. cit.

p. 199   *. . . Professor Alison Gopnik . . .*   Gopnik, A., Meltzoff, A. N., and Kuhl, P. K. (1999) op. cit.; Burk, L. (2002). *Infants and Children* (4th ed.). (1989) New York, NY: Allyn and Bacon, 500.

p. 201   *. . . Professor Myrna Shure . . .*   Shure, M. B. Preschool Interpersonal Problem Solving (PIPS) Test: Manual, 1974. 2nd edition, 1989 (revised, 1992). Alternative solutions for 4- to 6-year-olds.

p. 201   *. . . At Pennsylvania State University . . .*   Greenberg, M. T. (2003). Schooling for the good heart. In Coleman, D. (Ed.), *Destructive Emotions: How Can We Overcome Them?* New York, NY: Bantam Books.

p. 202   *. . . Professor Judy Dunn . . .*   Dunn, J., Brown, J., and Beardsall, L. (1991). op. cit; Shure, M. (1992). *I Can Problem Solve (ICPS): An Interpersonal Cognitive Problem Solving Program.* Champaign, IL: Research Press.

p. 202   *. . . less likely to be bullied . . .*   Rubin, K., with Thompson, A. (2002) *The Friendship Factor.* New York, NY: Viking, 142–153; Perry, D. G., Williard, J. C., and Perry, L. C. (1990). Peers' perceptions of the consequences that victimized children provide aggressors. *Child Development,* 61, 1310–1325; Hodges, E. V. E. et al., (1999). The power of friendship: protection against an escalating cycle of peer victimization. *Developmental Psychology,* 35, 94–101.

p. 202   *. . . radiate vulnerability . . .*   Gottman, J. M., Katz, L. F., and Hooven, C. (1996). *Meta-Emotion: How Families Communicate Emotionally.* Mahwah, NJ: Erlbaum, 23; Pellegrini, A. S. (1992) op. cit.

p. 203   *. . . just one good friendship . . .*   Hodges et al. (1999) op. cit.

p. 203   . . . *Sherryll Kraizer* . . .   Coalition for Children, Inc.; Sherryll Kraizer, Ph.D.; and the Levi Company (1996–2000). Retrieved from www.safechild.org/bullies.htm on 2/23/03.

p. 204   . . . *in school and in life* . . .   Raver, C. (2002). Emotions matter: Making the case for the role of young children's emotional development for early school readiness. *Society for Research in Child Development: Social Policy Report.* (Vol. XVI, no. 3).

CHAPTER 9

Singer, D., and Singer, J. (Eds.). (2002). *Handbook of Children and the Media.* New York, NY: Sage.

Singer, D., and Singer, J. (Eds.) (1992). *The House of Make Believe.* Cambridge, MA: Harvard University Press.

p. 206   . . . *encourages social development* . . .   Rubin, K., Fein, G., and Vandenberg, B. (1983). Play. In Mussen, P. (Ed.), *Handbook of Child Psychology, Vol. 4: Socialization, Personality, and Social Development.* New York, NY: Wiley; Berk, L. E. (2001). *Awakening Children's Minds: How Parents and Teachers Can Make a Difference.* New York, NY: Oxford University Press; Collins, W. A. (Ed.). (1984). *Development during Middle Childhood: The Years from Six to Twelve.* Washington, DC: National Academy Press.

p. 206   . . . *a (now classic) study* . . .   Sylva, K. (1977). Play and learning. In Tizard, B., and Harvey, D. (Eds.), *Biology of Play.* London, England: Heinemann; Cheyne, J. A., and Rubin, K. H. (1983). Playful precursors of problem solving in preschoolers. *Developmental Psychology, 19,* 577–584; Hughes, F. P. (1999). *Children, Play, and Development.* Boston, MA: Allyn and Bacon; Jarrell, R. H. (1998). Play and its influence on the development of young children's mathematical thinking. In Fromberg, D. P., and Bergen, D. (Eds.), *Play from Birth to Twelve and Beyond.* New York, NY: Garland Publishing.

p. 208   . . . *IQ scores* . . .   Athey, I. (1984). Contributions of play to development. In Yawkey, T. D., and Pellegrini, A. D. (Eds.), *Child's Play: Developmental and Applied.* Hillsdale, NJ: Erlbaum; Rubin, K. (1982). Nonsocial play in preschoolers: necessarily evil? *Child Development, 53,* 651–657.

p. 208   . . . *their children's lead* . . .   O'Connell, B., and Bretherton, I. (1984). Toddlers' play, alone and with mother: the role of maternal guidance. In Bretherton, I. (Ed.), *Symbolic Play: The Development of Social Understanding.* Orlando, FL: Academic Press.

p. 208   . . . *Professor Barbara Friese's lab* . . .   Friese, B. (1990). Playful relationships: a contextual analysis of mother–toddler interaction and symbolic play. *Child Development, 61,* 1648–1656; Moyles, J. R. (1994). *The Excellence of Play.* Buckingham, UK: Open University Press; Manning, K. and Sharp, A. (1977). *Structuring Play in the Early Years at School.* London, England: Ward Lock Educational.

p. 209   . . . *children's language progress* . . .   McCune, L. (1995). A normative study of representational play at the transition to language. *Developmental Psychology, 31,* 198–206.

p. 210   . . . *Professor Catherine Garvey* . . .   Garvey, C. (1977). *Play.* Cambridge, MA: Harvard University Press.

p. 211   . . . *in one study* . . .   King, N. R. (1979). Play: the kindergartner's perspective. *Elementary School Journal, 80,* 81–87.

p. 211   . . . Wall Street Journal . . .   Pereira, J. (2002, November 27). Parents turn toys that teach into hot sellers. *The Wall Street Journal.*

p. 212   . . . *"At times, I admit,* . . .   Marino, G. (2003, January 26). In (self-)defense of the fanatical sports parent. *The New York Times Magazine.*

p. 212   . . . *Susan Bredekamp, Ph.D.* . . .   Bredekamp, S. (1999). *Developmentally appropriate practice in early childhood programs.* National Association for Education of Young Children.

p. 212   . . . *academically oriented preschools* . . .   Rescorla, L., Hyson, M., and Hirsh-Pasek, K. (Eds.) (1991). Academic instruction in early childhood: challenge or pressure? In Damon, W. , (Gen. Ed.) *New Directions in Developmental Psychology*, 53, New York: Jossey-Bass.

p. 213   . . . *noted researcher Dorothy Singer* . . .   Singer, D. (2003) Personal communication.

p. 214   . . . *effects on their brains* . . .   Azar, B. (2002, March). It's more than fun and games. *Monitor on Psychology*, 50–51.

p. 214   . . . *Jaak Panksepp* . . .   Azar, B. (2002) op. cit.

p. 214   . . . *Professor Anthony Pellegrini* . . .   Azar, B. (2002) op. cit.; also see: Ladd, G. W., Birch, S. H., and Buhs, E. S. (1999). Children's social and scholastic lives in kindergarten: related spheres of influence? *Child Development*, 70, 910–929; Ladd, G. W., Kochenderfer, B. J., and Coleman, C.C. (1997). Classroom peer acceptance, friendship, and victimization: distinct relational systems that contribute uniquely to children's school adjustment? *Child Development*, 68, 1181–1197.

p. 215   . . . *communicated to others* . . .   Piers, M. (Ed.)(1973). *Play and Development*. New York, NY: Norton.

p. 215   . . . *Zero to Three* . . .   CIVITAS Initiative, Zero to Three, Brio Corporation. (2000). What grown-ups understand about child development. Published by CIVITAS, Brio, and Zero to Three.

p. 216   . . . *psychologist Holly Ruff* . . .   Ruff, H. (1984). Infants' manipulative exploration of objects: effects of age and object characteristics. *Developmental Psychology*, 20, 9–20.

p. 217   . . . *Professor Fergus Hughes* . . .   Hughes, F. P. (1999) op. cit.

p. 217   . . . *objects in* appropriate *ways* . . .   Hughes, F. P. (1999) op. cit.

p. 220   . . . *What can I do with this?* . . .   Vondra, J., and Belsky, J. (1989). Exploration and play in social context: developments from infancy to childhood. In Lockman, J. J., and Hazen, N. L. (Eds.), *Action in Social Context: Perspectives on Early Development*. New York, NY: Plenum.

p. 220   . . . *In one study* . . .   Baldwin, D. A., Markman, E. M., and Melartin, R.L. (1994). Infants' ability to draw inferences about nonobvious object properties: evidence from exploratory play. *Child Development*, 64, 711–728.

p. 222   . . . *Toddlers with a wide variety* . . .   Hughes, F. P. (1999) op. cit; Rubenstein, J. L. (1976). Concordance of visual and manipulative responsiveness to novel and familiar stimuli: a function of test procedures or of prior experience? *Child Development*, 47, 1197–1199.

p. 222   . . . *Professor Robert Bradley* . . .   Bradley, R. (1986). Play materials and intellectual development. In Gottfried, A., and Brown, C. C. (Eds.) *Play Interactions: The Contribution of Play Material and Parental Involvement to Children's Development*. Lexington, MA: Lexington Books; Rheingold, H., and Cook, K. V. (1975). The contents of boys' and girls' rooms as an index of parents' behavior. *Child Development*, 46, 459–463; Hartup, W. W. (1999). Peer experience and its developmental significance. In Bennett, M. (Ed.), *Developmental Psychology: Achievements and Prospects*. Philadelphia, PA: Psychology Press.

p. 222   . . . *having a range of toys* . . .   Bradley, R. (1986) op. cit.

p. 223   . . . *he takes some of the balls* . . .   Hughes, F. P. (1999) op. cit.

p. 223   . . . *Psychologists talk about "convergent"* . . .   Pepler, D. J., and Ross, H. S. (1981). The effects of play on convergent and divergent problem-solving. *Child Development*, 52, 1202–1210.

p. 223   . . . *one right answer* . . .   Hughes, F. P. (1999) op. cit.

p. 223   . . . *Amala and Michael* . . .   Pepler, D. J., and Ross, H. S. (1981) op. cit.

p. 225   . . . *research has shown* . . .   Dansky, J. L. (1980). Make-believe: a mediator of the relationship between play and associative fluency. *Child Development*, 51, 576–579.

p. 225   . . . *pretend play* causes *children* . . .   Rubin et al., (1983) op. cit.

p. 225   . . . *Professor Lorraine McCune* . . .   McCune, L. (1995). A normative study of representation play at the transition to language. *Developmental Psychology*, 31, 198–206; Spencer, P. E., and Meadow-Orlans, K. P. (1996). Play, language, and maternal responsiveness: a longitudinal study of deaf and hearing infants. *Child Development*, 67, 3176–3191.

p. 228   . . . *As David gets older* . . .   Unger, J. A., Zelazo, P. P., Kearsley, R. B., and O'Leary, K. (1981). Developmental changes in the representation of objects in symbolic play from 18 to 34 months of age. *Child Development*, 52, 186–195.

p. 228   . . . *David has trouble thinking* . . .   Flavell, J. H., Green, F. L., and Flavell, E. R. (1987). Development of knowledge about the appearance-reality distinction. *Monographs of the Society for Research in Child Development*, 51, serial no. 212.

p. 229   . . . *David Elkind* . . .   Elkind, D. (2001). *The Hurried Child*. Cambridge, MA: Perseus.

p. 229   . . . *they become "mommy"* . . .   Bodrova, E., and Leong, D. J. (1998). Adult influences on play. In Fromberg, D. P., and Bergen, D. (Eds.), *Play from Birth to Twelve and Beyond*. New York, NY: Garland.

p. 229   . . . *beautiful hotel* . . .   Garvey, C. (1977). *Play*. Cambridge, MA: Harvard University Press.

p. 230   . . . *in pretend play* . . .   Bodrova, E., and Leong, D. J. (1996). *Tools of the Mind: The Vygotskyan Approach to Early Childhood Education*. Englewood Cliffs, NJ: Prentice Hall.

p. 230   . . . *Vygotsky said* . . .   Vygotsky, L. S. (1967). Play and its role in the mental development of the child. *Soviet Psychology*, 12, 6–18; Vygotsky, L. S. (1978). *Mind and Society: The Development of Higher Mental Processes*. Cambridge, MA: Harvard University Press.

p. 230   . . . *real crying* . . .   Bodrova and Leong (1996) op. cit.

p. 231   . . . *two sisters at play* . . .   Vygotsky, L. S. (1967) op. cit.

p. 232   . . . *Professor Greta Fein* . . .   Goncu, A., and Klein, E. L. (2001). Children in play, story, and school: a tribute to Greta Fein. In Goncu, A., and Klein, E. L. (Eds.), *Children in Play, Story, and School*. New York: Guilford.

p. 232   . . . *events as they wish* . . .   Vygotsky, L. S. (1967), op. cit.

p. 236   . . . *Professor Marjorie Taylor* . . .   Taylor, M. (1999). *Imaginary Companions and the Children Who Create Them*. New York, NY: Oxford University Press.

p. 236   . . . *Those who played as children* . . .   Quereau, T., and Zimmerman, T. (1992). *The New Game Plan for Recovery: Rediscovering the Positive Power of Play*. New York, NY: Ballantine.

p. 237   . . . *Professor Ageliki Nicolopoulou* . . .   Nicolopoulou, A. (1993). Play, cognitive development and the social world: Piaget, Vygotsky, and beyond. *Human Development*, 36, 1–23.

p. 239   . . . *pediatricians now recommend* . . .   Santrock, J. (2001). *Life-Span Development*. New York, NY: McGraw Hill, 142.

p. 240   . . . *20 percent of a child's playtime* . . .   Collins, W. A. (Ed.) (1984). *Development during Middle Childhood: The Years from Six to Twelve*. Washington, DC: National Academy Press.

p. 241   . . . *Laura Berk* . . .   Berk, L. (2001). *Awakening Children's Minds*. New York, NY: Oxford University Press.

p. 242   . . . *Jane Brody* . . .   Brody, J. (1992, October 21). Personal health. *The New York Times.*

p. 242   . . . *way to play the game* . . .   Hughes, F. P. (1999) op. cit.

CHAPTER 10

p. 244   . . . *"Because raising children* . . .   Schoenstein, R. (2002). *My Kid's an Honor Student, Your Kid's a Loser.* Cambridge, MA: Perseus.

p. 244   . . . *Einstein needed little* . . .   Retrieved from www.einstein-website.de/biography on 5/28/03.

p. 248   . . . *Jerome Bruner* . . .   Bruner, J. (1961). *The Process of Education.* Cambridge, MA: Harvard University Press.

p. 248   . . . *Jean Piaget* . . .   Ginsburg, H., and Opper, S. (1988). *Piaget's Theory of Intellectual Development* (3rd ed.). Englewood Cliffs, NJ: Prentice Hall.

p. 255   . . . *Fred Rogers* . . .   Rothbart, D. (2003, February 28). A friend in the neighborhood. *The New York Times.*

p. 262   . . . New Yorker *cartoon* . . .   Cheney. (2002, September 23). *The New Yorker.*

p. 263   . . . *require that preschool teachers* . . .   National Association for the Education of Young Children (NAEYC) position statement. Early learning standards: creating the conditions for success. Retrieved from www.naeyc.org. on 3/13/03.

p. 266   . . . *Reggio Emilia* . . .   Reggio Emilia: Some Lessons for U.S. Educators by Rebecca S. New. Retrieved from http://ericeece.org/pubs/digests/1993/new93.html on 3/14/03.

INDEX

Boldface page references indicate illustrations. <u>Underscored</u> references indicate boxed text.

emotions and, 172–73
environments for, stimulating,
    92–93, 95–96
expansion, 94
gazing and, 73–74, <u>74</u>
gestural, 66, 73–74, <u>74</u>
grammar, 79–81
individual differences and, 63–64,
    86–87
instinct and, 64–67
intelligence and, 134
inventing language and, 66
language acquisition device and, 64
left hemisphere of brain and,
    19, 23
listening while in womb and,
    67–68, <u>68–69</u>
name, knowing own and, 71–73,
    <u>72</u>
negotiation process and, <u>62–63</u>
nonverbal, 66, 73–74, <u>74</u>
orchestra analogy and, 76
parent's role in, 88–92
parenting strategies for
    improving, 93–96
pointing and, 73–74, <u>74</u>
pragmatics of, 83–86, <u>84</u>
pretend play and, 225–28, <u>228</u>
process of
    in 1st year, 67–76
    in 4th year, 83–86
    pushing, 60
    in 2nd year, 76–79, <u>77–78</u>
    in 3rd year, 81–83
rules of language, 81–82, <u>82–83</u>
second, 29, 31, 96
sentences
    basic, 69–71
    complex, 79–81
social skills and, 201–2

storytelling and, <u>86</u>
stuttering and, 81
time periods for, 32–33
Universal Grammar and, 65
words
    baby's first, 76–77, <u>77–78</u>
    combinations, <u>80–81</u>
    recognizing, 71–73
Lateralization (specialization of
    brain's two halves), 23
Lavine, Linda, 113
Leading edge of competence, 145
Learning. *See also* Language skills;
    Math skills; Reading skills;
    Social skills; Writing skills
in context, 58–59, 256–57
"critical period" theory and,
    30–33
debate about early, 28–29
environment and, 26–30
field trip and, planning, 35–36
force-feeding academics and, 9–10
household items and, simple,
    36–37
independent, 3
letters, names of, 115–16
love of, creating, 253–54
memorization and, 32, 34–35
opportunities for, 15
personal desire for, 21
play and, 14, 58, 225, 248, 251,
    256–57
progression of, 138–40
receptive periods for, 31–32
repetition and, 34
rules
    through games, 237–38
    of language, 81–82, <u>82–83</u>
scaffolding and, 56–57, <u>145–46</u>
within reach, 251–52